BUNDU, THE BEAT
&
BEYOND

This is a pre-print copy
of my book & contains
a few typos & incorrect dates.
I have amended these in
pencil and hope that it
does not detract from
your reading experience.

John Lloyd
December 2013

BUNDU, THE BEAT
&
BEYOND

John LLOYD

authorHOUSE®

AuthorHouse™ UK Ltd.
1663 Liberty Drive
Bloomington, IN 47403 USA
www.authorhouse.co.uk
Phone: 0800.197.4150

© *2013 by John LLOYD. All rights reserved.*

No part of this book may be reproduced, stored in a retrieval system, or transmitted by any means without the written permission of the author.

The right of John LLOYD to be identified as the Author of the work has been asserted by him in accordance with the Copyright, Designs and Patent Act 1988.

Published by AuthorHouse   08/06/2013

ISBN: 978-1-4918-0039-3 (sc)
ISBN: 978-1-4918-0040-9 (hc)
ISBN: 978-1-4918-0041-6 (e)

Any people depicted in stock imagery provided by Thinkstock are models, and such images are being used for illustrative purposes only.
Certain stock imagery © Thinkstock.

This book is printed on acid-free paper.

Because of the dynamic nature of the Internet, any web addresses or links contained in this book may have changed since publication and may no longer be valid. The views expressed in this work are solely those of the author and do not necessarily reflect the views of the publisher, and the publisher hereby disclaims any responsibility for them.

CONTENTS

Foreword		ix
Glossary		xi
Chapter 1:	Early years and Africa	1
Chapter 2:	College and joining the Police	33
Chapter 3:	On the Beat	42
Chapter 4:	Good & not so good times	57
Chapter 5:	A new beginning	69
Chapter 6:	Stories from Crawley CID—1978-1982	97
Chapter 7:	Gatwick Airport CID	117
Chapter 8:	Singapore	143
Chapter 9:	Interpol	170
Chapter 10:	NCIS Re-Visited	217
Chapter 11:	The Serious & Organised Crime Agency (SOCA)	226
Chapter 12:	A Retirement Bombshell	243

This book is dedicated to Jackie, my wife of 35 years, who has always supported me in whatever I have chosen to do.

"Women and cats will do as they please, and men and dogs should relax and get used to the idea."

—Robert A. Heinlein

FOREWORD

I felt inspired to write this book after reading "Abo—a wee boy's progress", an autobiography by Alan Neill. He is, like me, a former Sussex Police Officer, although we have never met nor served together at the same place and time.

My prime motivation in writing this was for my own benefit and for that of my two sons, Gareth and Simon, so that they have a clearer picture of what their "old man" has done with his life.

My major problem in writing this was the fact that I have never kept a diary so I have had to rely on my memory. I am fortunate in that I have retained a small number of non-sensitive documents relating to my professional life which have been of great assistance when putting certain facts and incidents into perspective. However, some events may have been recorded slightly out of date sequence and any errors are mine alone.

I am indebted to my brother, Chris, who assisted me with some facts relating to our time in Africa.

When describing my Police career I have tried to include a wide variety of differing offences and scenarios so as to give the reader some idea of the range of matters I had been involved in investigating.

It is said that everyone has a book inside them—this is my effort. I hope that you enjoy reading it.

John LLOYD—2013.

GLOSSARY

AKEU — Anti Kidnap & Extortion Unit.
ATU — Anti-Terrorist Unit (Gatwick)
BAA — British Airports Authority
BA — British Airways
BCAL — British Caledonian Airways.
BEM — British Empire Medal.
BSAP — British South Africa Police—operated in Rhodesia until 1980.
BSP — Bank Settlement Plan—a financial clearing house for airline tickets.
CEOP — Child Exploitation Online Protection centre
CID — Criminal Investigation Department.
CJU — Criminal Justice Unit.
CPS — Crown Prosecution Service.
EOKA — Greek political and terrorist organisation active in Cyprus during the 1950's.
EUROPOL — Europe wide criminal intelligence organisation.
FBI — Federal Bureau of Investigation. (USA)
GP Car — General Purpose Police patrol car.
Guardia Civil — National Police in Spain.
HMRC — HM Revenue & Customs
HQ — Headquarters.
HR — Human Resources.
IATA — International Air Transport Association.
ICPO — International Criminal Police Organisation—Interpol.
ILOR — International Letter of Request.
IRA — Irish Republican Army.
Jo'burg — abridged name for Johannesburg.
KLM — Royal Dutch Airlines.

MCO	—	Miscellaneous Charges Order—a form of airline credit note.
NARPO	—	National Association for Retired Police Officers.
NCA	—	National Crime Agency.
NCB	—	National Central Bureau (Interpol)
NCIS	—	National Criminal Intelligence Service.
NI.CRO	—	Northern Ireland Criminal Record Office
RASC	—	Royal Army Service Corps.
RCMP	—	Royal Canadian Mounted Police.
RSPCA	—	Royal Society for the protection of cruelty to animals.
RUC	—	Royal Ulster Constabulary (Now the Police Service of Northern Ireland or PSNI)
SAAF	—	South African Air Force.
SAM	—	Surface to Air Missile.
SAS	—	Special Air Service.
SFO	—	Serious Fraud Office.
SKF	—	Swedish Ballbearing manufacturer.
SLO	—	SOCA Liaison Officer
SOCA	—	Serious & Organised Crime Agency.
SOCO	—	Scenes of Crime Officer.
SSOU	—	Serious Sexual Offences Unit.
TOD	—	Ticket on Departure.
UDI	—	Unilateral Declaration of Independence.

CHAPTER 1

Early years and Africa

My parents eloped from Surrey to Cornwall in 1946 just after the end of the Second World War and I was born in Redruth in November of that year. They had met during the war at a dance near Chertsey, Surrey, where my mother, Hilda who was born in 1921, lived with her parents and five brothers and sisters. My father, Herbert, was a Staff Sergeant in the Royal Army Service Corps (RASC) and had served with Montgomery's 8th Army in the Western Desert in Egypt. My father was never called Herbert but was always addressed as "Pat". I do not know just how he acquired this moniker but I believe that it was given to him by his Army pals in Egypt. Perhaps I might have been tempted to change my name had I been called Herbert.

My father was born in Chippenham in Wiltshire in 1912, the year that the Titanic sailed on its ill-fated maiden voyage. His family home was located in Chippenham where he had lived with his parents and elder Sister Winifred and younger brother Reginald who were born in 1907 and 1915 respectively.

The war altered many people's lives forever and those fortunate enough to survive it unscathed found themselves untethered from local ties and the population became a great deal more mobile.

And so it was with my father. The war had interrupted his legal career but it seems that he had little or no desire to return to Chippenham after the war especially after having met my mother. I believe that prior to the outbreak of war in 1939 my father had been married to a lady from Bristol called Phyllis but, having met my mother, it seems that

John LLOYD

he became estranged from Phyllis. I suspect that my parents moved to Cornwall to escape the family pressures in Surrey and because, at that time, divorce and all that goes with it was really frowned upon within society as a whole and in particular by my maternal grandparents who had been raised in the Victorian era with all the morals and strict social rules applied to that society.

My parents married in Truro in July 1947 which meant that I had been born out of wedlock which again helps explain why my parents eloped because the shame of being pregnant without being married in those days would have been too much to bear, both for my parents and grandparents. A family scandal no less. So, at the time of my birth I was a bastard. Some people might still view me in that light.

I assume that my parents had been able to marry in 1947 as a result of my father securing his divorce from Phyllis. This was never a topic of conversation in our house so the full facts were not known to me.

Hilda and Pat were very good parents and I always remember being loved by them in equal measure. I always felt secure and never wanted for anything. This is not to say that I was spoiled because I was not and I always knew where the boundaries were in any given situation. We were never rich but we always had sufficient to eat and enough clothes to wear etc. This was in "Austerity Britain "at a time when some things were still rationed and most things hard to come by. I remember that "Make do and mend" was a popular phrase.

In 1950 my brother, Christopher, arrived by which time we were living in Stoughton, an area of Guildford, in Surrey where my father was working as a Solicitors Managing Clerk in a local solicitor's office. The firm of solicitors was called Smallpiece and Merrimen or "Littlebits and Jollyboys" as my Mum often quipped. It was also around this time, probably in 1951, that I contrived to break my right arm in several places whilst falling out of a tree which I had climbed as a result of a dare from some older boys. I was taken to St Luke's Hospital in Guildford where my arm had to be re-broken before it could be straightened and put into a plaster cast from above my elbow to my wrist. I was kept in hospital for a week or two and spent the first couple of nights in a male surgical ward until space became available in a children's ward. I do not think that I particularly enjoyed my stay in hospital probably because of my tender years. The stitch marks are still visible all these years later.

A year or so later, probably in 1953 we moved to a village called Brookwood in Surrey. Our house was located on the outskirts of the smallish village in Lye Road and near to a small running stream.

I was very happy in Brookwood and Chris and I had many happy times roaming the nearby fields etc and playing with Marjorie and Roland Yates who lived next door and who were about the same ages as Chris and I.

I assume that by 1950 peace had broken out between my parents and my maternal grandparents because we did see them quite a lot at their Chertsey home on Eastworth Road.

My Grandparents, Frank and Daisy Cole, were lovely people and always treated Chris and I with kindly love and affection. Unfortunately I only have a little recollection of my Grandfather as he died in 1951 when I was very young but my abiding memory of him is being seated on his lap whilst he sat on his chair next to the fire place. I believe that he died so young as a result of being gassed during his Army service in the First World War in France which had left him in poor health. His experiences in that war had also included a terrible situation in which both his pals, either side of him, were shot dead during an advance on enemy positions. This had had a profound effect on my Grandfather as a result of which he suffered with a nervous disposition thereafter. He had managed to make a good living as a piano tuner and repairer, certainly sufficient to raise and support six children. He was a very talented man and was competent playing on numerous different musical instruments. He obviously had an excellent ear for music even though he could not read a musical note.

My mother often told me that theirs had been a happy close knit family and, like me, she had been raised with much love and affection albeit shared between her two sisters and three brothers. I suspect that things were somewhat cramped in their household as the three sisters shared

John LLOYD

one bedroom, the three brothers in another leaving Daisy and Frank in the front bedroom. Within my memory there was no electricity on the upper floor nor was there an indoor bathroom. There was an outdoors toilet which I remember being freezing in winter so any visits there were of short duration. I believe that baths were taken once a week in a galvanised iron bath which was taken off its peg in the kitchen and filled by means of boiling kettles on the Gas Stove. A laborious but a necessary process.

We did socialise with my mother's brothers and sisters and their families. There was Uncle Jack and his wife, Gwen and children, Uncle Arthur and his wife, Edith, and their children David, Sheila, Jean and Ronnie, Uncle Rich and his family who we did not see much of because they had moved to Yorkshire after the war had ended. We also saw my Auntie Lily and her husband Tom and their daughter Janet as well as my Auntie Ethel, her husband Charlie and their children, Peter (who was my age), Frank, Jeffrey and later my cousin June arrived.

I cannot remember the reasons why but I have no recollection of meeting my father's parents but this may have been because they had died when I was very young. We did see his brother and sister from time to time. Uncle Reg and Auntie Wyn were both unmarried but lived together for reasons of companionship and economic necessity. After the Second World War they lived in London E17 but later moved to Godalming in Surrey where they ran a corner shop together.

In our time in Brookwood I was a member of the Church Youth group and sang in the Church Choir but there came a time when I had to choose between the choir and the Wolf Cubs which both met on the same evening. I chose the Wolf Cubs so my stay in the Church choir was a relatively short one. The Cubs met at a hall in the nearby village of Knaphill which was within easy walking distance from our House. It was around this time that I became acquainted with two boys called Timothy and Jeremy Hawk whose mother was called Monica and they also lived in Brookwood.

Bundu, the Beat & Beyond

In 1955 my parents decided to emigrate to Africa. This was in common with a lot of other Britons who left the UK after the war to find a better life abroad and to leave austerity Britain behind.

My father flew out to Northern Rhodesia in Central Africa in a four-engined Bristol Britannia Aircraft, which I believe took about 24 hours of flying. He had secured a position with a firm of solicitors called Longman & Co in the northern copper belt town of Kitwe located near the border with the Katanga Province of the Belgian Congo.

My mother, Chris and I remained in Brookwood for a few months whilst my father arranged a suitable house for us and generally got settled pending our arrival.

During this time my father wrote to us on the blue coloured flimsy airmail letters which were to become so much part of our lives. I remember one of his letters ending with the question, "Do you like Fanta"? None of us had heard of Fanta as it was not then available in UK. We did not even know what it was.

I recall being involved, in a small way, in assisting my mother in packing up all our belongings into various boxes and tin trunks etc which were to be sent on to our new African home. They would be sent by sea and would take 2-3 months to arrive as their somewhat tortuous journey would involve them being sent by rail to Southampton where they would eventually be loaded onto a ship bound for Cape Town in the Union of South Africa where they would be off-loaded and then sent by rail to Johannesburg on South African Railways and then by another train to Bulawayo in Southern Rhodesia and then by Rhodesian Railways onto Kitwe in Northern Rhodesia, a total journey of some 8500 miles.

Eventually our time for the beginning of our great adventure arrived and I recall being at Heathrow Airport which was then a collection of Nissen Huts and tents etc. (there may have been some more substantial brick built buildings but I do not remember seeing any) We then boarded our aircraft which was to fly us to Northern Rhodesia. To me the aircraft looked huge but in fact it would have been somewhat small. It was a Vickers Viking aircraft which was basically a civilian version of a wartime

John LLOYD

bomber called the Wellington which had been a twin piston-engine medium bomber. I believe that it carried about twenty four passengers.

The three of us were seated in two seats facing another two seats with a small table in between. So my brother sat next to my Mum whilst I sat opposite them. At that time my brother was not a good traveller and was sick at the slightest bit of movement on buses etc.

The Vickers Viking was a relatively slow aircraft and only operated at altitudes below 10,000 feet or so because the cabin was unpressurised. The aircraft would not fly at night which meant that our journey would take several days and would necessitate night stops en route. This particular aircraft was operated by a company called Hunting Clan which was later absorbed by British United Airways, but more of that later.

We took off from Heathrow and flew to Nice on the French Riviera where I remember landing on the airstrip which was located parallel to the beach. All the passengers trooped of the aircraft and whilst it was being refuelled we were given lunch on the terminal building veranda overlooking the runway and the Mediterranean Sea beyond.

We re-boarded the aircraft after lunch and flew on to the island of Malta where we stayed overnight in a local hotel close to the airport.

The following morning after breakfast we took off bound for Benghazi in Libya where we landed at Benina Airport for lunch. After lunch we flew on to Wadi Halfa in Egypt where we spent the night on a Nile river boat. That location was later transformed and is now under water as part of the Aswan Dam project.

The next morning we flew on to Khartoum in the Sudan where I think we stayed at a local hotel and I recall that my brother and I got into some trouble with the Hotel staff for repeatedly pulling the bell rope which summoned hotel staff for room service etc.

The next day we flew on to Entebbe in Uganda. We were scheduled to land at a remote town called Juba en-route to Entebbe for re-fuelling but the flight deck crew decided that they had sufficient fuel to reach

Bundu, the Beat & Beyond

Entebbe where we landed in the late afternoon having flown directly over Lake Victoria which, we had been told, was infested with crocodiles.

The next day we took off from Entebbe and our route took us over the Belgian Congo which seemed to be experiencing a lot of Bush fires as a lot of smoke could be seen rising from the ground. It was the heat from these bushfires meeting the cooler air from the upper atmosphere which created very unstable air through which we were flying. This, in turn, created air pockets which would not support the heavy aircraft, and our flight became very very bumpy, so much so that my poor brother Chris had his face permanently buried in a sick bag. My mother was wearing a dark two piece suit on this day and I remember that all of a sudden and without warning we were forced to stand up as the aircraft plunged vertically downwards at an alarming rate. I had this vision of a black blur as my mother involuntarily stood up with the force of the vertical drop. After what seemed an eternity but was actually only some seconds the aircraft hit stable air and the crew managed to halt its downward motion.

Things were not helped by one of the adult male passengers screaming, "We're crashing, we're crashing."

Eventually normality was restored and we found ourselves flying through stable air once more. I recall the pilot informing us via the tannoy system that the aircraft had plunged 1,000 feet straight down in a matter of a few seconds. A somewhat scary event and one that I would not care to repeat.

After this we had an uneventful onward flight to N'dola, the main international airport for the copper belt in Northern Rhodesia where we had a joyful re-union with my father who was there to meet us and drive us the 40 miles or so to Kitwe.

We arrived at our new home in Empire Crescent which was a large three bed-roomed colonial style bungalow. The house had a large garden to the back and front with servant's quarters at the rear. Behind the servants quarters was a lane called a "sanitary Lane "down which the dustbin lorries would trundle on their weekly visits to collect the household rubbish.

John LLOYD

To the side of the house was a huge Anthill about seven or eight feet in height and about twelve feet in length. This subsequently became a favourite play area for Chris and I as we constructed road ways along the sides of the anthill for our Dinky toys and generally had a good time. We made friends with Keith and Geoff Wainwright, two brothers of about my age, who lived directly opposite us in Empire Crescent and often played with them in a nearby stream as well as on our huge Anthill in our garden.

Northern Rhodesia was part of the Federation of Rhodesia and Nyasaland, a political union formed of Southern Rhodesia (now Zimbabwe), Northern Rhodesia (now Zambia) and Nyasaland.(now Malawi). I am not too sure just how well this Federation worked nor how equitable it was. It seems that most of the power was centred in Salisbury, Southern Rhodesia, which is where all the centres of Government were located.

Upon our arrival we were introduced to the "Colour Bar" in which all African males, irrespective of their age, were addressed as "Boy" The colour Bar in the Rhodesias was nowhere near as severe as the system of apartheid found in South Africa but none the less it was restrictive for the indigenous black Africans. We had two servants, a Cook/Houseboy called George and a Garden boy called Rastron. George was responsible for keeping the house clean and tidy, washing and ironing plus doing some occasional cooking. Rastron kept the garden tidy and the grass cut short by using a thin metal blade of about three feet in length with a curved and sharpened business end. It was hard work but he seemed happy enough. In return they were given a basic wage plus foodstuffs such as Sadza or Maize meal (a staple of African diet), Kapenta (a small dried fish caught locally in abundance and similar to whitebait), sugar, salt and other basic foods. They were supplied with uniforms which actually looked quite smart. What they thought of them I do not know. George stayed in the servants quarters at the bottom of the garden which consisted of a small combined bedroom and living room plus a sanitary toilet and washing facilities.

He cooked his food on an open fire outside the front door of his quarters. These servants' quarters were called Kyas. When an African

Bundu, the Beat & Beyond

addressed my father he called him Bwana (master), my mother was addressed as Madam and we boys were called Picannin Bwanas (small masters).

I never quite got used to this class system but being the age that I was I suppose that I just accepted the status quo.

Chris and I got on quite well with George and we had long conversations with him when he let us and had nothing better to do. We found that he had a good sense of humour which is a quality I have always admired in people.

Most of the servants employed by my parents spoke reasonable English so communicating was seldom a problem however we were introduced to a lingua franca of Central and Southern Africa called Fanagalo, locally known as Kitchen Kaffir. This language was developed by the Mining Companies in South Africa to enable their workers who came from any one of the hundreds of tribes throughout Central and Southern Africa, each of which had their own language, to communicate with one another.

Chris and I came to understood a smattering of Fanagalo, such as "Ini wena funa"? (What do you want?) or that very useful phrase, "Hamba lapa lo Kya kawena." (Go to your home).

In the meantime our Nan sent us out monthly parcels from the UK consisting of the monthly overseas editions of the Daily Mirror newspaper printed on thin flimsy paper plus the Eagle comic for me which I enjoyed reading (Dan Dare & the Mekons etc), and the Beano comic for Chris.

Chris and I were sent to Kitwe Primary School which was about two miles distance from our house. We, in common with most other school children then, cycled to school. The roads were all tarmacked and well maintained with very deep storm drains at either side of the roadway to cater for the very heavy rain storms which hit us from time to time. We all wore the school uniforms comprised of grey shorts and shirt together

John LLOYD

with a grey felt trilby hat to ward off the strong sunshine which shone most days.

In common with most other children of our age in Africa we did not tend to wear shoes and socks apart from when we were at school or for special occasions. I found this very liberating, although, initially the soles of my feet were a little sore from coming into contact with small stones etc. Eventually, however, our feet hardened somewhat and we could walk virtually anywhere without any ill-effects.

For sports or other leisure activities we wore variants of plimsolls. These were generically called "Takkies". This was many years before the modern sports training shoes were developed.

In general the weather was very temperate in African terms and the sun shone virtually every day together with Cumulo-nimbus clouds which seemed to be ever present. The temperatures were generally acceptable at around 25-30 degrees apart from October which was known as "suicide month" when temperatures could vary between 30-40 degrees. The winters were very mild in comparison with Northern Europe and mainly the only adjustment needed was to wear a jumper or jacket in the evening when it could feel a bit chilly. Kitwe was at an altitude of just over 4,000 feet above sea level. The weather seemed to operate like clockwork in that sunrise was at 0600hrs and sunset was at 1800 hrs. There was no dawn or dusk period, one minute it was light and the next it was dark. However, when it rained it really did rain in absolute torrents. Thankfully, the rainy season was reasonably short and during that period it normally only rained for about an hour a day after which the sun shone. Sometimes I could see the wall of rain driving slowly down the road towards me like a steadily advancing grey sheet. It was a phenomenon I have never seen before or since.

Due to the weather being so good we enjoyed a mostly outdoor life and engaged in most forms of sports. Kitwe was formed of two townships, Kitwe was the commercial and private part of town and Nkana was the mining township where all the personnel employed at the Rhokana Copper Mine lived in Mine houses which were quite distinctive in design

Bundu, the Beat & Beyond

and only varied in shape and size according to the status of the occupant within the mining hierarchy.

We were permitted to use the Rhokana Olympic size swimming pool located in Nkana and it was there that I learned to swim becoming quite an accomplished swimmer at all levels. I think I inherited my swimming skills from my mother who, although small in stature, had been an accomplished swimmer in her youth.

There was a reasonable shopping area in Kitwe with large department stores such as Standard Trading Co and Economy Stores which were later joined by OK Bazaars. In addition there were the usual array of Jewellers, bespoke Gents outfitters and ladies fashion shops etc.

My father had bought a brand new Morris Minor 1000 saloon car which was black in colour with red leather upholstery. Its registration number was NK6434, it's curious how my brain retains such useless information all these years later!

Being fully mobile we spent at least one day every week-end taking trips to various places outside Kitwe such as Mindola Dam and Dad's farm which had a large lake where we could swim and have the now usual Braaivleis (see below) and have a generally good time.

We also visited an elderly widow at her home in the township of Itimpi (later re-named as Garneton) about 15 miles out of Kitwe. My father had befriended her through his legal work and we paid her occasional visits at her large house almost in the middle of nowhere. This lady, whose name I cannot remember, had arrived in Northern Rhodesia with her husband in the 1920's and had somehow bought a sizeable estate of 30,000 acres of land which was mainly used for agricultural purposes. I remember being impressed by the sheer size of her estate and that she fussed over Chris and I making sure we had small treats, cakes and biscuits which certainly endeared us to her.

At this time my father had become friendly with another solicitor called Jack Corey who had recently arrived from the UK with his wife Cynthia and two children. At week-ends we would often visit a spot known

John LLOYD

locally as "Tinkers claim" which had a small stream running through it. We would build a small fire and make tea and have a braaivleis with steaks, chops and sausages. Great adventures for us children.

A braaivleis is a South African tradition and is called a Braai for short. The word Braaivleis is an Afrikaans word and literally means Burn (braai) meat (Vleis) A Braai is roughly the equivalent to a Barbeque which is now popular in the UK but was an unknown concept to most UK residents in the 1950's. The braai normally consisted of cooking various meats such as steaks or chops together with the ubiquitous Boerewors (a delicious spicy Afrikaans sausage) Boere = Farmer and wors = sausage) The letter W is pronounced as a V. To enhance the flavour of the meat a Braai was then always cooked over an open outdoor flame consisting of wood and/or charcoal.

We enjoyed similar food to that available in the UK but there did not appear to be any shortages of anything apart from fresh milk which was unavailable due to their being no milk pasteurising plant in the area. Instead we used powdered milk called KLIM (milk spelled backwards) which came in large tins and you mixed the contents, in proportion, with water to make acceptable milk. Due to the heat all fresh produce had to be refrigerated to prevent it from being spoiled. Refrigerators were not commonly available in UK so this was a novelty to us at the time. I believe that fresh meat was relatively cheap in comparison to the UK and so we always had something "nice "to eat each dinner time. I recall that we had a wonderful Bakers in Kitwe called Fullers Bakery from which my father would bring home a lovely tasting white loaf each day and from which Chris and I would gleefully cut off slices to be devoured with butter and jam (which also came in tins from South Africa and was delicious). We were later introduced to the delights of Peanut Butter and Golden Syrup sandwiches which we devoured with some glee. Some years later a new bakery called Bamfords opened in Kitwe which also produced wonderful loaves of fresh white bread and my father's favourite, custard slices, which he would bring home for all to savour.

A lot of the food we had was imported from South Africa, especially canned goods like delicious Jams and fruits with such brand names as Koo and All Gold.

Bundu, the Beat & Beyond

We also delighted in tasting locally grown tropical fruits such as Mangoes, Guavas, Grenadillas (passion fruit) and Paw-Paws (Papaya). At that time these were unknown in the UK. We could also have locally grown oranges, lemons and bananas.

Chris and I also explored tasting a new variety of soft drinks called Hubbly Bubbly which had delicious fruit flavours but I am sure were full of sugar. This was before the days of diet or calorie free drinks. From time to time we also delighted in drinking a non-alcoholic ginger beer called Ting-a-Ling which came in brown bottles with yellow writing.

The currency in Northern Rhodesia was based on British Sterling with pounds, shillings and pence but all the notes and coins were produced locally. The denominations of the notes and the coins was the same as in the UK but the one penny coin had a hole drilled into the centre of the coin and the threepenny bit was called a Tickey which I thought was just a marvellous name for a coin. There is no modern equivalent for a threepenny bit but it represented half a sixpence which in today's money represents two and a half pence. We could buy quite a sizeable amount of sweets for a tickey in those days.

For the first time in my life I also began to take notice of the large variety of private cars used by the locals. In addition to British and French makes there were also a substantial number of very large flashy American cars such as the Chevrolet Impala and Ford Fairlane etc. They were very impressive to me as they had a lot of chrome features which always flashed brightly in the ever present sunshine.

You may recall me mentioning Monica Hawk who my parents had known in Brookwood, Surrey. Monica had given my parents the contact details of her twin sister and family who lived in Nkana, the mining township of Kitwe. My parents duly made contact with Dorothy and John Glazier at their home and subsequently became very good lifelong friends with them. John had been a prisoner of the Japanese during the war and had endured much hardship and privations. He was a real gentleman and all round good man but I do recall that he did not like anything Japanese and, understandably, disliked anything or anyone emanating from that country. Many years later he showed me

13

John LLOYD

his wartime diary which he had secretly kept which detailed much of the awful treatment suffered by most of the Allied POW's during that period. I felt very privileged to read it and suggested that he may wish to enlarge upon the contents with a view to having it published. As far as I know he never did and I suspect that he was just pleased that someone had read his diary and had understood the meaning and relevance of its contents.

The Glaziers had two daughters, Jennifer who was older than me and who I never met as she was at Boarding School in South Africa and later left for the UK for Nursing training, and Frances who was a few weeks older than me. At that time Frances was also at Boarding School in King Williams Town in South Africa but I did not meet her until a few years later.

We had one cinema in Kitwe called the "Astra" and some few months after our arrival from the UK our parents allowed Chris and I to go the Saturday morning session which was aimed primarily at children. We were delighted and paid our one shilling (five pence today) and sat in our seats. The main attraction was a Marilyn Monroe film called "Bus Stop". We sat through a number of cartoons, a travelogue film and an exciting episode of an American crime serial after which all the cinema lights went up and seemingly everyone got up to leave. Chris and I followed suit and made our way home thinking that the show was over, not realising that this was the interval during which most of the audience visited the toilets or the café snack bar for refreshments. We did not make that mistake again and became regular attendees every Saturday morning.

There was no television service in Northern Rhodesia at that time.

There was a smaller cinema in the mining township of Nkana located next to the Mine Mess which was run by a man called Ernie Rogers. Chris and I did not often go to the Mine cinema as we preferred the Astra.

I cannot be sure of the year but it would have been around 1958 or 59 my parents decided that we would all return to the UK with a view to re-settling back there. Accordingly they sold up everything apart from

Bundu, the Beat & Beyond

personal belongings and we took the train on Rhodesia Railways from Kitwe to Bulawayo via the Victoria Falls where we changed trains onto South African Railways travelling to Johannesburg where we took yet another train to Cape Town. As I recall that took about five days. We then boarded the Union Castle ship Edinburgh Castle and sailed away from Cape Town to Southampton, a voyage which lasted 14 days. I recall enjoying the voyage immensely as there were many other children on board and we just played and played and amused ourselves including partaking in the Crossing the Line Ceremony when crossing the Equator. We occasionally sneaked into First Class to use their indoor swimming pool much to the chagrin of some of the ship's staff.

There was only one stop en route and that was at the island of Madeira located off the north west coast of Africa. I recall going ashore and was absolutely amazed at how expensive some things were. For example in Northern Rhodesia we would pay six pence for a bottle of Coca Cola but in Madeira we were charged two shillings and sixpence or five times the amount we were used to paying. We only purchased these drinks once in Madeira.

Upon arrival in Southampton we went to our Nan's house in Chertsey who had kindly agreed to put us up for a time. I do not remember too much about this period apart from being able to meet most of my cousins on my mother's side including Janet Storey who was a few years older than me and Peter, Frank & Jeff Martin who were all around our ages. I recall walking from my Nan's house to the Martin's house in Fernlands Close, Chertsey which involved a walk of 2 or 3 miles across the open countryside to the rear of my Nan's house before arriving at their house and enjoying lots of games and antics on the open green outside their house or in the area a short walk away called the "Ruins" which I believe were the ruins of an old country house and in which we had some good times.

The walk I mentioned from my Nan's house to the Martins is not achievable any more as in later years someone decided to build the M25 motorway between the two houses.

John LLOYD

After some few months, I cannot recall just how many, my parents decided that the UK in the late 50's was not for them after all and so we reversed our early sea voyage this time on the Stirling Castle. I think that I celebrated my 13th birthday on board ship and remember being spoiled by the dining room stewards who gave me extra portions of just about everything including chips, so I was a very happy boy.

During that voyage Chris and I participated in a Fancy Dress contest on board ship. I was dressed up as "The Old School Tie" in long trousers, white shirt, a huge tie my mother had made plus a large top hat and wearing a monocle. Chris was dressed up as a nurse in drag as made popular in a film of the time called "Carry on Nurse".

We arrived back in Kitwe and secured another house in which to live, this time I think we lived in a series of Mine Houses called "Leave houses" the occupants of which had gone on extended leave for six months or so leaving their house fully furnished etc. We did this for a year or so before finally settling in a Mine house in 8th Avenue, Nkana, which my mother was entitled to as a result of her securing a position with the Copper belt Power Company in Nkana.

By this time I had started at Kitwe Boys High School which was an excellent school at that time and I had also met Frances Glazier by then who was a pupil at Kitwe Girls High School and we became very good friends with a shared interest in 60's pop music and I recall listening to her extensive collection of vinyl records whilst our mothers had tea and chin wagged as only ladies can do.

My brother, Chris, had experienced some problems at Kitwe Primary School which I believe involved some overbearing behaviour from one or two of the teachers as a result of which my parents moved him to the local Convent School.

At home, my brother Chris and I devised a small game for two which we called Pit-a-Pat. Like most good games this was a very simple operation in that we sat at either end of an internal corridor, the floor of which was highly polished, and using a ball like object fashioned from a bundle of

Bundu, the Beat & Beyond

rags we attempted to pat the "ball" passed one another by the use of one hand only scoring points when successful. It kept us amused.

It was around this time that the really brutal civil war broke out in the Belgian Congo, the southern border of which was only 60 or so miles from us. (distances in Africa are so huge that 60 miles is deemed as just around the corner). I remember that my mother, father and I went to the local social hall most days during that period to render what assistance we could to the thousands of Belgian refugees fleeing the bloody atrocities in Katanga province. My mother was later awarded a silver tea tray and service by the Union Miniere Company in the Belgian Congo as she had been their only telex link with the outside world for many days and had supplied valuable assistance during that difficult time.

In late 1960 or early 1961 my parents had decided that the education standards at the High School in Kitwe were falling and one of my Mum's work colleagues, Dorothy Myburgh, recommended a private Boarding School for Boys in South Africa at which her son, Toby, was a pupil.

Therefore arrangements were put in place for both Chris and I to start at Broadlands Private Boarding School for boys in the small "dorp" (village) of Meyerton in the Transvaal State of the Union of South Africa.

We had to be kitted out in the smart new uniforms for Broadlands which must have cost a small fortune as apart from the number one uniform (worn on formal occasions) we had to have six everyday uniforms, sports clothing and kit etc etc which all had to have our personal name tags sewn into them for identification at laundry etc. The school blazers and badges were only obtainable from a Johannesburg Department store in South Africa called John Orrs and they therefore took some time to arrive. We were each given a huge black tin trunk which were easily filled with our new clothing and other personal items and we had our names and contact details painted in white on the outside of each trunk.

This was before the days of affordable mass air travel. Flying was considered as an expensive option mainly reserved for the wealthy. It was therefore decided that we would travel the 1500 miles to school by train.

John LLOYD

Eventually the day of our departure arrived and our parents drove us to Nkana Railway Station where we boarded the Rhodesia Railways train and made our way to our second class compartment which had six sleeping bunks therein together with washing facilities. Our huge tin trunks were accommodated in the Guards Van at the rear of the train. On average there were usually about 25 such coaches in each train which had First, Second and one or two third class coaches. In the middle of the train was located a Restaurant Car which supplied first class silver service dining for breakfast, luncheon and dinner. I seem to recall that dinners cost about 5 shillings (about 25pence today) which sounds ridiculously cheap now but was in fact the going rate at the time.

Due to the times at which we travelled the passengers on the trains were mainly school kids like ourselves as a result of which we generally had a complete ball. Things got even more interesting when the opposite sex entered my thinking and it seems to me now that the main priority of the train crew was to maintain some distance between the boys and the girls, not always with success. If possible it seems that the train operators tried to place the girls on one side of the restaurant car and the boys on the other. It did not always work.

After leaving Nkana the train, which was normally pulled by one, and sometimes two, Garrett steam engines, chugged its way to the next station at around 20-25 mph. The journey to N'dola, the next stop from Nkana was only 40 miles by road but took around two hours by rail. Some of this slow speed might be down to the fact that the rail lines rarely went in straight lines but in a series of steeply curving bends. The rumour was that when the lines were built earlier in the century the workers were on a daily rate of pay and so it was in their interest to create the meandering tracks which exist today.

After dinner the train crew would come into each carriage offering bedding for hire. I forget just how much this cost but it would not have been very much. The bedding arrived in large canvas sacks secured with straps and buckles. The sack was opened and unrolled onto your bunk to reveal crisp clean sheets and warm woollen blankets and a pillow. Very cosy and very comfortable as the slow motion of the train tended to rock you to sleep at the end of each day.

Bundu, the Beat & Beyond

The following morning saw us arrive in Lusaka, the capital of Northern Rhodesia, where the engine crews changed and water taken on etc. There was normally a stop of around an hour or so to enable departing passengers to disembark and joining passengers to find their allotted compartments.

From Lusaka the train continued its way southwards towards Livingstone and the Victoria Falls via smaller stops such as Mazabuka, Choma and Broken Hill. Crossing the Victoria Falls Railway Bridge was always an experience I will never forget. Such a wonderful sight even if it was the dry season and the falls were at their lowest levels of water it was still a spectacle to behold.

From Livingstone we entered Southern Rhodesia and turned south—eastwards towards Bulawayo. We travelled through the Wankie Game Reserve after dusk so we did not get to see any animals. In the middle of the next morning we arrived at Bulawayo Railway Station where we had to change trains onto South African Railways. However the SAR train did not leave until sometime in the afternoon so we had some hours to while away in Bulawayo. Our normal routine was to put our tin trunks into the left luggage office and then make our way to Platform One where we could each take a hot bath for the sum of 2 shillings and sixpence (12 and a half pence in today's money) where we could rid our bodies of the dust and train soot etc accumulated over the previous two days travel even though we were able to wash in our compartments on the train.

Feeling refreshed after our baths we then walked into the centre of Bulawayo, a good 30-40 minute walk and found a convenient watering hole called the Empire Café which supplied good wholesome meals at reasonable prices and which had a wonderful loud Jukebox which played all the latest pop songs. We noted that the main streets in the City Centre were very wide and we were told that the reason for this was so that in the19th century and early 1900's the wagoner's could turn their carts around whilst being pulled by oxen in the roadway. Seems a good enough reason to me.

John LLOYD

After satisfying our hunger we re-traced our steps back to Bulawayo Railway Station, reclaimed our tin trunks and took them to the platform where the South African Railways Train awaited us. We then deposited the trunks with the guards van and found our way to our allotted compartment where we settled awaiting the departure time.

Upon leaving Bulawayo the train headed south westwards towards the border with Bechuanaland (now Botswana) where it crossed the border at a town with the pretty name of Plumtree. On entering Bechuanaland the train headed due south stopping at various places with such names as Mahalapye, Palapye and Francistown where there was normally an African band playing European style instruments for our entertainment. They did expect small tips from us in return which was fair enough. We also stopped en route at the capital of Bechuanaland which was called Gaborones.

The train continued on southwards into the night until it reached the town of Lobatse at 4am. We always knew that it was 4am because shortly after arriving at Lobatse Station our compartment door would be flung open, light from the corridor would flood the darkened compartment and a large suitcase would be flung inside. This was immediately followed by a school chum from Broadlands called Peter Nel who always greeted us with those immortal words, "Haazit you ou's?" This roughly translates as "How are you chaps?"

After leaving Lobatse the train continued south towards the South Africa border which was crossed at the town of Mafeking (of Boer war fame). After Mafeking we continued south before arriving in Johannesburg during the late afternoon. A distance of some 1500 miles took us four days and 3 nights which is laughable by today's standards but it was gentle and relaxing with little or no pressure you will find in today's modern Air terminals but that's progress.

On one southbound train journey when we were travelling through Bechuanaland the train came to a sudden juddering halt where it remained for at least an hour, perhaps longer. There was no explanation from the train crew as there was no public address system throughout the train. Looking out of the train windows did not offer any possible

Bundu, the Beat & Beyond

explanation. Eventually the train began its slow progress and we eventually arrived at the spot where the front steam engine had stopped. I was amazed to see the half body of an elephant lying just to one side of the track. I assume that the other half was on the opposite side. It appears that the train had hit the elephant as it crossed the railway line at the exact moment the train was passing. The elephant came off second best in that contest.

At Johannesburg we were normally met by the School Governor (and owner) Mr Royce-Shewring who drove us at breakneck speeds in his huge American green and white Oldsmobile which impressed us no end. The 30 miles or so from Johannesburg to Meyerton normally took only 20 minutes or so depending on the traffic conditions. This was quite quick when you bear in mind that there were no motorways in those days.

Broadlands was quite a small school and catered for only 200 boys of all ages from 5 years of age to 18. As I was 14 at the time I started in Standard 7 whereas my brother, Chris, who was just 10, started in Standard 4. Our teachers were a mixed bunch with a variety of differing abilities and character. The Head Teacher was Mr John Holman who was quite a strict disciplinarian and canings were a weekly occurrence for a variety of infractions. His teaching ability seemed very sound and he did encourage the senior boys under his tutelage to study hard as well as play hard at sports.

The school was a microcosm of Apartheid South Africa in which the majority of the pupils and teaching staff were white but we did have a number of Chinese and Japanese students who boarded with us because apparently, due to the crazy race laws applicable at the time, they were classed as being white. What I can say is that all the students seemed to get along very well together irrespective of race or ethnic background. One of my Chinese classmates was Poi Yin Ming with whom I got along very well.

One of the older Prefects in Standard 10 was a Japanese boy called Johnny Wai who was an extrovert character with a larger than life personality. He was very popular.

21

John LLOYD

Our Head boy at the time was a South African named Vincent Van Buuren who seemed to excel at anything he did. He was a first class student and excelled at Soccer and cricket. More importantly he was a really nice young man and always had the time to talk to anyone irrespective of their age or status. After leaving school he went to University and after graduating he did his National Service in the South African Air Force but was sadly killed in a flying accident whilst operating a Harvard Trainer which was used by the SAAF at that time.

School lessons began early in the morning just after breakfast but were finished for the day around 1.30pm and so after lunch we were free to indulge ourselves in any of the many sports activities available. The school punched well above its weight in sporting terms when you consider the relatively few boys available for selection. We put out teams at all age levels between 12-18 in Soccer, cricket, hockey, Athletics, water polo and tennis. We also teamed up with the girls from a Convent in the nearby town of Vereeniging to compete in the areas local swimming galas.

We did our homework in our classrooms immediately after dinner during the early evening for a period of an hour or so.

I met Gavin Bosse when I started at Broadlands. He was my age and in the same class. We took an instant liking to each other and he always invited me home at week-ends whenever possible. He lived with his parents in a very elegant apartment in the then stylish suburb of Johannesburg called Hillbrow and Gavin was always very good at introducing me to his friends and showing me the sights of J'oburg. His father, Claude, had been a paratrooper during the war and now worked as a Schools Inspector whilst Gavin's mother, Joan, was the manageress of a high end ladies fashion shop in the centre of Jo'burg. I was introduced to the wonderful world of drive-in cinemas which were a novelty for me. The one I remember had been built on the top of a mine dump (mine waste). These mine dumps were huge and covered many acres of land. Drive in cinemas were such a novelty because this was well before the days of Videos and DVD's. Television was not introduced in South Africa until the mid 1970's so the experience of a family driving to a drive in cinema and parking up whilst viewing the latest films and eating

Bundu, the Beat & Beyond

a meal of Hamburgers and fries (or whatever you chose from the cinemas restaurant) was very popular.

I maintained contact with Gavin long after we left school when he had become an Officer in the SA Air Force flying Mirage fast jets and later becoming a pilot with South African Airways where I met up with him again some years hence.

Being schoolboys we often got up to schoolboy pranks and adventures. These included scaling out of our first floor dormitories around 0100 hrs using homemade rope ladders and making our way into the plantation of gum trees adjacent to the school where we would light a small fire and have our own unofficial Braai (BBQ) cooking our portions of Boerewors and consuming bottles of coke purchased from the village of Meyerton the previous afternoon. Eventually the school Authorities discovered what was going on and later had burglar bars fitted to the dormitories to keep out unwanted visitors but we all knew that the real reason was to keep us in.

We also conducted the occasional night time raids on another private boarding school called Longwood House, located about a mile away through those very same woods, which was a mixed school of boys and girls. These raids were not malicious but we did cause sufficient noise to awaken the sleepy residents and on one occasion we "borrowed" the Longwood House School bell and had it inscribed "Broadlands Raid 1963" after which the bell was returned to Longwood house. As far as I know there was never any official reaction from the staff or pupils at Longwood House and our raids were never reciprocated which perhaps says more about the lack of sprit or daring amongst the pupils of that school. (or perhaps they had better things to do at night but that is speculation).

Overall I really enjoyed my 4 years at Broadlands interspersed with the lengthy, but enjoyable, train journeys to and from home in Northern Rhodesia. The long school holidays gave us a chance to renew our relationship with Mum & Dad as well as catching up with friends in Kitwe like Frances, Chris & Wendy Turner, Michael Hall and Peter Kemp who later joined us as a pupil at Broadlands.

23

John LLOYD

I cannot remember exactly when but it may have been in 1962 during one holiday period I accompanied Michael Hall and his friend Diana Stock to a local Social Club Hall in Kitwe where we thoroughly enjoyed an evening of live Rock n' Roll as performed by Mickie Most and his Playboys who played mostly covers of Buddy Holly songs which I really loved at that time. In years to come Mickie Most went on to become one of the UK's foremost music producers and impresarios. Sadly he died in 2003.

Both Chris and I knew that Mum and Dad had made quite a financial sacrifice in sending us to Boarding School but I know that they were happy to do it. It is something that I will always be grateful for because the overall education and experiences we enjoyed did prepare us well for adulthood and certainly taught us a good degree of independence, sufficient for us to stand on our own two feet.

In 1961 I went on a school trip to the Drakensburg Mountains in South Africa to a place called Mont Aux Sources which had been part of the location where the film Zulu had just finished being filmed. It was a spectacularly beautiful region and if you have seen the film you will know exactly what I mean.

South Africa is sometimes called "The world in one country" and there is a lot of truth in that assertion. There is such a wide variety of different scenery and experiences to enjoy.

In 1962 my father had bought a very new Austin Cambridge car with a very small short gear stick, very ahead of its time then. As a family we drove to the port of Beira on the Indian Ocean which was then part of Portuguese East Africa (Mozambique). After spending a few days there enjoying the sun, sea and sand, our car was loaded onto the Union Castle liner called "Rhodesia Castle "(I didn't know that Rhodesia had a Castle) and we then boarded the ship where we had a comfortable cabin (they were called cabins in those days and not staterooms). The ship then set sail on a southerly course heading down the east coast of Africa.

I met a young girl on board who was the same age as me. Her family had embarked at the Kenyan port of Mombasa and were emigrating to South

Bundu, the Beat & Beyond

Africa. We got along very well but it proved to be a very short friendship as she and her family disembarked at the South African port of Durban some days later. I don't know why this short liaison stuck in my mind. I cannot even remember her name but I do know that we got along very well.

Before reaching Durban the ship stopped at the capital city of Portuguese East Africa called Lourenco Marques (now Maputo) where we stayed for a day or so. I remember that my brother, Chris, was a very keen fisherman then and he joined a few crew members fishing for small sharks at the stern of the ship. They did catch some whilst Chris, using only a line, a hook, and some bread as bait, caught a large amount of Mackerel which the seamen used as bait whilst fishing for the larger sharks. Chris did have a very enjoyable day though and I can still remember the joy on his face during that day. It was almost like he had reached fisherman's heaven.

After Lourenco Marques we sailed for Durban where I said farewell to my young friend and after that we sailed to Port Elizabeth before finally sailing into Cape Town where we all disembarked and our car was off-loaded. Our parents were continuing this holiday by driving from Cape Town back to Northern Rhodesia via the Garden Route and Johannesburg. In the meantime it was time for Chris and I to return to school so we were put onto the overnight train to Jo'burg, a thousand miles to the north, where we were met by school transport and taken to school. The train journey took about 24 hours.

A couple of weeks later our parents drove into the school to meet the Governor, Mr Royce-Shewring and Mr Holman, the headmaster. I assume that they were discussing the progress of their "boys ". In the meantime our car was the subject of much interest from many of the other school boys who greatly admired this state of the art vehicle.

This was also the year of the Cuban missile crisis when, during October and November 1962 the world held its breath whilst the two super powers, Russia and the USA, went head to head in a diplomatic and military stand-off when Russia threatened to place nuclear weapons on Cuba just 90 miles from the US Coast. Even at our young age I can

John LLOYD

recall being able to appreciate the potential dangers this situation held and it was the main topic of conversation amongst the senior part of the school. I think that we all issued a collective sigh of relief when Prime Minister Krushchev blinked first and backed down thereby averting what could have turned into a nuclear war.

I played a lot of sport at Broadlands including soccer (I lacked technical ability in soccer but was very enthusiastic), hockey, water polo, competitive swimming, athletics and cricket. I enjoyed all these sports very much and, apart from soccer, I played to quite a reasonable standard although the good weather enhanced that experience. I played hockey for the school 1st team and cricket for both the school 1st and 2nd teams. We played in the Transvaal schools league as well as friendly matches. I represented the school at water polo and our team was so well regarded that we were invited to represent the nearby town of Vereeniging as their junior team which saw us play a variety of sides in the Transvaal.

Also in 1962 the double winning side of the 61/62 season in England, Tottenham Hotspur, came out and toured South Africa playing their wonderful style of soccer which amazed and entranced all the football fans in South Africa. I have followed "Spurs" since that time.

During 1963 and 1964 I became friendly with another class mate called Geoff Du Preez who lived in Pretoria. Geoff was then the South African Junior roller-skating champion and some week-ends he took me home with him where I stayed with his family in their large house in a suburb called Arcadia. On at least one occasion during the week-end breaks we would visit his local roller-skating rink which was a motor garage during the week but somehow converted into a skating rink at week-ends. Geoff really was a talented roller-skater and whilst I could skate reasonably well I was not at all in his class.

It was at this roller-skating rink that we heard the dreadful news of the assassination of President JF. Kennedy on 23 November 1963. That news shocked and stunned us all.

In my last year at Broadlands I was selected to play for a Transvaal State Schools Water Polo team at the Maccabi Games held in Johannesburg

Bundu, the Beat & Beyond

in 1964. I do not remember the score but I know that we did beat the Maccabi side by quite a margin and I even managed to score a couple of goals.

I matriculated at the end of 1964, left school and returned to Northern Rhodesia which had, by now, achieved independence from the UK and had been re-named Zambia. Chris stayed on at Broadlands but left in 1965 after encountering some internal school problems. He transferred as a Boarder to the General Smuts High School in Vereeniging where he remained for his last few years at school.

I had left school with no idea of what I wanted to do with my life. University was not an option as it was very expensive and so I had to get a job upon my return to Kitwe. My good friend, Chris Turner, worked with a company called S.K.F. (Svenska Kullager Fabriken) which produced and retailed a large variety of Ball and Roller bearings used in heavy and light industry. SKF had a base in Kitwe and Chris arranged to get me an interview with the Boss, Peter Bluett, as a vacancy had arisen. Good timing for me.

I started at SKF as a stock controller/counter jumper. This meant that I was responsible for maintaining adequate stock levels of a huge variety of Ball and Roller bearings which were used in the Mines and heavy industry etc. The stock had to be ordered from our parent Company in Sweden and normally took 2-3 months to arrive by sea and rail. I found this challenging work as it was a continual juggling act trying to ensure that we had sufficient stock to cater for immediate and medium terms orders as well as trying to predict our future needs. Generally I was reasonably successful at this but occasionally we would have a run on some bearing such as CRL52's (a giant bearing only required on an occasional basis). In these circumstances I would try and obtain the required bearing from our sister company in Salisbury, Southern Rhodesia, and if that failed I might have to arrange one of these monster bearings to be airfreighted at huge cost from Sweden. I was also responsible for all the counter sales which put me right in the front line whilst meeting people from all walks of life but mainly Engineers etc and so I had to develop, in reasonable quick time, the ability to talk at their level about matters which I had little or no knowledge. It got better in time.

John LLOYD

By then I had purchased an MGA white sports car with a convertible soft top. Chris Turner had a hard top version in red. This was my first ever car and I loved driving this around town and being a sports car it was real fun.

The annual Agricultural Shows were very popular with local residents and were held at the Kitwe Show Grounds on the outskirts of town. In addition to the usual agricultural and animal exhibits and displays these shows also offered a variety of other displays and shows including gigs by local amateur Pop Groups. I recall one particular group from Kitwe who called themselves "The Planets" performing at this show one year and putting in a creditable set of Rolling Stones material including "Paint it Black". I did have an acoustic guitar at that time and was able to pick out some chords and tunes with reasonable accuracy such as "Guitar Boogie" as made famous by Bert Weedon who was a renowned Guitarist in the UK during the 50's and 60's. I did not have any formal guitar lessons which was really my undoing as I was unable to progress a lot further from the fairly basic level I did achieve.

Sport always played a big part in most people's lives on the Copper belt as it did in most parts of southern Africa. Rugby was the winter game played by most of the white males whereas soccer was a game played mostly by the African population. There were two rugby teams in Nkana who were very close rivals and games between these two sides attracted large crowds to watch them slug it out. These teams were the Diggers and the Pirates who played to a very high standard. I remember being in the audience watching several of these games delighting in the standard of their play which was heightened by the intense rivalry between the two sides.

My parents had obtained an Alsatian dog by this time who we called Kim. He had a lovely personality but was also a very handy guard dog if necessary. I would frequently take him in my MG and drive to the edge of town where we would enjoy lengthy walks into the Bundu (bush) during which he had a fantastic time running here, there and everywhere taking in all the sights, sounds and smells which dogs find so vitally interesting. On reflection we were, perhaps, fortunate, not to have encountered any wild animals or snakes which were then in abundant

Bundu, the Beat & Beyond

supply. We did see snakes around our household gardens on occasion and I recall one particular afternoon when my mother was cultivating her small vegetable and flower garden at the rear of our house when she was disturbed by a quick rustling sound at her feet at which point she looked down at the ground in time to see a very large snake (not further identified) slither quickly past her and strike at a nearby frog about three feet away from her. My mother was normally a calm person but I think she got a bit of a fright on this occasion.

In 1964 the Federation of Rhodesia and Nyasaland was broken up and Northern Rhodesia officially became Zambia on the 24th October 1964 and whose first President was Dr Kenneth Kaunda. At first the remaining white population was a little nervous as to how things might change but under the President's stewardship it was a fairly seamless changeover and matters continued much as they had before.

I had continued my sports activities when I returned to Kitwe after leaving school, playing hockey initially for Kitwe Playing Fields 2nd eleven in a domestic league, I normally played on the right wing and had the occasional run outs with the first team. I suppose my big achievement came in 1965 when I was selected to play for the Zambian national Under 21 side against Egypt. This game was played at a nearby town called Luanshya and we came out on top by three goals to one and I somehow contrived to cut in from the wing and score a goal in the second half.

I also joined the Kitwe Badminton Club where I played to a reasonable club level with my friend Chris Turner. I found this to be a very sociable game and I met some lovely members during my time there including a married lady with the wonderful name of Ida Boosey. Ida had a really outgoing personality and was full of fun. I later realised that she ran a shop, just opposite the SKF premises where I worked, selling velocettes (small motorised scooters).

Also in 1965 Ian Smith the Prime Minister of Southern Rhodesia proclaimed Unilateral declaration of Independence (U.D.I.) from the UK. This caused international consternation and there was some talk of the UK Military invading Rhodesia to restore the status quo. Thankfully

John LLOYD

this never happened but the UK government did send a squadron of RAF Fighter jets to Zambia where they were based in Lusaka. Fortunately they were never used in anger against the Rhodesian Forces. The UK and other governments also initiated economic sanctions against the Rhodesian regime including an oil embargo. The oil embargo had a direct impact on Zambia because all our oil was imported via the rail links through Rhodesia. As a result petrol was in very short supply and was rationed. The normal motorists like me only received a few gallons of petrol a month which really meant that I had to all but cease using my MGA. However my friend Chris Turner and I did resolve to find a solution to this issue by having a tandem pedal cycle made up in the SKF workshops from two old cycles. This worked quite well and Chris and I used this contraption to cycle to and from work. We even made the top Zambia newspaper, the Northern News, which featured our picture astride the tandem and a short piece of narrative attached.

SKF entered a team in a Hockey tournament open to all local businesses in the Copperbelt which was played at Kitwe Playing Fields. Chris Turner and his girlfriend (later wife) Marsha, were part of the team and Marsha had invited her close friend Caroline along to play for the SKF side. Caroline lived in a town called Chingola (about 40 miles away in the direction of the Congo border) and when we met there was an instant attraction and before I knew it we were going out together. We got on really well but because we lived so far apart we could only see each other most weekends.

It was late on a Sunday evening at the end of one of these week-ends when I was driving the 40 miles or so back from Chingola to Kitwe that my old MGA failed me and broke down about half way home. The night sky was quite black and there was little or no ambient light as I was quite literally in the middle of nowhere. This was well before the days of mobile 'phones and there were no public telephones located on this road. My only hope lay in the occasional passing motorist. After about an hour or so with no passing traffic I managed to flag down a driver who was travelling from Chingola to Mufulira. The town of Mufulira was not on my way home but the driver kindly offered to telephone my home and try and raise some help for me. My mother was at home but my father was away at the time.

Bundu, the Beat & Beyond

About two hours later I was really relieved to see a car approaching from the direction of Kitwe which stopped and out got one of my mother's work colleagues, Roger Hampson, who lived next door to Mr & Mrs Glazier. After securing my car as best we could, Roger kindly drove me home where I got to bed around 0300hrs, tired but relieved that I had got home safely.

I arranged for my car to be collected the next day and fortunately it was still in one piece and had not been vandalised or worse. It was towed back to the SKF workshops where one of the Engineers who was also a qualified motor mechanic diagnosed that a "con-rod" had broken and had gone crashing through the crank case. This meant a new engine. This was expensive but my engineer friend managed to find me a re-conditioned second hand engine which I could afford and he very kindly spent two week-ends removing the broken engine and replacing it with the re-conditioned one.

My relationship with Caroline ended soon after this.

I had always maintained my good friendship with Frances and we became quite close in the months after that. I was only 19 at the time and the thought of a serious long term relationship had not really entered my head. Frances and I had always got on really well together and we had so many shared interests. She, by this time, was studying to become a teacher at a college in Bulawayo and when she came home for holiday breaks I would drive my MGA to N'dola to collect her from the train station and drive her home to Nkana thereby saving her several hours on the somewhat tortuous train journey. I think that the train used to arrive at N'dola around 6am or so and we would be back at her home well before 7am where her Mum usually supplied a hearty breakfast. My Mother drove passed the Glazier's house on her way to work just before 7am and often remarked that I must have flown from N'dola to Kitwe. It was her gentle way of telling me to drive slower, I suppose.

In mid 1966 I decided that I wanted to travel to the UK in order to take a course in English Law with a view to following in my father's footsteps in the legal profession. It was hard leaving my parents and Frances but I knew that this was something I had to do.

John LLOYD

I had sufficient savings to buy my one way air ticket from N'dola to London and fund my courses but my big regrets were having to sell my beloved MGA sports car and leaving Frances. My Dad had generously agreed to give me a monthly living allowance for the duration of the 2 year course which was really decent of him.

I made some fond farewells and left Frances my sizeable collection of 60's records as I knew that she would appreciate the music and look after them as best she could. I flew from N'dola on a Zambian Airways DC8 (leased from AliItalia) to London via Rome. I was met at Heathrow by my mother (who was in UK on a short holiday) together with her best friend Ann. I was introduced to Watneys Red Barrel which I did not take to and thought it was very watery compared to the Castle Lager I had been used to in Africa.

In 1967 Frances flew to the UK for a holiday during a break from her Teachers Training College in Bulawayo, Southern Rhodesia. She stayed with her Aunt Monica in Brookwood where I visited her and we enjoyed a fond reunion. She reminded me recently that it was snowing at this time and very cold. I also met her again in London where we enjoyed the normal sightseeing tour visiting St Pauls Cathedral with its whispering gallery and Carnaby Street then at the peak of iconic 60's fashion. She had just turned 21 in the September and she returned to Africa to resume her last year of Teacher Training in 1968.

CHAPTER 2

College and joining the Police

I had arrived in the UK in September 1966 just after England had won the World Cup and I found it to be very different to the life and society that I had grown up with.

My Mum had arranged digs for me with a Mr & Mrs Parrott in the village of Hassocks in Sussex. They were a very friendly couple and did all they could to make me welcome. Mr Parrott was a retired Metropolitan Police Officer who was then working as Chief Security Officer for Miles Aviation at Shoreham Airport.

The only college in the Brighton area offering the subjects I wished to study was, curiously enough, Brighton Technical College and it was there just near the Level in Brighton that I commenced my studies in the General Principles of English Law and The British Constitution.

I found English civil law very dry and dull and the thoughts of civil torts etc did not excite my interest overly much. I found the course on the British Constitution (unwritten in case you were wondering) a great deal more interesting.

After a few months I arranged to leave Mr & Mrs Parrott and move in with a student friend, Paul Nicholls, who lived with his parents and younger sister in the Sussex coastal town of Seaford. I joined Seaford Hockey Club and played for their first team during the 1967/68 season. However I found that playing on the soft, muddy, uneven pitches of England a very different prospect from the dry, hard, flat pitches we enjoyed in Central Africa. I have retained a fixture card from Seaford

John LLOYD

& Blatchington Hockey Club for the 1967-68 season and I see that we played a total of 29 matches in the Sussex area winning 13, losing 10 and drawing 6. Three matches were cancelled due to weather or waterlogged pitches and we also played against a team from Cheltenham which we won 2-0 and a team called Sphinx Hockey Club from Coventry which we also won 2-1. Fairly average perhaps?

I had become (and still am) an avid supporter of Brighton & Hove Albion Football team and I remember attending my first game at the old Goldstone Ground in Hove which was a night match against First Division Coventry City in the League Cup. The game ended in a 1-1 draw but I was hooked and during my college days I did manage to see most of their home games even though they were then in the old third division.

The Nicholls moved from Seaford to the ancient village of Alfriston and I moved along with them. They had bought a three bedroomed flint stone cottage with a delightful garden. Paul and I shared a bedroom which we decorated in our own unique style with a copy of an Aubrey Beardsley print which we painted directly onto one of the bedroom walls. I am not sure just how much his parents appreciated that but I do not remember them making any direct comment.

Paul and I shared many happy times together and we visited his girlfriend, Margaret, at her parent's home in Peacehaven most week-ends. They did not seem to mind me tagging along with them when we went out at night and we got along very well together. The three of us even took a holiday together when we drove up to Edinburgh via Gretna Green. Paul and Margaret married a couple of years later and I was his Best Man. They still live happily in Seaford today.

Whilst at College I attended a couple of lively social events organised by the Students Union of the nearby Sussex University. One was at the University main hall in Falmer and was a concert given by the legendary Chuck Berry. I remember standing in the queue outside the main entrance to the hall when I turned round to look behind me in time to see none other than Chuck Berry himself walking towards the entrance with his uncovered guitar slung over his shoulder. There were no airs or graces with Chuck. He just seemed like one of the lads and had no

Bundu, the Beat & Beyond

pretensions even though he was an internationally renowned rock star at the time. His concert was just sublime.

The other occasion was a much grander affair organised as part of Rag Week and called the Rag Ball. It was held in the very large Brighton Centre and I would estimate that there were about two thousand students in attendance to dance to and appreciate the music of two live groups, The Spencer Davis Group and Geno Washington and his Ram Jam Band. A very memorable occasion for me.

I finished my college course after 2 years by which time I really knew that I did not want to spend every day cooped up in a solicitor's office so I looked around and decided that I could use my basic legal knowledge as well as having a more active job by joining the Police Force. I applied to Sussex Constabulary (as it was then) sometime late in 1968 at which time I was living with my Nan in Eastworth Road, Chertsey. My application took many months to process because all my references were located in Zambia which slowed the process down to a slow crawl.

Having established that there would be a significant delay in my Police application I managed to obtain a local job in Chertsey with a firm called CCL Ltd working in their accounts department. I was engaged in general book-keeping which I found reasonably easy as I had done a course in Book-keeping whilst at Broadlands so the general principles were no stranger to me. I did find the work fairly dull and monotonous but the routine was spiced up a little by our Office Manager, a quite elderly gentleman, whose name was Dudley. Dudley had a very engaging and lively personality and considered himself something of a ladies man even at his advanced age (he must have been approaching 70 or so). His attempts at chatting up all the youngish female staff in the Accounts Office was always worth at least a smile but give them their due all the ladies seemed to treat him as quite harmless and gave back as good as he gave them. Being the only other male in this department gave me the opportunity to witness these antics on a daily basis which were good entertainment value.

In early 1969 I received a letter inviting me to attend Police HQ at Malling House in Lewes for an interview. I duly attended at the given

John LLOYD

time and date and was interviewed by the Deputy Chief Constable, George Terry. (Later Sir George Terry who later became the Chief Constable of the newly named Sussex Police).

I found Mr Terry to be no nonsense straight talking man with an engaging and affable nature. The interview seemed to go quite well I thought and it ended with Mr Terry offering me a position with Sussex Constabulary as a Police Officer, subject to a satisfactory medical. I accepted immediately and after the interview concluded I was ushered into the presence of the Force Medical Officer whose name I do not recall.

The medical examination did not last very long and seemed to me to be fairly perfunctory. I had the impression that as long as I had four working limbs and could see and hear okay then that was all that was required. Needless to say, I passed the medical and was in. I was then just 22 years of age which, in fact, was older than the minimum joining age for the Police at that time which was 19.

I returned to Chertsey and awaited a date and joining instructions from the Police. This duly arrived and I was asked to present myself at Lewes Police Station on the 1st April 1969 (who was the fool?).

I was to spend 2 weeks at Lewes pending the commencement of my initial Training course at Sandgate in Kent which was to last 13 weeks.

I handed in my notice at CCL Ltd who had been very good to me. I was taking a 50% pay cut so I didn't join the Police for the money. At 0900hrs on the 1st April I presented myself at Lewes Police Station. I was wearing a civilian suit and tie as I had yet to be issued with my uniform. I had, however, purchased a set of Military style boots which I had polished and bulled up as best I could and intended to wear them with my uniform.

I was directed to an Inspector Jeff Green, a uniformed Officer, who was responsible for the running of the prosecution department at Lewes. I assisted him, at his direction, with reviewing various criminal and traffic prosecution files.

Bundu, the Beat & Beyond

Two other new joiners started at this time, Angela Livingstone and Bob Batey. Later I got to know Bob quite well.

During this 2 week period I was also issued with my uniform at Lewes HQ Clothing store. This comprised a heavy winter uniform tunic and trousers and a lighter weight summer issue. In addition I was given a helmet and a flat cap, a couple of black ties, white cotton gloves (for ceremonial occasions I was told) and half a dozen cotton collarless blue shirts plus attachable collars. These collars were attached to the shirt by means of two brass studs. One at the back of the neck and one at the front of the throat. They were quite different to anything I had ever worn before and I did not find them overly comfortable. I was also issued with a large raincoat and a cape which I thought looked very smart indeed but I did not wear the cape very often.

I was also issued with a wooden truncheon complete with a leather strap fitted at the top. The truncheon slipped very easily into a specially designed long pocket of the uniform trousers just to the side of the normal trouser pocket. I never had occasion to use this in anger but it was sometimes a useful tool for making a forced entry into premises or for dispatching animals which had been badly injured after being hit by a vehicle.

My Nan insisted that I spend my weekends with her which was lovely and she further insisted that I bring my uniform home and show it off to her. I duly did this and posed for a few photographs in her back garden. At the side of her back garden was a narrow lane leading from Eastworth Road to a graveyard at the rear of her house. Whilst I was posing for these photographs a man poked his head over the garden fence and thinking that I was a fully qualified Police Officer he asked if I would assist him in getting the funeral cortege and vehicles out of the lane and back onto Eastworth Road.

What could I do but agree? I somewhat nervously stepped out into the middle of Eastworth Road wearing my uniform for the first time whilst knowing that I was not only untrained but that I was a Sussex Officer "working" in Surrey which had its own Police Force. I managed to wave my arms about with reasonable authority and was somewhat amazed

John LLOYD

when the traffic actually stopped at my command whilst I was nervously hoping that a real Surrey Officer or Police vehicle would not happen by. The funeral cortege emerged from the lane and went on its way and the traffic was permitted to resume its business by one very relieved rookie. I had got away with it.

Sometime during these two weeks, Angela, Bob and I were taken to Lewes Magistrates Court where we took the Queens Oath and were sworn in as Police Constables. I was assigned the warrant number of AL605. The letter A denotes that I am male, L is the first letter of my surname and 605 was my warrant number. Female Officers were given the warrant number beginning with the letter B followed by the first letter of their surname so Angela's warrant number began BL followed by three numbers. This was a system unique to Sussex I believe.

I also spent a couple of days during those two weeks as an Observer in a Lewes town Panda Car driven by an experienced PC whose name, I think, was Colin McKenzie. I was quite excited at the prospect but also somewhat nervous at the same time as I did not know quite what to expect.

The reality was a bit of a let-down as all I remember us being called to was a stray cow which had wandered onto the main road leading from Lewes town to Malling House Police HQ. We did our best to calm the animal and herd it away from the traffic before the farmer arrived to reclaim his errant beast.

Surely there must be better things for us to be involved with? There were, but more of that later.

I also accompanied Inspector Jeff Green to Uckfield Magistrates Court on one of these days where he was prosecuting the list of offences up for that day before the local Magistrates. Most of the matters were fairly routine Traffic cases but one case sticks in my mind involving a young, very attractive, blonde woman, no more than a girl really, who had been charged with prostitution related offences. This really opened my somewhat naïve mind as I could not understand why such an attractive young lady should be associated with prostitution. The explanation was quite simple and yet brutal. She had got in with a new boy-friend with whom she was besotted and he introduced her to the delights of cocaine and heroin so much so that she had become an addict. She had been forced by her so called boyfriend to prostitute herself in order to pay for the drugs and supply a cut to her boyfriend who was no better than a pimp. Welcome to the real world.

After two weeks of relative routine calm I made my way to Number 6 District Police Training School at Sandgate in Kent. I arrived late on a Sunday afternoon in time for me to be shown to my dormitory shared with three other men. I unpacked all my belongings and uniform just in time for dinner.

Sandgate was a large former country mansion house and was quite well suited to the function of training new Police recruits. It had a large parade ground on which we learned to march in the Police style. Our drill Instructor was a former Royal Marine who was now an Officer with Kent County Constabulary. His name was Sgt Pond and he drilled our squad relentlessly on a daily basis for an hour or so before we adjourned for classroom lessons.

Sandgate had extensive grounds and located just behind the main building was a very high hill which we called "The Hill". Part of our daily physical exercise involved running up and down "The Hill" This was very challenging but most of us survived the ordeal.

My course colleagues were from all the South East region forces of Surrey, Sussex, Kent and Hampshire. I got on well with most of them as they were a sociable crowd and always up for a laugh once lessons had finished for the day.

The Sussex contingent included John Minall, John Daniels, Keith Bray, Bob Batey and a man called Dave Roseblade who was later sacked after having been featured in a News of the World newspaper article involving wife swapping and other sexual adventures.

It was here at Sandgate that I learned the theory of all the relevant laws that I needed to know about. They were divided into three broad categories of General Police Duties, Traffic and Crime.

John LLOYD

I found General Police Duties (GPD) quite interesting, Crime very interesting but Traffic rules and regulations left me cold even though I knew that they were important. For example the Construction & Use regulations was a vital bit of legislation but trying to learn all the relevant weights of differing vehicle types etc really eluded me.

We were supplied with a small buff coloured booklet in which were printed all the relevant definitions a Police Officer would need to know. I, as well as many of my colleagues, managed to learn these by rote which helped later in examinations

We were taught all the rudiments of criminal, traffic and general law together with practical exercises and report writing. The main reference book was called Moriarty's Police Law. It made for very dry reading but it was full of useful and relevant information.

There was a little bit of scandal whilst I was at Sandgate as one of the Senior Students was allegedly having an affair with the Commandants wife which I thought was either extremely brave or extremely foolish. The Commandant was a Chief Superintendent from Kent County Constabulary and his wife appeared to be somewhat younger than he and quite attractive. I do not know just how this matter ended but I suspect if came to a natural conclusion when the Senior student finished his course and returned to his home force.

There was one other item of note from my time at Sandgate. In one of the other dormitories was a man whose nickname was Zebedee (after the magic roundabout character). Apparently Zebedee had some aversion to water and washing with the inevitable result that he suffered with very poor hygiene and body odour. This was obviously to the detriment of his room-mates. At first they tried encouraging him to wash, shower and/or bath but to no avail. They then sat him down and pointed out the error of his ways. This had no effect. Finally after a few weeks they had had enough and took matters into their own hands. They and some other students isolated Zebedee, stripped him of his clothing and marched him into the shower block where he was unceremoniously washed and scrubbed from head to toe with soap and water. Zebedee did not come back for a repeat performance and we were told that he did, from then

Bundu, the Beat & Beyond

on, make an effort to stay clean and less smelly to the satisfaction of his room-mates.

One man of note on my course was called Gary Julian from Surrey Police who had previously been an Officer with the British South African Police (BSAP) in Rhodesia. He and I had quite a bit in common in view of our respective backgrounds. At that time the BSAP were engaged, together with the Rhodesian Security Forces, in a counter insurgency war against Black terrorists trying to infiltrate that country from Zambia and Mozambique. They say that one man's terrorist is another man's freedom fighter and so it was in Rhodesia. Gary showed me some photographs taken by the BSAP in the bundu (bush) some of which were quite shocking. Let there be no mistake this was a very nasty little war and one in which a great number of people were killed or maimed. I did not keep in touch with Gary after we left Sandgate but some years later I learned that he had left the Police and had re-trained as a Barrister. Indeed I came across his name many years later when he was head of the Extradition Section of the International Crown Prosecution Service in London.

One of the requirements for Police in those days was that you were expected to have the ability to swim and save lives, if required. This was especially relevant for those Forces which had a coastline. Accordingly we spent one period per week in the local indoor swimming pool during which time I qualified for my Bronze Medal Certificate in Lifesaving. On the 1st of May it was deemed as being summer and we switched to the open air pool which was absolutely freezing.

At the end of thirteen weeks I successfully passed the course and passed out with most of my colleagues. We had a passing out parade at which the Band of the Royal Marines played their wonderful music to which we marched up and down the parade ground for the benefit of the wives, sweethearts and families of the students who were watching from the grandstand and side-lines.

During my time at Sandgate my Force had contacted me to inform me that my initial posting was to be to Hove. I was quite delighted with this news as I knew that Hove (next door to Brighton) was a busy station with a variety of differing Policing problems.

CHAPTER 3

On the Beat

I had been assigned digs with an elderly lady who lived in Hangleton, Hove. The digs were very comfortable and my landlady was very kindly and understanding. The only slight difficulty was that Hangleton is nearly an hours walk to Holland Road, Hove where the Police Station was located. This was not normally an issue during the day or evening as I could get a bus but on early turn I had to report to the Station no later than 0545 in time for the days briefing and there were no buses from Hangleton to Holland Road at that time of the morning. Later I was able to get a lift from one of my shift mates, Mal Pepper, who also lived in Hangleton and had a Mk1 Ford Cortina.

I presented myself at Hove Police Station in Holland Road at 0900 hrs on a July Monday morning as directed. I was ushered into the office of Chief Superintendent Lou Weeding the Commander at Hove Sub Division. He welcomed me to Hove and told me that my services were needed because the Police were under strength and were in need of all the help they could get.

The Sussex area was divided into separate Operational Divisions or areas. Brighton was E division subdivided into two sub divisions. Hove was the sub-divisional Station for D Division which also included Shoreham and Lancing. Hove was therefore designated as DH or Delta Hotel whilst Shoreham was DS or Delta Sierra.

Police pay was very poor in 1969 and I remember that my first monthly pay cheque was for £50 which was less than half of what I had been earning at CCL Ltd. I was never going to be rich but there was sufficient

Bundu, the Beat & Beyond

to pay for my digs and food which left me with just enough to pay for social occasions, clothing and the like.

In those days the Uniform Officers were divided into four Sections (or columns). Each Section had its own designation ie: A, B, C & D. I was assigned to C Section at Hove.

After meeting with C/Supt Weeding I met my Section Inspector, Ernie Ewens, who had previously been an Inspector of Police in Cyprus during the EOKA civil war in that country and prior to that had been with the British Police in Palestine when Britain held the mandate before it became part of Israel.

He was a very affable man and made me most welcome. I then met my two Section Sergeants. Bill Adams was one of them. He was an ex-military type (in common with many Police Officers at that time who had joined just after World War 2 in 1945/6.

I met most of my fellow PC's on C section including, Mick Russell, Chris Candler, Peter (Conky) Moore, John Bartlett, Chris Cooper, Ron Chillingworth, Malcolm Pepper, Terry Chinchin, Bert Jennings, Terry Clothier, Dick Starnes, Dick Viner, Dennis Johnson, John Packham, Geoff Stafford and several others whose names elude me as I write.

In the months to come I was joined on C section by other new recruits including John Bishop, Tony Baker and Andy Fogden.

You may have noticed that all these names are male and that female names are noticeable by their absence. In those days there was a Policewoman's Department which operated quite separately from the male Uniform Sections. They dealt exclusively with child issues, missing children and similar problems as well as being used as "Matrons" who looked after any female prisoners in the cell block at Hove. They worked different hours and only received 9/10's of a male Officers salary because, over a calendar month, they worked less hours than the men.

The Officer in charge of the Policewomen at Hove was a Sgt Gloria Kevis who, years later, changed her name to Geoffrey. Gloria was a

John LLOYD

competent Officer and seemed to operate an efficient department. The other Women Officers I recall from that period at Hove were Maggie Phillips, Jan Prior, Wendy Cowie, Jackie Barnes and Val Brenchley.

Without exception my Section colleagues made me feel welcome and I was assigned to shadow Mick Russell who was to be my tutor Constable for six weeks or so. I remain indebted to Mick who was a good practical Copper and he taught me a great deal of basic Police work which I had not been taught at Sandgate. At that time we used Morris Minor "Panda" Cars as Beat patrol vehicles to supplement the Foot Officers on each beat. The Morris Minor or Moggie Minors as they were affectionately known were splendid cars and although they would never win a speed race they were ultra-reliable even with the pounding they took from my colleagues.

After the six week period with Mick I spent a further two weeks acting as Observer on the General Purpose Patrol Car (GP car). The GP car was not restricted to any one beat area but could patrol anywhere within the Hove Divisional boundaries. It was normally double crewed by a driver and an observer who operated the car radio and generally tried to keep his eyes open for anything of note. The Observer was also responsible for operating the Blue Lights and two tone horns during an emergency. These were known as "Blues & Twos".

One notable incident I remember from my 2 weeks on the GP car was during a set of night duties when a car failed to stop in response to our requests which resulted in a frantic car chase all over the Mile Oak and Portslade area of the Hove division. I put in a call for assistance from other mobile units in the area and some considerable time later the errant vehicle was finally stopped and the driver detained. A case of both a stolen vehicle with the driver over the drink/drive limit. The GP cars then were old Austin Cambridges and whilst comfortable they were not particularly fast and certainly not designed as a pursuit vehicle. Somehow we managed to keep pace with the speeding suspect car sufficient for it to be boxed off by our colleagues who had approached from our front in the opposite direction.

Bundu, the Beat & Beyond

Police discipline in those days was a great deal tighter than it appears to be today. For example if I wanted to see the Inspector for any reason I would have to go through the shift Sergeants first and if I wanted to see the Sergeants I would have to knock on their Office door before being permitted to enter. The majority of ranking Officers were former Military men who had seen service in the Second World War and, to some extent, their sense of military discipline found its way into Police life. All Officers had to be properly dressed at all times with helmets, if on foot patrol, and caps if on car patrol. Today Police discipline appears to be a lot more relaxed to the extent that some Officers do not wear any headgear at all and others appear to be unapproachable in their para-military style uniforms.

One service that the Police offered the public in those days was known to us as F&U's or Furnished and Unoccupied. When a house resident was planning an absence from his house for a week or two, perhaps because of holiday or a business trip, they had the option of reporting their intended absence with their local Police who would record details of the relevant dates together with details of a nominated key holder who lived within reasonable striking distance of the empty property. The Night Duty Uniform section would then undertake to visit each of these houses at least once each night and record the times of their visit on a record sheet kept for each house. We were obliged to check both the front and rear of the premises to ensure that the house remained secure.

As far as I know this service is no longer offered.

After completing the GP duties I then started out on my own operating initially on number one Beat in Hove Town Centre off Western Road. I recall walking down a road just off Western Road one sunny afternoon when I heard the sound of a female voice singing at the top of her voice. She seemed to be singing Salvation Army type hymns. Her singing was interspersed with foul and obscene language which was a bit of a contrast. Suddenly there was a loud crashing sound as a number of china plates and steel cutlery were hurled from a first floor window of a terraced town house on the opposite side of the road.

45

John LLOYD

I made my way to the house and up the stairs to the first floor flat from where the noise was emanating. The door to the flat was open so I entered and found the solitary occupant, an elderly lady of about 70 years or so who was dressed, somewhat bizarrely, in a see through baby doll nightie.

It was immediately apparent to me that this poor woman was probably a sandwich short of a picnic and was possibly suffering with some mental health issues. I radioed my control explaining the situation and requesting that an Ambulance be summoned so as to take her to hospital and have her medically examined.

An Ambulance arrived quite shortly afterwards and I somehow managed to persuade the woman to come with me and into the Ambulance. I sat beside her in the back of the Ambulance as she was still very agitated and displaying some signs of violent intent. Accordingly I felt obliged to hold her wrists with my right hand but she was having none of that. She immediately plunged her hands downwards into her groin area which left my right hand in a somewhat precarious position. I managed to maintain some physical control over her without hurting her too much and eventually we arrived at the Royal Sussex County hospital in Brighton where the lady was examined and sectioned under the mental health act. I am glad that I did not have to deal with that sort of incident very often.

Another occasion I can recall is when another of the uniformed Sergeants named Pat Regan asked me to accompany him on a foot patrol around the George Street area of Hove. Pat was unofficially known as the "Nagasaki Greyhound" due to his slightly oriental facial features and because of his prowess as an athlete. As we walked down George Street I noticed the open shop door leading into a Bookmakers shop. Being quite fresh from Training School and quite up to date (or so I thought) with the law even relating to the operation of Betting shops. I noticed one or two minor transgressions within the Bookies from the street and told Pat of what I had seen. He looked at me a bit straight but agreed that I was correct. He instructed me to remain outside whilst he went inside the Bookies to "deal "with the matter.

He returned a few minutes later and told me that these matters had been sorted out. I suspect that what he really told the licensed Bookie was that he had with him a really keen rookie Officer and perhaps he might like to amend the views from the street so as to avoid any formal action.

The Uniform Sections operated on a three shift system in those days, Early Turn which was from 0600hrs-1400hrs, Late Turn from 1400hrs to 2200 hrs and Night Turn from 2200-0600hrs. We had to report for duty at least 15 minutes prior to the commencement of each shift for a briefing on current events and incidents on the sub-division. We were not paid for these 15 minute briefing periods which was a bone of some contention for some of the more militant Officers.

The shift pattern commenced with Night duty on a Monday evening and lasted for seven nights after which we had two days off ie: the Monday and Tuesday (the first rest day mainly consisted of sleeping to recover from the night duties). Late Turns would commence on a Wednesday afternoon and would last for seven days after which we would have two days off ie: Wednesday and Thursday. The final shift in the rota was Early Turn which commenced on a Friday morning for seven days finishing at 1400 hrs on the following Thursday after which we had a long weekend of three Rest Days before starting back on Nights again the following Monday evening. The shift pattern was not ideal from the individual Officers point of view. Most of us found it to be very tiring and contrary to normal social hours. This was later recognised in the early 1970's with the Edmond Davies report on Policing which awarded the Police a substantial pay increase to take into account such factors as the anti-social hours worked by most Officers.

For the first two years of my Police service I was on probation as was the norm in those days. We "Probationers" were obliged to attend monthly one day Probation classes at John Street Police Station in Brighton where we received refresher tuition on a whole range of subjects both legal and practical. Two of the instructors who took these classes at that time were Dennis Care and Doug Raines. There was also a male instructor who favoured placing any female officers at the front of the class and we could only speculate as to the reasons for this but perhaps short skirts and black tights may have had something to do with this.

John LLOYD

I really enjoyed working at Hove which had a large variety of differing housing at all social levels, from expensive good class dwelling houses to somewhat run down Council Estates with the majority of housing falling in between those two categories. The expensive houses were always a target for the burglars whereas the Council Estates were often the source of many social problems which often spilt over into problems in which the Police became involved.

This is not to say that the people living on the Council housing estates were all criminals because the vast majority were hard working decent people but some of the housing conditions did create circumstances which lead to incidents of unrest and what is today called Anti-social behaviour. These were sometimes difficult to deal with especially at times when smallish gangs of unruly youths got together intent on causing mischief. The Police presence was spread quite thin and to deal with gatherings of unruly youths would require a deployment of a number of us at once so as to be able to quell any situation which threatened to get out of hand.

I quickly learned that one important aspect of Policing was the ability to interact with members of the public at all levels of society and to listen to what they were telling you rather than the accent in which they spoke. In other words just because someone spoke with a posh upper class accent did not necessarily mean that they were trustworthy neither did someone speaking in a cockney accent mean that they were dishonest. Another important aspect of policing is the ability to judge another's character and size people up within a few seconds of meeting. This is not an exact science but with practice and experience most Police Officers become pretty adept at this.

One other lesson I learned was to periodically look above my eyeline. Whilst most activity did take place at ground level it was also important to be aware of what was happening above you.

One aspect of our work involved dealing with domestic disputes between neighbours or spouses. Our involvement was needed to prevent a breach of the peace (or worse) and on numerous occasions I found myself at the tender age of 22 years and a single man trying to give suitable advice on

Bundu, the Beat & Beyond

marital matters to couples who were much older than I. I do not know what these couples thought of my advice or my relative tender years but overall they seemed to respect the fact that I was trying to help them rather than me casting blame on one party or the other.

I was to be fairly lucky throughout my Police career in that I was never seriously physically assaulted. Like all other Police Officers I had encountered my fair share of scuffles with various miscreants and others who objected to being arrested but I was only assaulted once to any notable degree. This happened when I arrested a young man in Portslade for malicious damage. He was also drunk. Whilst I was waiting for Police transport to take us to the Police Station he decided to award me a "Glasgow Kiss" and head-butted me in the mouth area causing a split lip plus some bleeding and swelling. I had not been issued with handcuffs and so I had to physically restrain him from any further violence until such time that my Police transport arrived. The CID Officers were delighted as they charged him with Assault Occasioning Actual Bodily Harm (ABH) on me plus the malicious damage offence. As ABH was a recordable crime they had an easy detected crime on their books.

In early 1970 I received news that my good friend Frances had become engaged to Jim who she had met after just having started working as a Teacher having graduated from Teacher Training College in Bulawayo. Jim lived in the flat next door to Fran's which must have been convenient.

Jim's full name is James Jansen Van Vuuren, an old Afrikaans name. Due to the expanding Guerrilla war in Rhodesia Jim had been called up for Military service and had been posted up to the border near the Kariba Dam and was tasked with monitoring the movement of insurgents crossing the border from Zambia. Fran and Jim were married in Bulawayo in January 1971 and my mother was able to attend the wedding. I was really pleased for Fran and I knew that she would make a delightful bride and wife for Jim.

About a year into my Police service I was working an Early Turn on one of the central town foot beats when I received a call from our Sub-divisional control room asking me to attend a local primary school

49

John LLOYD

where the caretaker had opened up the school and had found evidence of an overnight break in. I got the call around 0800hrs and as it was a nice sunny day I walked the mile or so to the school in fairly slow time.

When I got to the school I met the caretaker outside who showed me the broken window in one of the class-rooms and through which entry appeared to have been gained. I walked into the school building and began searching each of the classrooms beginning with the one in which entry had been gained. The caretaker left me to it and it was in the third classroom I checked that I found a man of the road aged about 55 years or so hiding underneath the teacher's desk. I am not sure who had the bigger fright but I managed to maintain my equilibrium and fell back on my training. I took hold of the man, who fortunately did not offer any resistance, and told him that he was under arrest on suspicion of burglary. He did not protest and I called for mobile assistance to take my prisoner back to Holland Road Police Station.

The Police vehicle arrived within a few minutes or so and my prisoner and I were taken to the "nick" where I booked him in with the Station Sergeant in the cell block. It transpired that my prisoner had stolen some small items from the school when he had entered the building the previous night but had fallen asleep before being disturbed by my search. He was charged with burglary and later appeared at Court.

I was the butt of some friendly banter from my colleagues for having arrested a prisoner for burglary on an Early Turn which was normally a fairly quiet period of the day for that type of matter. The CID were happy because they had a detected crime and I understand that they managed to "clear up" other similar matters in the area.

I can recall some names from Hove CID in those days including Mick Bennison, Dave Fickweiler, Don Mobbs, Tony Matthews, Dave Tomlinson and Jan Timpson. Jan was the former wife of Rodney Timpson, a Traffic Policeman based at Chichester, who later married the actress Penelope Keith.

Another totally different type of matter the Police were involved with then was dealing with "sudden deaths". We called them G5's after the

Bundu, the Beat & Beyond

form number which we were obliged to complete after attending such an incident. These incidents came about when a person died in unexplained or sudden circumstances or one in which the Doctor was unable to certify the cause of death. Although I became used to these situations I was never really comfortable with them. Most of these matters did require a degree of common sense as well as a good degree of observation plus the ability to deal with distraught relatives in a composed and dignified manner.

On one such occasion I was called to an address in Mile Oak in response to an Ambulance being called by the parents of a very young baby who they had been unable to awaken after a night's sleep in its cot. I got to the house before the Ambulance and went upstairs to the baby's bedroom. The poor infant was lying on its back as if it was asleep but I could feel no pulse nor detect any signs of breathing or body heat. I was certain that the baby had died at some time during the night and well prior to my arrival. Shortly after that the Ambulance crew arrived and one of them believed that the baby was still showing signs of life as a result of which the baby was rushed outside to the Ambulance where it was driven off to the Royal Sussex County Hospital in Brighton about 5 miles distant.

Prior to the arrival of the Ambulance crew I had told the distraught parents that I believed that the baby was dead and they seemed to have accepted that until the Ambulance crew arrived and decided otherwise.

I kept in contact with the hospital and was later informed that the baby had been declared dead upon arrival at the hospital. Quite what the Ambulance crew had thought they had detected I will never know but it was I who was left at the house trying to comfort two very upset parents whose hopes had been falsely raised and then dashed.

One other notable "sudden death" I attended was in a block of flats in Hove where neighbours reported the sounds of a distressed woman screaming and shouting for help. When I arrived at the front door of the flat I could hear the somewhat faint screaming of a feminine voice shouting for help. There was no key to the outside door of the flat so I had to break in by forcing the door which luckily was not very substantial.

John LLOYD

I went inside and made for the sounds of female agitation which was coming from the bedroom. I will never forget the sight that greeted me.

In the bedroom was a double bed with no over bed clothes. On the bed were two figures. On top was the naked and lifeless body of a very large elderly gentleman face down. Underneath the man I could just see the figure of a much younger woman who was very petite and slender. I could see her upturned face which seemed to be very agitated, upset and enormously embarrassed. I guessed what had happened and had to prise the body of the lifeless male off the young woman who was also naked. The woman was totally embarrassed yet also very grateful for my assistance as she had been unable to move the considerable bulk of her lover from her position below him.

It seems that the man was not her husband but a local worthy who had seduced the young woman and had been conducting an affair with her for some months. Fortunately for everyone involved the dead man's Doctor was able to confirm the cause of death as he had been treating him for heart disease within a few days prior to his death. This meant that there was no requirement for a Coroner's Inquest at which all the sordid details would have emerged. The Press would have had a field day! What a way to go but what an awful experience for the young woman.

One offence which was not very common in those days was that of Robbery. At that time there was a fur shop located in Church Road, Hove, which dealt in very expensive furs and fur coats etc. This was before the time when it became unfashionable and unacceptable to deal in, or wear, fur coats.

One day a general call went out to all patrols concerning a robbery which had taken place at the fur shop in Church Road. I was quite nearby that location and I was first on the scene. As I arrived I saw numerous fur coats strewn across the pavement and roadway outside the shop. It seems that the shop had been raided by a gang of three men and the two female staff stood no chance having been threatened with violence by the gang. The gang members had then grabbed as many fur coats as they could before making their getaway outside where a driver and car was waiting

Bundu, the Beat & Beyond

for them. In their panic to escape the scene before the arrival of Police the men had managed to drop many of the coats they had stolen.

Fortunately a bystander had witnessed the events and had had the presence of mind to record the registration number of the getaway car. Amazingly this vehicle was not a stolen or cloned vehicle but was registered to a known criminal. Hove CID did not have too much difficulty in tracking down and identifying the gang members and most of the stolen property was recovered. The four men were charged and later appeared at Lewes Quarter Sessions and pleaded not guilty. I was called to give evidence to describe the scene upon my arrival at the fur shop. This I did and other witnesses gave their evidence as to what they had seen etc. The gang were subsequently found guilty of Robbery and sentenced to a term of imprisonment.

I had moved from my digs to the single men's quarters located on the top floor of Hove Police Station. This was very convenient for work and the accommodation supplied rooms for about a dozen single Officers. In addition to the rooms we had a communal lounge and TV plus a shower/bath/toilet block. I enjoyed my time there. Other residents I recall at that time were Tony Howard who was a talented goalkeeper, John Packham, Dennis Johnson, Peter Crossley, Barry Massey and Martin Richards.

It was Tony Howard who christened me with the nickname of "Bongo" due to my habit of tapping out drumming on any available surface when music was being played.

The only downside to living in the Single Men's Quarters above the Police Station was that at the rear of the backyard were a set of dog kennels in which, periodically, stray dogs were placed pending collection by their owners or the RSPCA. This was fine unless their incarceration began out of hours during the evening or night time periods because most dogs once locked up alone will bark and howl incessantly until they are released. This caused us some degree of sleeplessness.

It was during my time at Hove that I encountered a certain Superintendent Nicholas Jelf who seemed to have origins in the upper classes of society in that he spoke with a very upper crust accent. He

John LLOYD

was quite a portly gentleman and did not seem to fit the usual profile of a British Police Officer. I did not know him at all well and had little contact with him.

Some of my senior peers told the story from some years earlier about a Uniform Inspector who led a section of Uniformed Officers on a drugs raid against the country house of a well-known Pop Star. His section had to approach the house across an open field at night but as there was a full moon shining, the Inspector had instructed his men to turn their helmets sideways on their heads so as to avoid the moonlight shining off their helmet badges and thereby giving away their presence to anyone who may have been watching! I cannot vouch for this story as I was not there but my peers assured me that it was true.

A sad event affected us all at Hove Police Station during that time when a very popular Officer called Dennis Perry contracted Leukaemia and died within a few months. He was just 22 years of age. He had been a talented footballer and I had known him quite well as a genial very pleasant young man with his life's prospects ahead of him.

In the hot summer of 1970 I completed my Probationer Continuation Course at the Police Training Centre at Nutfield in Surrey where, as well as the Home County Forces, we were also joined by some City of London Officers.

It was in 1971 that I was operating a one man road block on a small road just outside Hove which led to the Devils Dyke and also to a back way onto the main A23 road leading from Brighton to London. This was in response to a series of daytime burglaries in good class dwelling houses in which the CID felt it possible that the Burglars were from outside the Brighton and Hove area and were possibly using back roads to exit the main town area and make good their getaway onto the main London road.

This road was not busy with traffic in the late afternoon with only the occasional passing car. I saw a green Morris Minor approaching me from the direction of Hove and making as though to travel in the direction of the A23 road. I stepped into the road, made the stop sign at which

Bundu, the Beat & Beyond

point the vehicle stopped just in front of me. I walked to the driver's door where I could see that the male driver was a black man. There was a black lady in the passenger seat with two young black children in the rear seat.

At that time there were virtually no black people in the Brighton and Hove area and I had not come across black people during the course of my Police duties before now.

This was to be a small but defining moment for me especially as I was schooled in apartheid South Africa.

I decided that the only way to proceed was to treat the occupants as I would any other person.

I explained to the driver the reasons for my stopping his car and also called him "Sir" After a few minutes I realised that this was a well brought up family from south London intent on having a good family day out at the seaside. They were all very polite so, after taking a cursory look into the car's boot, I bade them farewell and they went on the merry way.

The reason that this small incident has stuck in my mind is that this was the first time that I had ever called a black man "Sir" and I realised that I did not feel either inferior or superior in this situation but was somewhat gratified that I was able to treat people as equals irrespective of their colour or ethnic background. Today this type of situation is commonplace and is quite unremarkable but to me in 1971 this was a moment that defined some attitudes for me which exist to this day.

In those days the Police were also responsible for the registration and monitoring of foreign "aliens" and Hove had a full time Aliens Officer who worked mainly 9-5—Monday to Friday and I was "selected" to stand in for him during his absences on Annual Leave or periods of sickness etc. The job was almost entirely office based and consisted of receiving and interviewing foreign nationals at the Police Station and ensuring that their registration was completed satisfactorily and that they were complying with the conditions of their registration. It was

John LLOYD

not particularly onerous but it was important. How I won this job I will never know but it did give me the opportunity for a little more of a social life as well as being able to meet more of the staff at Hove Police Station, especially those on other shifts. It was around this time in 1970/71 that I met a young woman Police Cadet called Linda Nightingale who was seconded to Hove with another female Cadet, Linda New.

CHAPTER 4

Good & not so good times

Linda hailed from next door Brighton where her parents were the proprietors of a Jewellers shop at 14 Duke Street called F. W. Stuck. Linda and I began seeing each other and I met her parents, Tom & Gwen, who made me most welcome. I also met her older sister, Ann, as well as an elderly gentleman and original owner of the Jewellers shop, Mr Frederick Stuck. The premises were an old town house with the ground floor converted into shop premises. The family lived in the other three floors which included a basement area.

Tom Nightingale had met Gwen Brewer during the Second World War when he served with 601 County of London Squadron (Hurricane) at the RAF fighter base at Tangmere in Sussex. Gwen lived in nearby Chichester. Tom was Lancashire, born and bred, and was a genuinely nice man although he did tend to see life in either black or white. There were very few shades of grey in Tom's world.

When Linda reached the age of 19 she applied for, and was accepted, into the Regular Police Force and was sent to complete her Initial Police Training Course at Ryton-on-Dunsmore near Coventry.

I was invited to attend her end of course Ball and made my way by train to be with her. I was delayed by some hours due to the train breaking down en route in the middle of nowhere. I managed to arrive half way through the evening to find a very upset Linda who was relieved to see me in good shape having thought that I had been involved in something nasty. This was well before the days of mobile 'phones at a time when communications were somewhat haphazard.

John LLOYD

Linda and I became engaged and by a stroke of good fortune she was also posted to Hove (I think that some pressure was exerted somewhere).

Around this time I had acquired a Triumph Herald with a convertible soft top. It was a lovely car being very clean and reliable. However, one night whilst taking Linda home after a function at Hove Police Social club, we were involved in an accident whilst driving along Western Road. We approached a set of traffic lights at a four way junction, the lights were green in our favour and as I drove across the junction a car driving in the opposite direction turned right across my front intending to turn to his right. As he did so he collided with the front offside of my Triumph resulting in severe damage, so much so that my car was an economic right-off. Fortunately neither Linda nor I were hurt but the downside was that we lost our lovely little car. A further twist to this was that a Brighton Police Officer attended the collision and recorded details. As was the practice then I was issued with a form HO/RT1 requiring me to produce my vehicle insurance certificate, MOT certificate and Drivers Licence at a Police Station within seven days.

I elected to produce these documents at Hove Police Station but when I came to get these documents together I was horrified to see that my MOT Test Certificate had lapsed nine days previously.

I went to see the Station Sergeant, Harry Norton, who was a real old time Copper and good all round bloke. I produced my driver's licence and Certificate of Insurance and showed him the out of date MOT test certificate. He was as embarrassed as I was but he did the only thing that he could do and that was to record the details of my valid documents and report me for the offence of using a vehicle without a valid MOT certificate.

I went to see Bob Allen, the Superintendent in charge of Hove at that time and told him what had happened. In his usual gruff manner he said, "What do you want me to do about it?" I replied, "Nothing, I just wanted you to know the situation before you found out about it from some other source." He seemed satisfied with this and I left his office. Despite his gruff exterior Bob Allen was an excellent Police Officer and always led from the front.

Bundu, the Beat & Beyond

I was later summoned to appear at Brighton Magistrates Court. I did not appear in person but I wrote a letter to the Court explaining the full circumstances. I was fined £2 for this offence which was not a lot even in those days but more importantly I had learned a salutary lesson.

A few weeks before our wedding I received a telephone call from my father in Zambia informing me that he would be unable to travel to UK to attend our wedding. He sounded dreadful and it was not the voice I remembered. He did not explain why he was unable to attend but I accepted what he told me even though I was disappointed. I knew that my mother was, at that time, in South Africa making arrangements pending their intended move south.

I told the Duty Inspector, Bert Stevens, about my concerns over this telephone call but I was assured that my father probably just felt "a little under the weather"

Some days after I had received the telephone call from my father and on a day in August 1972 I was on Late Turn engaged in single man Traffic control on a busy main road called Old Shoreham Road in Portslade. The Traffic Lights at a four way junction had failed and I was conducting the traffic for some hours before being relieved. During that time I received a radio message from Hove Control informing me that a Telegram had arrived for me. I acknowledged and said that I would collect the telegram at 1700hrs when I was scheduled to return to the Police Station for my refreshment break.

I returned to Holland Road around 1700hrs and collected my telegram from the front Office staff. I opened the telegram and read and re-read the few lines of its contents. The telegram was from David Houston-Barnes my father's former boss in Kitwe and the words went something like: Regret to inform you that your father Pat Lloyd died last night. His remains are held at Kitwe General Hospital:

At first I was unable to take in this dreadful news but then I thought back to his telephone call some days previously and how awful his voice had sounded. What was I to do? There was only one thing that I could do and that was to travel to Zambia and to finalise his business and

John LLOYD

personal effects. With my mother in South Africa it would be unfair to expect her to do this.

I went to see the Duty Inspector, Ernie Ewens, and informed him of the events and advised him that I intended to travel to Zambia at the earliest opportunity to settle my father's affairs. He was very understanding and arranged special compassionate leave for me. I then made a very hurried visit to a local Travel Agent who managed to book me on a flight to Zambia departing the next day. My outward flight was on a British United Airways VC-10 from Gatwick Airport which was routed via Entebbe, Uganda on its way to N'dola and Lusaka in Zambia.

The VC-10 was met at Entebbe by a smart, attractive young lady in what was to become the tartan uniform of British Caledonian Airways which was in the process of taking over BUA at that time. I arrived in N'dola later that day where a car was waiting for me to drive me to Kitwe.

I stayed with some friends of my father, Bob and Joan Stewart, who were very helpful and kind to me. Bob was an anaesthetist at Nkana Hospital and Joan was a nurse. I remained in Kitwe for a couple of weeks sorting out my father's financial affairs and papers. I managed to dispose of his car by sale to a local Asian man for a good price. I had valuable assistance in tidying up my father's affairs from Mr Coutts, his Bank Manager, who was able to steer me in the right direction in all sorts of matters.

I later learned that my father had been working with a solicitor named Nobby Clarke who, as it turned out, was something of a rogue. It appears that Nobby Clarke had fled Zambia owing about 50,000 Kwacha in business taxes to the Zambian Authorities. This had led to my father carrying the can and I think that the strain, stress and shame were just too much for my father to bear. This situation appears to have had a direct bearing on my father's state of health and his subsequent death.

Shortly before I returned to the UK my father's remains were cremated and I was handed his ashes in a small card board box wrapped in greaseproof paper. A short religious ceremony was held in a Kitwe Church where the large congregation bore testimony to the high regard in which my father was held.

Bundu, the Beat & Beyond

I returned to London Heathrow clutching the box containing my father's ashes. I was met by my mother and Linda. My mother had travelled from Johannesburg so as to be at our now imminent wedding.

My father's ashes were interred in a plot we purchased at the rear of St John's Church in Church Road, Hove. He was just 58 years of age.

I have always felt a sense of guilt for not having reacted to my father's telephone call, maybe I could have done something which may have saved him, maybe not. I will never know. He was a good man and I still miss him all these years later.

Linda and I were married in Brighton in 1971 and we lived in Police flats in Abergavenny Gardens in Hove, just a short walk from Hove Police Station as well as the shops in Western Road.

We took our honeymoon in Spain in a resort called Tossa De Mar. Linda was not at all keen on flying and so we went by train which was a novel experience. As I recall the journey took about two days and we shared a mixed compartment for sleeping at night. Not exactly the ideal for a honeymoon couple but we coped. We enjoyed a good ten days or so in the resort where we stayed at quite a reasonable hotel before making the return train journey to England.

1972 also saw the centuries old tradition of Assize and Quarter Session Courts come to an end to be replaced by the newly named Crown Courts. I was Court Officer for the very last Assize Court held at Lewes in 1972 which was marked by a short ceremony by the Judges and Barristers with T. C. Williams, our Chief Constable, also in attendance.

Later that year I began to feel unwell and continually suffered with severe stomach pains. In the summer of 1972 these stomach pains culminated in me vomiting blood. The Doctor was called and after examining me he arranged for an Ambulance to take me to Brighton General Hospital where I was admitted to the Male General ward for further examination.

Due to the severe loss of blood, things were a bit touch and go for a time. I was given a blood transfusion.

61

John LLOYD

Linda accompanied me in the ambulance and stayed with me at the hospital for as long as she could before being ushered out by the Ward Sister. She went to her parents' house in Duke Street where she stayed for some time. Her parents insisted that she telephone the hospital to advise the staff of her altered whereabouts so that contact could be made if there was a need. Linda refused on the grounds that if the hospital staff did not know where she was then I would be alright whereas if they did know where she was then I would not be alright. I did not find out about this until very recently but her ploy certainly worked.

I was diagnosed with severe abdominal ulcers but fortunately the medical staff decided that an operation was not necessary and I was treated with drugs and put on a strict diet and was not permitted to have any fried food or food with any excess acid etc.

Linda was in an advanced stage of pregnancy by this time and apart from visiting me in hospital which she did every afternoon and evening she also had to continue life at Abergavenny House and at her parents' house. She reminded me recently that she travelled twice every day to visit me travelling by bus. It was, according to Linda, a long hot summer

I received a large basket of fruit from my Section Mates together with a get well card containing some humorous and ribald comments which cheered me up no end. I recall that the fruit and card were delivered by a member of my section called Doug Penry who also lived in Abergavenny House with his wife who was also pregnant. When their son arrived I believe that they were considering calling the child Henry but in the end they selected another name. Wise choice.

The hospital ward was quite large and catered for about 2 dozen male patients in two rows along each wall. Beside each bed were a small bedside cabinet and a small cupboard in which the patient's personal effects and clothes were stored. There was a toilet and bathroom block at the far end of the ward. The patients were a mixed bunch of people but we mostly got on well enough. There was an elderly gentleman in the bed opposite to mine named Mr Hutt. He was somewhat eccentric and sometimes appeared confused. One night after lights out he got out of bed and turned to his left as if to make for the toilet block. He walked

Bundu, the Beat & Beyond

past two beds and then turned left again, opened the patient's cupboard door and proceeded to urinate inside. The Night duty Nurse managed to intervene but not before the interior of the cupboard received a soaking.

I was well looked after by the medical staff at Brighton General who were, without exception, very caring people. The nursing staff also included a couple of young South Korean ladies who spoke excellent English but with heavy accents. I remember them delivering my lunch one day and one of them said to me, "Mr Royd, do you want Jerry and custard for runch?" Their inability to pronounce the letter L was always the source of good fun and humour for me. They were excellent nurses however and never failed to get their priorities straight.

One point which struck me about hospital life was just how noisy the ward was, especially during the daytime when cleaners would be pushing motorised floor polishers around for what seemed like hours. This was not the place to be for a restful time.

I have an aversion to needles and I became to dread the times (almost daily) when the blood nurse would come to my bed requiring a sample of my blood. In the end I called her the "Vampire" which she took in good humour.

I remained in hospital for a couple of weeks or so before being discharged but I was signed off sick for some weeks after that and was only able to go back to work on light duties. This saw me working in the Administration Office at Hove under Sergeant Jock Crawford and his team of ladies on a Monday-Friday 9-5 regime.

In October 1972 our son Gareth was born and was the source of much delight to all the family.

He was a very bonny baby and he was loved dearly by Linda and I as well as his grandparents and we enjoyed many happy days taking him to parks and other similar venues during my days off work.

In early 1974 I was successful in applying for a rural beat at Yapton, near Bognor Regis. This was to be a very different role and experience to

John LLOYD

that I had enjoyed to date at Hove. It also required that we move from Hove to the Police House at Yapton which adjoined the Police House for the Officer responsible for nearby Barnham. In those days one of the requirements for a posting to a rural beat was that the applicant had to be married.

We moved to the three bedroomed Police house in Yapton which was joined to the Barnham Officers house by a Police Office in between the two houses.

I was part of a small network of rural Officers operating in this area with Dave Robinson at Barnham, Ron Leahy at Eastergate and Roger Pavey at Fontwell. We all worked separately and had differing shifts most days such as 0800-1600 or 1800 to 0200. During the late shifts we were also responsible for patrolling and dealing with any incidents on the adjoining beats. We were all under the direct supervision of a Sergeant Ray Jones based at Bognor who came out to see us periodically. He was an old time Copper with old time values but we got along well enough.

The work had similarities to town policing but also differences. The most obvious difference was that I mainly operated alone and had no immediate back up in the event that something went wrong. If I needed assistance I would have to call up on the Force Radio network to the main Force control room in Lewes who would try and identify other Police units within a reasonable vicinity. This, however, could take up to twenty minutes or more to arrive (if you were lucky).

I also had some gypsy encampments located on my patch. Today these people are called "Travellers" Contrary to popular belief these gypsy communities were not a continual source of problems. Granted some caused me problems and some were thieves but the same can be said for other communities. In general I found that if you treated the gypsy community with a degree of respect they would respond accordingly. Not once did I encounter any physical violence with them although there were times when opportunities may have arisen to provoke that type of response.

I suspect that this situation has vastly changed today.

Bundu, the Beat & Beyond

Most of the gypsies lived in modern caravans that were immaculately clean and tidy. Some lived in modern brick houses but most in Caravans. I managed to develop quite a reasonable relationship with most of them but it did take some time to earn their trust and a degree of respect. I did learn some lessons, one of which is "never assume anything ". On one occasion I had to execute an arrest warrant (with bail) on a gypsy male named Johnson. After entering his house I found him in his armchair beside the fireplace. I explained to him the reason for my visit and showed him the warrant and ended by saying "You can read it if you want to" This was a big mistake as he came straight back at me saying that he could not read which left me embarrassed with egg on face. I read the warrant to him and gave him the option of coming with me in my Police van or following me to Bognor Regis Police Station in his own vehicle. Unsurprisingly he opted to follow me in his own vehicle. We drove to Bognor in convoy and upon arrival I formally arrested him and he was bailed to appear at Court. Honour more or less even.

In November 1974 I received the very sad news that my dear old Nan had died. I was unable to attend her funeral about ten days later because I was required as a Witness in a case being heard at the Magistrates Court. Neither the Defence nor the Prosecution would release me so I had no choice but to turn up at Court only for the Defendant to plead Guilty at the very last moment. To say that I was angry, frustrated and disappointed would be an understatement but that was the sheer lunacy of the Court proceedings in those days. Court time and defendants' rights were sacrosanct to the apparent exclusion of anything else.

Christmas time in Yapton brought some surprises for us not least of which was that on Christmas day morning we found a number of wrapped Christmas presents on our front doorstep. These were from grateful, but anonymous, local residents. The presents were not for Linda or I but for young Master Gareth. The locals knew that I could not accept any form of gratuity so they bent the rules a little and gave small gifts to Gareth. A really nice gesture and also very unexpected which I thought illustrated one of the differences in attitude from the public between town and country policing in those days.

John LLOYD

We were still not well paid in 1974 and I can admit now that I took a small part time job in a Yapton garage on my days off to supplement our income which was tight especially as Linda had resigned from the Police before we left Hove so we were reliant on my income alone. I was unofficially employed rubbing down the body work of damaged vehicles which had come in for bodywork repairs. This was very tedious hard graft as it was all done by hand with very fine sand paper. I never earned a fortune but it did help with our household bills. This was strictly against the rules but it was needs must in those days. Did it compromise my position in the local community? I don't think so because I knew that the two owners of the garage were honest and trustworthy and they never attempted to take advantage of my position as a Police Officer at any time.

It became apparent around this time that our marriage was in trouble and we were not getting along like we should have been. We had frequent arguments and disagreements and it was obvious to me that something had to give. Part of our problem perhaps, is that both Linda and I have fairly strong characters and we both had strong views on a range of matters, few of which seemed to align with the other. I thought also that Linda began to struggle a bit when we moved to Yapton because this was the first time that she had been removed from the support of her family. I think that she struggled with that fact and perhaps I did not, or could not, give her all the support that she needed in our new situation.

Our relationship carried on in this vein for some months before it became obvious that we either had to make significant changes to our relationship or consider the parting of the ways. The first option was not really viable due to the strength of our personalities which tended to clash when in continual and close proximity with each other.

Linda reminded me recently that she went to the Doctors surgery in nearby Barnham as she was, at that time, suffering with depression. The medical advice from her doctor was that she should go home and read her Bible. I am not surprised that she was disgusted by this so called advice which was certainly unhelpful to our situation.

Bundu, the Beat & Beyond

Eventually we came to realise that we would have to part which was extremely difficult for both of us and compounded by the fact that we had a young child. We told Linda's family of our problems and they were naturally very upset and tried their very best to dissuade us from separation and divorce.

We both knew that our relationship probably could not be mended and we decided that the best thing for us to do was to seek a divorce. These matters were then placed in the hands of lawyers but fortunately for both of us Linda and I still were on good terms with each other and we mutually agreed a financial package to support Gareth. The papers were submitted to Brighton County Court and we divorced some months later.

Prior to this I had to inform my bosses of my impending divorce which meant that I could no longer continue working in Yapton. A few weeks later I was given the option of transferring to either Gatwick Airport or Worthing. The policing role at Gatwick Airport had transferred to the responsibility of Sussex Police on the 1st April 1975. HM Government had decided that because of the rise of international terrorism and aircraft hijackings the old British Airports Authority Police (BAA) were not sufficiently equipped and resourced to cope with the new demands and threats.

I decided to opt for Gatwick as I thought that it would offer a whole new range of challenges and experiences. I was not wrong. Life is all about choices and this turned out to be one of my better ones for a whole raft of reasons but more of that later.

The period leading up to our divorce and immediately afterwards was very traumatic for me (and, no doubt, for Linda). I disliked the whole process intensely but, on balance, it was the right choice albeit a painful one.

I missed the day to day contact with Gareth and I know that I missed out on a lot of his childhood which is something I will always regret. Due to the fact that Linda and I were still on quite good terms we were able to agree suitable arrangements to permit me access to Gareth on my

John LLOYD

Rest Days. I am eternally grateful for that as it meant so much to me. It was not the same and would never be the same as living together as a family under one roof but I think that we did make the very best of a very bad job.

When he was a little older Linda agreed for me to take Gareth on holiday to South Africa where we stayed with my mother at her home in Germiston. There was never any question of me not returning Gareth to the UK as we always had mutual trust in each other.

A year or so later we did try again by which time Linda had a flat in Brighton and we lived together again for a few months but the same underlying problems were still there and in the end we decided to call it a day, this time for good.

I will always be grateful to Linda because we did have good times together and she had produced a miracle called Gareth which was a real blessing. We are still in contact all these years later and we are still on good social terms whenever we meet up with her and her husband, Dick. Perhaps we were two people who got on very well as good friends and should have remained that way.

Some years later when Gareth was a young adult it became apparent to me that he seemed to have some difficulty in committing to relationships. I blamed myself for this as I thought that the separation of Linda and I followed by some years of living without a father figure may have been a contributory factor in those commitment issues.

Many years later this situation did get much better however but more of that later.

CHAPTER 5

A new beginning

I presented myself at Gatwick Police Station at the end of May 1975 to be told that I was on C Section (again).

At that time a large new modern Police Station was being built at Gatwick and the Police Station consisted of a series of linked Portakabins situated close to the airside fence and close to the one (and only at that time) Terminal building.

Sussex Police had not had much notice of their taking on the Policing role at Gatwick prior to the 1st April and so most of the Officers were young and single and were accommodated in a series of hotels in the Gatwick area. Some were put up in 4 star hotels which served Gatwick and were nicely off thank you. Perhaps I drew a short straw as I ended up in a 2 star hotel situated in Southgate, Crawley called the Barrington Hotel. It was clean and comfortable enough and was managed by a Geordie lady called Sally who had two young daughters in their early teens. Sally had a very good heart and was very flexible in her dealings with us. One slight downside to living at the Barrington was that we had to share, two to a room, which for a recently married man used to home comforts etc came a bit hard. I shared a room with Chris Penfold who was on D Section so we did not get to see too much of each other due to conflicting shifts. So things worked out alright in that regard.

Policing at Gatwick was a whole new experience for every Sussex Police Officer as it was very different from the type of policing we had been used to. There were a number of former BAA Police Officers who remained at Gatwick after the takeover including John Cobb, Dave Ellis,

John LLOYD

Mick Bevan, Roy Stagg, Dave Shepherd, John Watkins, Bill Bounds BEM (whose nickname was Bungalow Bill because there was not a lot upstairs!!), Ian Till, Bob Donaldson, Dick Lock, Dave Osborne, Pete Parker and Dave (Cozy) Powell. There were others whose names escape me as I write. I recall that the ex-BAA Officers always referred to Heathrow as being "the big Airport", which when compared to the size of Gatwick at that time was an accurate description.

In general the Sussex Officers got on well with the former BAA Officers and we looked to them for guidance in respect of Airport procedures and by-laws.

The prime thrust of the Sussex Police presence at the airport was counter terrorism. Part of the strategy involved the carrying of firearms by uniformed Officers whilst on patrol, mainly in the Terminal building. Before being authorised to carry firearms the selected Officers had to pass a Firearms Course held in the Firing Range in the basement of John Street Police Station in Brighton.

In those days Sussex Police used the Walther PPK 9mm automatic pistol but we trained on the .22 version which had less of a recoil. I suspect that this was due to finances and the savings accrued by using .22 ammunition instead of the more costly 9mm bullets. The downside to this was that the training weapons were really well used and virtually worn out. Having received instruction on how to handle the weapon and how to stand and point etc we were given a strict briefing on safety procedures which was fair enough.

Then the time came for me to actually fire my weapon down range to target at a distance of 25 yards. I aimed carefully and squeezed the trigger expecting there to be some recoil. The very strong recoil took me completely by surprise and I then heard the tinkling of glass as the neon light above my head and about five yards down range shattered at the impact of a .22 bullet.

I thought to myself that there is no way that I could have missed the target especially under ideal conditions. The instructor ordered me to unload my weapon which I did and upon removing the magazine we

Bundu, the Beat & Beyond

found that three cartridges had been expelled from the weapon in one firing. One had hit the target, the second had hit the ceiling just in front of the target and you know what happened to the third one. It transpired that this particular weapon was so worn and over used that it had fired the three rounds in automatic mode. All in all a really interesting introduction to Firearms. We were also trained on the Sterling 9mm Sub Machine gun as well as being given the opportunity to fire other weapons such as shotguns and the like.

Most of the students on our course appeared to be quite competent using firearms and equally importantly using the safety drills. There were two exceptions, one male Officer had real difficulty with accuracy and was unable to pass the course. The other was a female Officer of slender build who had great difficulty in operating the slide on the Walther which is used to cock the weapon and pull a round into the firing chamber. She was given additional tuition and permitted to continue on the course. I make no further comment on that save to say that I am pleased that I never had to work with her on any armed duties.

I managed to pass with the grade of marksman which I was quite pleased about. We later went on a tactical firearms course at an old Country estate near Horsham and we practiced using firearms both outdoors and in. During one of the indoor exercises I was tasked with being the nasty armed terrorist and was instructed to hide myself away in part of the Country house whilst a dedicated armed search team came looking for me.

I walked down one particular corridor which had a kink in it half way down the corridor which made a sort of chicane. To the immediate right of the kink was a cupboard facing down the hall. The cupboard had two doors, a lower and upper door leading into two separate compartments. I was much slimmer and fitter in those days and I managed to secrete myself behind the upper door, the bottom of which was about five feet above floor level, I closed the door behind me and waited, loaded gun in hand (blank ammunition).

Some considerable time went by but I could hear the sounds of the search team heading in my direction until they finally reached the cupboard in which I was hiding. They gingerly opened the lower door

John LLOYD

and found the compartment beyond to be empty. I fully expected them to open the upper door and find me there. They did nothing of the kind but continued on their way down the corridor in the belief that no one would be hiding in the upper part of the cupboard. How wrong they were.

When I gauged that they were about ten feet or so beyond the cupboard and heading away from me I opened the cupboard door and squeezed off two shots in quick succession above their heads.

The noise in the confines of a narrow corridor was immense as was the shock given to the search team. They seemed very subdued as I climbed down from my hiding place and at least one of them displayed signs of needing the toilet. Lessons were learned, however, which was the main point of the exercise.

We were obliged to undergo frequent Refresher Courses so as to ensure that our marksmanship, gun handling and tactical awareness were up to scratch. On one such Refresher course we had a rather elderly looking Uniform Sergeant from Gatwick as one of the students. I will call him Sylvester.

Sylvester did not fit the usual profile of a British Police Officer from those times in that he looked much older than he probably was, had thinning silvery grey hair brushed back over his head, he wore spectacles and had a rather portly figure. In Police terms he would not have been out of place in some rural backwater.

Sylvester also had the ability to devise his own language which members of his Section eventually came to understand and almost revere. He would talk about the "Perrymeter Road" (Perimeter Road) or the Multi-coloured Car Parks (Multi-storey Car Parks) as well as "Articled Lorries" (Articulated lorries) and so on and so on.

One aspect of the Refresher Firearms Course included each student being faced with a large video screen on which were portrayed a variety of different scenarios and against which the student was expected to react in a quick and decisive manner. Sylvester's turn arrived and he assumed

Bundu, the Beat & Beyond

the crouch position with his arms extended to his front with his firearm pointing towards the video screen and his large belly pointing downwards towards the floor.

The first scenario which popped up on the screen for Sylvester was of a group of armed criminals who were firing at him from open cover with no other "innocents" within range. The criminals continued to fire at Sylvester for some seconds with no reaction or return fire from Sylvester. There came a point at which a somewhat exasperated Instructor said to him, "What are you doing Sylvester?" Sylvester replied, "I am assessing the situation."

Some Police Officers were just not cut out for carrying and using firearms.

The armed duties at Gatwick were a 24 hour, seven day a week role. In general they were fairly boring duties as, in theory, we were not supposed to involve ourselves in anything other than our security role. We operated in pairs and to help pass the time we did chat to each other about a whole range of topics whilst keeping our eyes and ears tuned in to what was going on around us in the busy terminal.

On one occasion I was paired with an Officer called Pete Desimone and as I was going out with a Nurse from Great Ormond Street Hospital at the time I was explaining to Pete how our relationship worked and where she worked etc. There came a point in which I was saying "And she is a Nurse at Great Ormond . . ." At exactly the same time as I said that a very attractive young lady came into our view just a few yards away. She was well endowed in the chest department and our conversation reached a natural break. From then on whenever we saw an attractive young lady Pete would always say something like, "Look at those great Ormonds!!!" Childish I know, but it kept us amused.

We did engage with Airport staff and tried our best to foster good relations with all the various commercial companies operating on the Airport. This had obvious benefits for us because it permitted good relationships to be developed and for a good degree of trust to be formed. This in turn meant that companies, staff and individuals were more

John LLOYD

likely to provide information of interest to us and have the confidence to report matters of concern to them. It was a two way street.

We also engaged with some of the passengers when circumstances warranted. By definition they were a transient presence who were only in the airport for as short a time as they could get away with.

I found ~~that~~ the American passengers to be very outgoing and naturally friendly, they could be quite loud at times but were, almost without exception, very polite. They loved having their photographs taken with us and we obliged when we could. One morning on early turn I was standing in the Arrivals Hall at the Immigration Desks together with WPC Judy Cunningham when a whole line of American Tourists came down the ramp and turned right before walking towards us. I heard one of the middle aged female tourists say in a very deep Southern accent, "Gee honey, look there's a gen-yew-wine British Bobby (pointing at me) and look (now pointing at Judy) he has a Bobbette with him."

The American people have developed a great nation and it is said that we are two countries divided by a common language. This has some truth to it and in my experience when the American don't have a ready word for something they seem to make one up.

We were not on permanent armed duties and we alternated between general patrol duties and real Police work and the armed duties. Some of our Officers did not take to the Policing role at Gatwick and yearned for a transfer back to normal policing elsewhere. For others, me included, I did enjoy most of my time on Uniform duties at Gatwick.

I had only been at Gatwick for a few weeks when I came across two 12 year old boys from Crawley who were walking into the Terminal building from the direction of the east side car parks. They were in possession of a number of anti-tank missiles and two smoke grenades. To say that I was slightly alarmed would be an understatement. The boys told me that they had found these items in a copse about 150 yards south of the Car Hire Offices. This area was, at that time, undeveloped land. They showed me where they had found the ordnance and I could see that there were other similar items buried beneath the small excavation made by the boys.

Bundu, the Beat & Beyond

The ordnance found by the boys was left on top of the remaining suspect items. The boys were taken back to the Police Station to await collection by their parents whilst I requested the attendance of the Army Bomb Disposal unit.

The bomb disposal unit arrived and eventually made the area safe. They discovered that there was a substantial ordnance and ammunition dump secreted in a shallow burial pit and it transpired that this was a leftover from the Second World War era when Canadian troops had been based in the area.

As part of our anti-terrorist role the Gatwick Police also conducted periodic joint exercises with the Military including the SAS who based themselves at Gatwick Police Station for the duration of the exercise which lasted 24 hours or more. The SAS men tended to keep themselves apart and my main recollection is that most of them were fairly short in stature but very broad in build and were, without doubt, very tough looking. I certainly would not wish to have looked for any trouble with any of them and I was glad that they were on our side. Previous and subsequent incidents in which the SAS were involved have proved just how professional and competent they were and continue to be.

Whilst staying at the Barrington Hotel I met an Officer from Brighton who had been transferred to Gatwick by the name of Terry Gatland. Terry was a very useful amateur boxer and was very handy to have around in any physical confrontations. On several occasions whilst on night duties at the Airport Terry would surreptitiously bring in his .22 air-rifle to work and we arranged to be crewed together on the Police Land Rover. This Land Rover was equipped with a powerful search-light mounted on the roof. In the early hours of the morning and at a time when there were no incoming or outgoing flights we would make our way to the south side of the runway near what was the old Laker Airways Hanger and drive onto the large grass area adjoining the runway.

I would drive and Terry operated the searchlight and within just a few minutes he was able to spot many hundreds of rabbits grazing on the grassy area at which point I stopped the vehicle. The rabbits seemed transfixed by the glare of the powerful light and Terry would take aim

John LLOYD

with his rifle and shoot one or two rabbits which he would later "paunch" in the Police Station toilets and take them back to the Barrington Hotel where Sally, the hotel Manager, would cook them for him as a rabbit stew or whatever took his fancy. I have never liked rabbit so I cannot say just how good they were but Terry always seemed to enjoy his rabbit meals. These antics were not really legal and we could have been in some trouble if any of the Airport Authorities had found out but they never did.

A very sad footnote to this is that a few years later Terry transferred to the Metropolitan Police in London and I never saw him again although I did hear that he fell into difficult times and resorted to an attempted robbery. His getaway vehicle was a bicycle and he was caught in quick time. This resulted in him being dismissed from the Police and being handed a prison sentence. A very sad end to what should have been a promising Police career.

In 1976 I moved out of the Barrington Hotel and moved into a large two bed flat above a large house in the nearby village of Rusper. The flat had been found by a PC on D Section called Dave Sawyer and we moved in together and had complete independence. His WPC girlfriend, Fran Piercey, moved in with us and on a social level things were just fine.

We then moved to a three bedroomed house in Mannings Close, Pound Hill, Crawley where we were joined by Barry Wood a Gatwick Customs Officer who had previously trained to be a fast jet pilot with the RAF before he was invalided out on ill health grounds.

We subsequently moved to a four bedroomed house in Grisedale Close, Southgate, Crawley where Dave and I shared the house with Barry Wood and Liz Hanson who worked for Gatwick Handling at the Airport. Shortly after this, we were joined by a PC on my section called Mick Stone who was going out with Liz. They later married and they now have two strapping sons and live in the nearby town of Horsham. I still see them from time to time.

It was here in Grisedale Close that the four of us began sharing cooking duties, mainly for the evening meal. At that time I was not an

Bundu, the Beat & Beyond

experienced cook although I could normally prepare something suitable for myself and never went hungry. (Vesta Curries were always an easy and tasty option) There came a time when I was cooking the evening meal for the four of us and I decided to prepare a Lasagne for dinner. By the time I got around to assembling all the ingredients all the shops had shut and there were no late opening corner shops in those days. I then discovered that we had run out of milk, nor did we have any milk powder with which to make the creamy sauce. I was in a real quandary as I had already started cooking the meat and some other ingredients. I frantically inspected all our kitchen cupboards and all I could find to what I thought would be a fairly close milk substitute was a canister of custard powder.

My logic said to me that if I used a small amount of custard powder in diluted form with water I would be able to create something akin to milk. I proceeded accordingly.

I presented my splendid looking Lasagne to the other three with a flourish and proceeded to divide the results of my culinary efforts between the four of us. I didn't mention the custard.

We all took a first mouthful and it was obvious that my "milk solution" had not worked. The Lasagne had a really strange taste, so much so that the other three were giving me quizzical looks as if to say, "What the hell is in this"?

I had to come clean and told them what I had done. My Custard Lasagne was not a success and was never repeated.

Even today, whenever we meet up they never fail to remind me of my Custard Lasagne.

Although we were all on different shifts (except Mike who was on C Section with me) we did manage to socialise together on many occasions.

It was in late 1977 that I took a lone holiday to visit my mother in South Africa which I enjoyed very much. We took this opportunity to visit Mr & Mrs Glazier at their home in Khumalo North, Bulawayo, Rhodesia,

John LLOYD

and I was also able to meet up with my long standing friend, Fran and her husband Jim who I met for the very first time. They lived in an area of Bulawayo called Newton West where they were developing a lovely house right on the outskirts of the town where it meets with the Bundu. Fran told me that she had her own private game park view to the rear of her house. Mum and I had quite a hairy journey from Johannesburg to Bulawayo. This was at the height of the Rhodesian Bush war and Military intelligence at the time suggested that one element of the terrorists had obtained or were just about to obtain some Surface to Air Missiles (SAM). Indeed, within a year in 1978 the terrorists shot down two Air Rhodesia Vickers Viscount civilian aircraft killing all those on board including those passengers who survived the crash who were killed in cold blood on the ground.

As a result all flights from South Africa took evasive precautions whilst landing and taking off in Rhodesia. We flew on a South African Airways Boeing 737. Also on board was the Transvaal State Rugby team who were travelling to Bulawayo to play a competitive match against Rhodesia who had a pretty strong team at that time. On the landing approach the aircraft went into a very steep dive a couple of miles from the runway and then levelled out just before touching down on what looked to be very short runway. It was almost hearts in mouth time again but we landed safely and were met at the airport terminal.

In common with most other men of his age Jim was an Army Reservist with the Rhodesian African Rifles and was called away on anti-terrorist duties periodically for weeks at a time. Some time later he was wounded in the foot but fortunately recovered with, seemingly, no long term effects.

It was wonderful to meet up with Mr & Mrs Glazier and Fran after a gap of so many years and to catch up with all their news. I think that my Mum was in seventh heaven as she and Dorothy Glazier always got on so well.

Sadly, all good things come to an end and that included that holiday and I returned to the reality of life in the UK.

Bundu, the Beat & Beyond

I was temporarily transferred to the Gatwick Plain Clothes Unit which carried out anti-crime surveillance at the Airport including shoplifters of which there were many as well as pickpockets who mainly seemed to be South Americans based in London who travelled to Gatwick for the rich pickings.

One of my Sergeants at that time was Derek "Geordie" Fermor who seems to have identified something in me because he strongly suggested that I apply to the CID. (Criminal Investigation Department)

In 1977 I successfully applied to be an "Aide to CID" which entailed me being attached for a three month period to Gatwick CID so as to learn the ropes in basic Detective work as well as coming to terms with the piles of paperwork associated with Crime investigation.

The Gatwick CID Office then comprised a Detective Inspector, two Detective Sergeants and six Detective Constables. The Detective Inspector was Ray White (formerly of the Regional Crime Squad) and one of the Detective Sergeants was John Alderson a former Colour Sergeant in the Royal Marines. He was a gentle giant, very experienced in policing and well respected.

Other Officers there at that time were Brian Wright, Simon Hill, Keith King, Chris Gillings and Brian Cartmell.

I was very lucky in that my mentor was DC Keith King, a very experienced Detective who was also well respected by his peers. Keith had a very strong sense of ethics and morals and was as honest a person as anyone would care to meet. He was also teetotal and whilst the rest of us were downing our beers or whisky he would be sipping his coffee. This is not to say that he was a dull stick in the mud, just the opposite. He was normally full of fun and had the type of personality which most people would warm to.

Keith managed to guide me through the myriad of paperwork when preparing crime prosecution files but also showed me the ropes on Interview technique and evidence gathering. He was always very courteous to everyone he came across and seemed to treat all people in

John LLOYD

a fair and equitable fashion. Together we dealt with a variety of different crimes, mainly theft and minor frauds. I remember one old lag that we dealt with for theft who, when appearing at Crawley Magistrates Court, said to the Magistrates "I would like to thank Detective King and his sidekick for the way they dealt with me" etc etc. This was the first time I had received public praise from a villain even though he did not remember my name.

One other notable case of that period involved an employee of Laker Airways who was systematically stealing anything and everything she could from the company. We had received a complaint from the Laker Airways Security Officer of sizeable amounts of items being stolen from the company offices and hanger on the south side of the airport. We arranged to insert covert security cameras in the vulnerable areas and did not have long to wait for results.

We viewed the results the following day after a 24 hour period and we identified the middle aged lady employed by Laker Airways who was seen to remove several items including cutlery, foodstuffs and table linen.

Keith and I arrested the woman at her home in Crawley at which time we searched the premises. We found a veritable Aladdin's Cave of stolen property mainly belonging to Laker Airways. She was later charged with numerous offences of theft involving property valued at around £5000 which was a lot of money in those days.

During this time Keith introduced me to one of his many friends, Jackie Walford, who worked for British Caledonian Airways as a Supervisor on the Ticket Desk at Gatwick. Shortly after this we began dating and within a few weeks we were engaged to be married. Talk about a whirlwind!

We quickly established that our respective backgrounds held so many common factors. Jackie had been born in Nakuru, Kenya but had lived most of her teenage years in Kampala, in Uganda which she always referred to as "home" Her father had died in Kampala at a rather young age and we also established that she had been on secondment from Gatwick to Entebbe at the time I had flown on BUA to Zambia after

Bundu, the Beat & Beyond

my father had died. This meant that she would have been the smart young lady in the Caledonian Tartan uniform who had met the aircraft in which I was travelling. Neither of us could therefore say that this had been love at first sight but what a coincidence. I also met her mother, Lelia, who was of French extraction but had been born and raised in the French Colony of Madagascar. Lelia met her future husband, Basil Walford, during the Second World War when he was stationed in Madagascar with the Kings African Rifles.

They had four children, Evelyne, Jackie, Eric and Denise. In time I met them all.

By this time Keith King had married Wendy Cowie who had been at Hove at the same time as me and as Wendy King she was now stationed at Brighton Police Station where she became involved in a number of high profile cases one of which was the notorious "babes in the wood" murder investigation.

It was around this time that Jackie introduced me to her long time friend, Sue Nash, who also worked for British Caledonian Airways at Gatwick. A little later Sue began going out with Ian Inglis also from BCAL. The four of would socialise together and indeed shared a holiday to the Far East where we stayed in the original Raffles Hotel in Singapore before it was re-developed and had a wonderful time enjoying the renowned curries in the Tiffin Room as well trying the famous Singapore Slings from the Long Bar.

We visited the world famous Bugis Street one evening where we sat at a café table in the street sipping our drinks whilst admiring the almost continual parade of Kai Tai's. These were men dressed as women and I have to admit that some of them were absolutely stunning whereas some of the others were really obvious and perhaps should not have bothered.

We also sampled authentic Chinese food at Newton Circus and from some of the street stalls. It was mostly delicious and nourishing as well as cheap. We moved on to Hong Kong where we visited a tailors shop called "Sam's" where we were all fitted out for new clothes which were made up within 24 hours. I think that Ian and I ordered some shirts

John LLOYD

whilst Jackie and Sue had some tailored suits made. Later we decided to treat ourselves and visit a very plush Chinese Restaurant in Kowloon The meal tasted delicious and we had an enjoyable evening together. Later that night I was struck down with a strong case of food poisoning and had to spend the next few days in my hotel bed recovering whilst the others visited various Hong Kong attractions including a trip to the Chinese Border.

We have remained very good friends with Sue and Ian and we later attended their wedding in Edinburgh where we thoroughly enjoyed the Scottish Country Dancing and met some wonderful Scottish people with whom we still maintain contact to this day.

Sue and Ian were to have three daughters, Shona, Lynsey and Hannah who have grown into delightful young ladies. We feel honoured that all three still address Jackie and I as Uncle John and Auntie Jackie even though we are not blood related and they are all now adults.

They now live in the West Midlands area where Ian is a Senior Airline Manager at Birmingham Airport. We still maintain regular contact with them and see them several times a year.

My three months of Aide to CID at Gatwick was soon up and I really wanted to progress and attain a permanent CID position. I made that fact known and was advised that I should seek another period of Aide to CID at a Station other than Gatwick in order to get a broader experience of criminal investigation work. Accordingly a few weeks later I commenced an Aide to CID at Crawley Police Station.

During the interim period I returned to uniform duties on my old C Section where I met a new transferee from Brighton called Nigel Godden. We were to become life-long friends. When Jackie first saw me in uniform at the Airport she did not recognise me until I removed my helmet at which point she burst out laughing.

Jackie and I also arranged a charity football match between members of Gatwick CID and the BCAL ladies. In order to level the playing field a little it was decided that the men's team, who were called the Gatwick

Bundu, the Beat & Beyond

Grabbers & Gropers, were to play in fancy dress costume and wear Wellington Boots to slow them down. The BCAL ladies team, known as Bristols United wore BCAL T shirts, shorts and normal football/hockey boots. Jackie and I prepared hundreds of programmes for this football match which we sold around the airport to staff raising several hundred pounds for our chosen charity, the British Caledonian Golden Lions Children's Trust who offered holidays for under privileged children.

We enjoyed a good game against the ladies and adjourned afterwards for a social evening. We additionally organised a second similar event the following year for the same charity.

I got on pretty well with my Aide to CID at Crawley and was involved in some quite good investigations involving Burglaries, thefts and assaults. At the end of those three months I was again returned to Uniform Duties at Gatwick but after a few weeks Detective Inspector Mick Bennison, head of Crawley CID accompanied by Detective Sergeant Mick Saxby, came to see me at Gatwick and informed me that they had been impressed with my attachment period at Crawley and were in a position to offer me a job as a Detective Constable at Crawley. I was extremely pleased with this and accepted immediately.

In early 1978 I left Gatwick Uniform and was transferred to Crawley CID where I began work again on C Section with DC Keith Menzies and DS Brian Foster. These were two experienced Officers and I learned a great deal from both of them.

Keith hailed from Brighton and lived with his wife, Jackie, and their two young daughters, Natalie and Jane, in Tilgate, Crawley. We formed a good friendship which still exists today. Keith has a keen intellect twinned with a sharp wit which I found to be an attractive combination.

We were later joined on C Section by Nigel Godden who had completed a successful Aide to CID and the three of us enjoyed a successful partnership both professionally and socially. Nigel was a very tall and well-built young man. He played rugby to a high standard and was a very useful asset to our CID unit. We also formed a strong friendship

John LLOYD

which has stood the test of time. Jackie and I still socialise with Keith and Jackie Menzies as well as Nigel and his wife Cherie to this day.

In those days most Police Stations had a Social Club or Bar. Crawley was no exception and it had a very lively Social Club and well run bar which was attached to the Police Station. We often adjourned to the bar after finishing Late Turn at 2200hrs for a few wind down "drinkies" before making our way home. There was a definite drinking culture within the CID in those days and we enjoyed numerous merry times after finishing work. It was a good place to unwind and also bond with your fellow Officers. Drinking was never a real problem for most of us but one or two did seem to drink more than they should and at some odd times of the day. We always adjourned to the bar at lunchtimes each week-end where we would be joined by our families or girlfriends.

This was before the days of political correctness was even a concept and many things happened then which would not be tolerated today. One small example was the manner in which some Policewomen were treated by some of their male counterparts. By this time the Police Women's Department had been disbanded and all the female Officers had been amalgamated into mainstream Policing in which the women worked alongside the men doing the same hours and receiving the same rates of pay. However there was an attitude amongst some of the male Officers that Policewomen were an inferior species within the Police family and that, with a few exceptions, the Police woman was unable to deal with all the matters traditionally dealt with by the men. This attitude led some Policewomen to be treated in such a way that they must have felt intimidated and unwanted. It was to be some years before this attitude lessened to a degree where it was no longer an issue.

Jackie and I married in September 1978 in Crawley with a lot of my CID colleagues in attendance including Keith Menzies, Colin Binstead, Adam Christie, Dave Bradley, Mick Saxby and Brian Foster.

Keith King was my best man and did a sterling job as one would expect from a man of his calibre.

Bundu, the Beat & Beyond

We used Jackie's airline concessions for our honeymoon and flew out to Malindi in Kenya via Nairobi. We stayed at a lovely beach resort called Tradewinds in Malindi which we found to absolutely idyllic. Sun, blue skies, long white beaches, warm water in which to swim etc etc. The only slight downside and cause of some embarrassment to us both was that when we arrived in our room we found that we had been given two single beds which really did not suit a honeymoon couple. I had a quiet word with the Manager and later that afternoon four African staff were seen by all the other hotel guests carrying a huge double bed across the lawn to our room where it was swapped for the two single beds. This was accompanied by some ribald comments from the hotel guests who witnessed this little pantomime.

We spent a very happy two weeks in Malindi after which we reluctantly returned to the UK and work.

During the next few years Jackie and I enjoyed numerous trips abroad for next to no money using her airline concessions. These concessions permitted air travel to staff at a fare of 10% of the full economy class fare but the downside was that this was on a space available basis so you could find yourselves stuck in some remote part of the world if the aircraft was full with fare paying passengers.

This only happened to Jackie and I once when we did a tour of the far east including the Philippines. On the day of are intended departure from Manila to return home to London we had reservations on Philippine Airlines. We turned up at the airport and checked in our luggage which was accepted. We were told that passenger space was limited and we had to standby until the flight closed about 20 minutes prior to boarding. That time arrived and went and eventually we were told that that we would not be accepted for travel that day. However our luggage and spare clothing etc was on the aircraft now bound for London. We had little alternative but to travel back into Manila, find a cheap hotel, wash our clothes and hang them to dry overnight and then return to Manila Airport the next day hoping to get on that day's flight. We repeated that procedure for the next three days and nights. We even

John LLOYD

went to see the Station Manager of Philippine Airlines who assured us that "there is no problem" However, there was a problem, so much so, that we were denied boarding for three days. Finally our patience ran out and we managed to purchase reasonably priced tickets on KLM who flew us to Amsterdam from where we caught a British Caledonian flight to Gatwick.

I think that it was during this particular trip that Jackie and I had visited Bangkok which I found to be a fascinating City of contrasts. We did the usual touristy things of visiting temples and the floating market and so on. Early one evening we decided to take a stroll before dinner and we found ourselves walking through the notorious red light district of Patpong. There were, at that time two Patpongs, with very original names of Patpong 1 and Patpong 2. I think that we found ourselves in Patpong 1 and we very quickly realised that we were in a very different area of Bangkok when young ladies of the night would approach me offering their services whilst completely ignoring the fact that Jackie was on my arm.

We found this rather amusing but after several minutes of similar behaviour we withdrew from Patpong 1 to continue our walk elsewhere.

I had maintained my weekly contacts with Gareth and he would often stay with us in our Police House in Brantridge Road, Furnace Green in Crawley. He also accompanied us on several overseas holidays abroad including a trip to South Africa. He did not know just where we going until the moment we boarded the aircraft when he saw the electronic sign announcing the BA flight to Johannesburg. We had a great holiday, visiting my mother at her home in Germiston and additionally travelling down to Durban to visit my brother Chris who was living and working there at the time.

Gareth seemed to enjoy himself immensely so much so that he would wake up quite early each morning and Jackie and I would sense a presence in our bedroom around 0600hrs and would awake to find Gareth just a couple of feet from our bed, staring at us intently just willing us awake. My brother Chris took him down to the beach a couple

Bundu, the Beat & Beyond

of early mornings where they enjoyed a touch of surfing which Gareth loved.

Jackie and I also took Gareth on holidays to other destinations including Florida and Disney World etc which we all thoroughly enjoyed.

My Grandfather, Frank Cole (right) and very tall friend with some of the musical instruments he was able to play. Circa 1920.

My mother in her early 20's.

My father in his early 20's.

The author at school circa 1954.

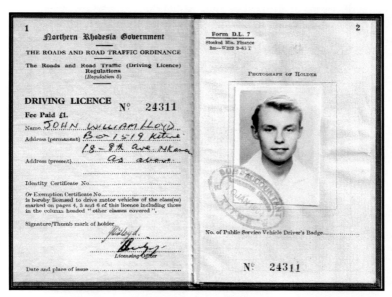

My Northern Rhodesia Drivers Licence January 1964.

My Zambia Registration Card December 1965.

Kim and the author, Nkana 1965.

My pride and joy - Author with his MGA, Nkana 1965

My Nan and me. First time in uniform and when I was asked to direct traffic. Chertsey 1969.

My son Gareth on Brighton seafront circa 1977.

Gatwick CID charity football team 1978, Back row L-R: Nigel Godden, Graham Bradley, Derek Fermor, Chris Gillings, Unknown, Bill Stepney, Bob Diplock, Martin Ripley (Referee), Front Row, Unknown guest, Author as a last minute replacement player, Unknown guest, Simon Hill, Keith King.

BCAL ladies charity football team - second match 1978. Back row L-R: Deidre Northcott, Linda Brown, Jan Kemp, Brenda Young, a rather camp trainer Ian Inglis. Front row (L-R, Sharon Alcorn, Marion Cursons, Sue Nash, Jackie Lloyd, Carol Mourton and in front lying on the ground is Jan Hammond.

CHAPTER 6

Stories from Crawley CID—1978-1982

One of the first investigations I dealt with at Crawley involved the theft of controlled drugs from Crawley Hospital. From the evidence and information available my suspicions fell on the Ward Sister in charge of the ward from where the drugs had been stolen.

She was the only common factor when comparing the staffs daily shift rosters against the dates and times during which the drugs had been unlawfully taken.

This was not rocket science nor was it particularly good Detective work but more a process of elimination.

Having obtained this Ward Sister's work roster from the Hospital I decided that the most prudent thing to do was to arrest her at her Crawley home at a time when she was not at work. This matter was the subject of much speculation and rumour amongst staff at the Hospital and I wanted to avoid an arrest in public which would raise the temperature even further amongst hospital staff.

On the morning of her next rest day a colleague and I went to her house where I arrested her on suspicion of theft. Her house was searched but no illicit drugs were found.

She was taken to Crawley Police Station where the Duty Sergeant booked her into custody. She was given the option of securing the services of the Duty Solicitor but she declined.

John LLOYD

She was aged about 40 years and had been quite a beauty in her youth, I thought, but that beauty was now fading and she was beginning to look somewhat haggard. I could not see any obvious signs of needle marks on those visible parts of her body but I just had the impression that she was showing signs of being a drugs abuser.

This was before the days of tape recorded interviews so I took contemporaneous notes of my questions and her replies which is quite a laborious process. After some time my lines of questioning were such that she started opening up and began to make small admissions. Eventually she admitted to stealing the morphine based drugs from the hospital for her own use. It appears that she had previously worked in hospitals in the Middle East where her addiction to morphine (heroin) based drugs had started.

Having admitted these matters she agreed to sign a written statement made under caution. She dictated that statement which I recorded after which she signed the written statement as being accurate.

At that time I was still not in possession of all the evidence from the hospital Authorities as they had been dragging their heels a little.

I was therefore not in a position to charge her with the offences at that time. I was also aware that she seemed to be in a somewhat fragile mental state and in consultation with D/I Mick Bennison it was decided that I should report her for these matters and submit a full file of evidence as soon as possible to Sussex Police Legal Branch for their consideration of charges.

I knew, as she probably did, that her medical career was most likely at an end and, in view of her somewhat fragile state, I decided to refer her to the Social Services Department immediately for assessment and for any support etc deemed appropriate to her circumstances.

I then submitted my, as yet, incomplete file with a full written report of what I had done. She was released from custody and Social Services intervened. I then went on two Rest Days.

Bundu, the Beat & Beyond

I was contacted by telephone the next morning by DS Mick Saxby who informed me that the Ward Sister had been found dead at her home earlier that day having apparently committed suicide. She had cut her wrists using a medical scalpel.

I was somewhat shocked by this news although not overly surprised because I had been aware that she was in a fragile mental state which was recorded in my report together with the intervention of Social Services.

I then had to write a statement for the Coroner pending the inquest into her death and my crime file was also submitted to the Coroner as it contained information relevant to her death.

The subsequent inquest ruled that her death was due to suicide when the balance of her mind was disturbed. I was not criticised in any way but in my mind this was an unsatisfactory conclusion to what should have been a relatively routine investigation. It also brought home to me just how careful all Police Officers need to be in certain situations.

Another story involving drugs that I was involved in investigating related to a young personable 18 year old lad who came from a very good home in Crawley and who had everything going for him if only he had not taken some wrong paths.

He had got himself involved with some lowlifes in Crawley who were part of the drugs scene. He had become a heroin addict fairly quickly it seems and needed a great deal of money to fund his daily habit.

He resorted to burglaries in residential homes around Crawley selling any items that he managed to steal.

I was investigating some of these burglaries and with the assistance of Roger Mason, our Scenes of Crime Officer (SOCO),finger-marks were developed from two of these burglaries which were later identified as those of my suspect who had only one previous conviction for a minor theft which meant that his fingerprints were on file.

John LLOYD

I arrested him and interviewed him during which he made some admissions. His parents were totally distraught at their son's behaviour and were at something of a loss to know what to do with him.

I did have sufficient evidence to charge him with four burglaries. He was duly charged and released on bail to appear at Crawley Magistrates Court four weeks hence.

I submitted my prosecution file and moved on to the next case. A week or so later I was told by another Officer that the 18 year old had been found dead as a result of an overdose of heroin.

I felt a little numb but my main thoughts were what a real waste of a very young life which had been cut so short by this vile habit. We never did find out who supplied him with the heroin on which he overdosed although we had some suspicions. His parents were naturally inconsolable but their influence on their son had been negated by his total dependence on heroin. Another human tragedy,

A significant proportion of crimes reported to us were committed by Drugs abusers or "Druggies" as we called them and we therefore often came into contact with that community for obvious reasons. On one such occasion my colleague Keith Menzies and I drove up to a well known "Druggies" house intent on arresting him for several burglaries for which he was suspected through good forensic evidence.

We pulled up outside the house and Keith went to the front door whilst I made my way to the back door of the house with a view to preventing our suspect from absconding that way. I realised that I was just a little too late because as I reached the back of the house I saw the figure of our suspect vaulting over the five foot fence to the side of the garden and disappear into next doors back yard. I shouted, "Come back here Martin. I can see you." If truth be known I couldn't see him even though I knew where he was. I was therefore most surprised and gratified when Martin clambered back over the fence into his own backyard and rather meekly surrendered to custody. I was gratified because I was wearing a brand new pair of flared trousers, which were fashionable at the time, and I did

Bundu, the Beat & Beyond

not really fancy clambering over fences and the like whilst giving chase to an errant burglar.

I found that very often Police life is sustained by humour which is very therapeutic for a variety of reasons not least of which is that it acts as a type of release valve permitting some of the tensions associated with sometimes stressful situations to be released.

Every morning at 0900hrs the CID held a briefing, normally conducted by the Detective Inspector, during which newly reported crimes were discussed and allocated for investigation as well as criminal intelligence disseminated on known active criminals operating in our area. These briefings were attended by all CID Officers on duty that day with the exception of the Late Turn Detectives who commenced duty at 1400hrs.

One of the DC's at Crawley at that time was Roger Buttle who was a very hardworking and dedicated Officer who was also a good "thief-taker". Roger worked some very long hours and no one doubted his commitment to the "job". Roger did have one failing however. He invariably had a problem in getting up in the morning or at least arriving into work in time for the 0900hrs briefing. He always seemed to have a ready excuse for his lateness, some more original than others. One morning we were well on our way to completing morning briefing when in walked Roger around 0915hrs.

DI Mick Bennison said, "Well, what's the story today then Rog?"

Roger explained that he had acquired a new Budgie which he kept in a cage in his bedroom but that he had inadvertently left the door of the cage open and at some point during the night his Budgie had flown out of its cage and had settled on his bedside alarm clock and must have turned it off which meant that the alarm did not sound at the normal time, hence his lateness. Roger got a round of applause for that one.

We also had some practical jokers in the CID office. Mark Hayler and Mick Saxby were two of these.

John LLOYD

On one occasion Mark Hayler filled his fountain pen with disappearing ink and "accidently" discharged this dark blue coloured substance over a brand new white shirt being worn by another DC called Ron Holmes. Ron did not see the funny side of this thinking that his brand new white shirt had just been ruined by Mark and his antics. Ron got up out of his desk chair and flew at Mark shouting various obscenities and threats. Fortunately Mark was a little fitter than Ron and managed to evade Ron's attempts at catching him which was probably just as well as Ron was threatening all sorts of nasty violence to Mark. At the same time Mark was protesting his innocence saying and re-saying "It's disappearing ink Ron, it won't stain "Ron was in a bit of a red mist and appeared not to hear Mark's protestations. It went on like this for some minutes before Ron realised that the "ink stain" had miraculously vanished and Mark was spared any serious violence.

Mick Saxby was in charge of the CID property Store in which all seized stolen property and potential Court exhibits were stored. It was his responsibility to ensure that the property register was correctly completed and up to date etc etc. Week-ends would often find Mick rummaging through this store to ensure that what was registered in the property book was physically in the store.

On one occasion he brought out a .177 air pistol from the store complete with pellets. He was examining the weapon and said to me, "I bet that you can't reach the end of the corridor before I count to five. If you don't I will fire at you." I weighed up my chances and thought that as the corridor was only about 12 feet in length the challenge would not provide too many problems for me. I was being naïve and too trusting.

I agreed and began running toward the end of the corridor during which time I heard Mick say just one word " five" after which he shot me in the back with the air pistol. It did not do any damage but it did sting a lot. I had learned another lesson much to the amusement of Mick and my colleagues.

One other "prank" which comes to mind was when some CID Officers were provided with headed notepaper from a local solicitors office and decided to use that paper to play a "joke" on one of our colleagues.

Bundu, the Beat & Beyond

Using the solicitor's note-paper they prepared a stylishly written typed letter detailing that Officer's affair with a local woman and citing him as the respondent in a forthcoming divorce petition lodged by the woman's husband. This letter was then signed purporting to be from a well known local solicitor and sent to the Officer at the CID Office at Crawley Police Station via the Detective Inspector. The DI handed the unopened letter to the Officer in question who opened it, read its contents after which he went as white as a sheet. He then excused himself and left the Office. We later learned that he had gone directly home to his wife and had admitted the affair to her plus one or two other affairs which nobody knew about. His wife was naturally furious but fortunately calmed down sometime later and forgave her errant husband. The Officers behind that "prank" were quite abashed and ashamed of what they had done. They had not foreseen the consequences of their actions and had not expected their target to take the action he subsequently did and had hoped to forestall any such action by informing him of what they had done before any harm was caused. Another lesson learned.

Every year the CID held a Christmas party to which we invited other professionals with whom we had contact throughout the year, such as Solicitors, Social Workers, Probation Officers, Ladies from our typing pool etc. These parties normally commenced just after 5pm and went on for some time. Those of us who had finished work by 5pm were able to attend and indulge in the vast quantities of alcohol available.

One year I had arrested a man for burglary and after interviewing him I put him into a cell and popped back to the Office just in time for the beginning of that years Xmas party. I had a few whiskies to greet the Christmas period and began enjoying the happy mood which prevailed. After an hour or so I got a 'phone call from the Duty Sergeant, Brian McArdle, who said something like, "What are you going to do with your prisoner?" I have to admit that the presence of my prisoner had slipped my mind which was by now somewhat soaked with strong spirit. I told Brian that I would be over shortly and my addled brain told me that I should prepare charge sheets which I began to type up myself in the CID Clerks office using two very slow and deliberate fingers. I am not sure that these charges made 100% sense but I hoped that they would suffice. When I had completed my typing efforts I managed to make my

John LLOYD

way to the Charge room where Brian had placed the prisoner awaiting my arrival. Fortunately Brian was also there and saw what state I was in. Brian was a calm and understanding fellow and he had to assist me in standing up straight whilst I read out the charges to the prisoner. The prisoner was then released on bail to appear at Court on a future date. I got away with that for a number of reasons.

That would not happen today as the Police culture is now quite different. There are no social clubs or bars in Police Stations anymore and drinking is not permitted on Police premises. There is a downside to this in that the bonding and camaraderie has less of a chance to develop.

By this time, our good friend Keith King had transferred from Gatwick to Burgess Hill CID but due to its close proximity with Crawley we often had need to visit their CID office for operational reasons. As I recall he was working with other CID colleagues at Burgess Hill including Steve Tuffin, John May, Nick Siggs and Ann Bilson. I was always impressed with Ann who always seemed to be very calm and composed whilst having a high degree of efficiency which I though was a good combination. I was to meet up with Ann some years hence when she had become Ann Rattray (upon marriage) and was working at Gatwick as a Uniform Inspector.

Crawley had, at that time, a small section dealing with Child Abuse matters, a forerunner of the Child Protection teams of today and they mainly dealt with reports of child sex and physical abuse. This small unit was semi-attached to the CID office but because of confidentiality it operated as an autonomous unit but answerable to the head of Crawley CID. This unit was headed by a Uniformed Sergeant, Tim O'Connor, a very genial Irishman who was always very charming and polite. Tim and I never worked together but he always gave me the impression of being a very competent Officer. Working with him was Gill Richardson and Judy Charlton who I knew very well. Judy went onto to later marry a really nice man called Barry Lovell who I had worked with on Gatwick Uniform some years before.

I was appointed the Divisional Drugs Liaison Officer in 1980 which meant that I was responsible for logging all the drugs seizures into the

Bundu, the Beat & Beyond

CID property store and was also the focal point of liaison with the Force Drugs Squad who included George Hedgecock and Nigel Kent among their members. This was not a particularly arduous task but I was pleased to have been given this responsibility because the Force Drugs Squad was a very good team who worked well together. They would visit Crawley once or twice a month and update me with their current activities and I would reciprocate if I had any local intelligence which I thought would be of some use to them. I only became involved in one of their Operations as they were a self contained unit and preferred to operate by themselves which was fair enough.

This Operation involved a local target who was a well known Drugs dealer where information had been received that a drugs drop was to be made on the M23 spur road leading into Crawley which was going to be collected by their Crawley target.

This was a difficult venue to maintain discreet observations and the actual drop was missed so we never could confirm the identity of the supplier however the target was later observed to approach the drop site and collect the drugs (heroin) after which he was immediately surrounded and arrested. A substantial quantity of heroin was seized and the overall result was satisfactory. The suspect later appeared at Brighton Crown Court and after a trial was found guilty and sentenced to a term of imprisonment.

During my time at Crawley CID I occasionally worked with other Officers based on other CID sections including Kelvin Robinson, Derek Chambers, Colin Binstead, Stuart Booth, Dave Swainston and Ron Holmes however as we worked a shift system I mainly worked with my shift partners Keith and Nigel.

After joining Crawley CID in 1978 I had to wait just over eighteen months before going on my initial CID Course at Lewes HQ. I believe that this was down to the large numbers of Officers awaiting their courses and the Training Staff could only cater for a fairly small number at any one time.

John LLOYD

I finally received my joining instructions to commence my CID course due to start in early 1980, between the 4th February and the 3rd April.

Others on that course included some Officers who I already knew like Gerry Cannan, Chris Gillings, and John Watkins. Others I met on the course were Janet Post, Jim Roden, Pete Desborough, Clive (Yaki) Brind, Alwyn Evans, John Bacon, Phil Helyer, Barry Gibson, John Bishop, Ken Scrase and Dave Smith.

This was an intensive ten week course and focused mainly on the criminal law which we already thought we knew but soon found out that there was a great deal more to learn.

We had guest speakers provide enlightening talks on such topics as pathology and odontology given by highly qualified professionals who, as a bonus, were really entertaining which made the lectures doubly good value. Additionally we had lectures on a range of other topics including paedophilia and child pornography. We were shown some child pornography material but I was not disappointed when the film projector broke down after a short time because witnessing children being abused is not my idea of the best way to pass an afternoon.

The tutors were a good social mix with DI Ron Bishop as Course Director assisted by DS George Divall and DS Dudley Reynolds.

We were accommodated in the blocks adjoining the class rooms at Lewes HQ and we ate in the Staff Restaurant on site. There was a bar and social club for the HQ staff which we were permitted to use.

The bar was run by a very camp man named Terry who was really great fun and helped make the 10 weeks go by a little easier.

We were permitted to return home at week-ends and Gerry Cannan, who lived in Sharpthorne at the time, kindly gave me a lift to and from my home in Crawley. He was not out of pocket as he was able to claim a mileage allowance for this.

Bundu, the Beat & Beyond

At sometime during the course each student had to deliver a 45 minute presentation to the Instructors and the remainder of the class. Each student could choose the subject of their talk.

I elected to talk about the Republic of South Africa although when I posted my theme I merely indicated that my talk was "Impressions of RSA" which lead to a deal of speculation by the staff and other students who thought that I might be talking about the Royal Society of Arts or something similar!

My turn came late one morning and I walked into the classroom clutching a gallon box of South African white wine which had been chilling in the fridge plus a sufficient number of plastic mugs. I placed these on the table in front of the assembled audience and I could see a degree of apprehension on the face of Ron Bishop but a sense of anticipation from the others.

I had brought the wine over from a recent trip to South Africa as boxed wine was not readily available in the UK at that time.

I began delivering my presentation and invited anyone who wished to help themselves to the wine. Slowly people began to leave their seats and took wine before returning to their seats, the DS Instructors included. After 20 minutes or so I could see that Ron Bishop was being tempted by the wine and he gave in shortly after that and helped himself. By the time my presentation finished the box of wine was empty and the class and Instructors were all in good spirits. For some reason my presentation received high marks.

During the time of my CID course the Rhodesian Authorities had come to an agreement with the African leaders including Robert Mugabe, plus the British Government, about handing over power to the African majority.

Plans were put in place where free elections open to all the people of Rhodesia would be held within a few weeks. As part of that process it had been agreed that around 600 or so British Police Officers would be flown out to Rhodesia to be present during the election process whilst

John LLOYD

trying to ensure that no intimidation took place. Almost immediately a general appeal was sent out to all UK Police Forces to supply a number of Uniform Officers for this purpose.

In view of my background DI Ron Bishop thought that I would be an ideal candidate to volunteer for this mission. I disagreed for somewhat selfish personal reasons not least of which is that the UK Police would be in Rhodesia/Zimbabwe for some weeks and as I was in the middle of my CID course I would not be able to qualify at the end of course examination which required a minimum 70% pass mark. I also felt that I no longer wanted to put on a uniform again having only relatively recently been awarded CID status. I declined to volunteer and other Sussex Officers formed part of the British contingent that travelled to Rhodesia/Zimbabwe. On reflection it was, perhaps, an opportunity missed but I was, and still am, comfortable with my decision.

We studied hard during the course and revised in the early evenings after dinner but we all met up in the bar around 2100 hrs for a few drinks prior to bed which helped us get to know each other really well.

The dreaded examinations arrived and we all did our best. I have never enjoyed exams which I viewed as a necessary evil. The end result was worth it however as I came a respectable third in class just a couple of marks behind Chris Gillings and Alwyn Evans. I am pleased to say that all my other colleagues passed as well and so we adjourned that evening for a really good end of course celebration at which most of us got quite inebriated.

It was back to Crawley CID the following Monday where the heavy work load carried on unabated. I assisted another of my Crawley colleagues, Kelvin Robinson, in dealing with a Welshman who I had dealt with previously for thefts of motor vehicles and allied offences. I had previously got on quite well with this Welshman but for some reason he got a real strop on when he saw me and I played second fiddle to Kelvin to enable us to deal with this stroppy individual in a proper manner.

Mick Saxby and I were seconded onto a Murder Investigation Team operating out of Brighton Police Station. The team were investigating

Bundu, the Beat & Beyond

the murder, by strangulation, of a middle aged woman whose body had been found inside her flat located just off the Lewes Road in Brighton.

Background information suggested that this woman, who lived alone, had a strong liking for sex as a result of which she had a large number of male visitors arriving and departing almost on a daily basis. There was no indication that she had been a prostitute.

Initially no prime suspect was identified and we therefore had to establish just who her male visitors had been and find out where they now were.

The Home Office Pathologists Post Mortem report included reference to her sexual organs which he described as being akin to a horses collar which I thought was a little unfair until I saw some Post Mortem photographs of the deceased woman after which I had to concede that the Pathologist did have a point.

This investigation went on for a few weeks until such time that her last known male visitor was identified and he could be positively linked to the scene and the deceased by forensic evidence.

He admitted strangling the woman in the throes of sexual passion. He was charged and later sentenced to Life Imprisonment.

Mick and I returned to our normal CID duties at Crawley.

We were frequent visitors to Crawley Magistrates Court either to give evidence or to assist the Prosecutor in understanding a new overnight case or, in some cases, to swear out a Search Warrant before a Magistrate in closed session. The Chief Magistrate in those days was the renowned and somewhat fearsome Mrs Brissenden who would truck no nonsense in her Court whether that be from the Police, witnesses, defendants and the lawyers. She was very strong in her handling of the variety of cases put before her but I always found her to be very fair.

The Magistrates were very ably assisted by the Court Clerk, Des Sturmer, who was also a strong character with a somewhat bluff manner, but I always found him to be very helpful and well balanced.

John LLOYD

One other case of note in which I was involved whilst at Crawley was at a time when a Welsh Male Voice Choir visited Crawley and gave a concert at the local Leisure Centre. They were, apparently, very good as Welsh Choirs tend to be. That night, after the show, the choir were put up in a local Hotel in Brighton Road. I was Night Duty call out CID and around 0100hrs I was called out to deal with an allegation of indecent assault at the Brighton Road Hotel.

I interviewed the distressed young lady victim who was a guest at the hotel. She told me that she had been in the hotel bar earlier in the evening having a couple of social drinks with a friend when, towards the end of the evening members of the Welsh Male Voice Choir had entered the bar to have a last pint or so before retiring for the night.

One of the choir members appears to have taken a shine to the young lady who had apparently rebuffed his advances. She then retired to her bedroom and got ready for bed at which point there was a knock on her door which she answered. Standing before her was the Choir member referred to above. It appears that he virtually forced his way into the bedroom whereupon he sexually assaulted the woman who resisted him physically whilst screaming at the same time. The noise of her screams plus her physical rejection seem to have put an end to the Welshman's advances and he left her room after apologising for his behaviour.

The matter was then reported to Crawley Police and I was called out to investigate. Having interviewed the victim I arranged for a Woman Officer to remain with her with a view to re-assuring her and calming her down a little after her traumatic ordeal.

I then enlisted the help of the hotel staff and the Choir's leader as a result of which we were able to identify the suspect.

I knocked on the suspect's bedroom door on the floor above and he answered and opened the door. I identified myself and he broke down virtually immediately. After he had calmed himself I asked him to get dressed and arrested him and took him to Crawley Police Station where he was interviewed.

Bundu, the Beat & Beyond

He made full admissions and after I had got the statement of complaint from the victim he was charged with one offence of indecent assault and kept in custody to appear at Crawley Magistrates Court later that morning. It was nearly 0900 hrs by the time I had finished preparing the crime process file by which time the early CID man (who came on at 0800 hrs) plus the general day men had arrived for work.

The Welshman had been given access to a local solicitor for legal advice and decided to plead Guilty at Court. He had no previous convictions and the Magistrates felt that, as it was a first offence, they would be able to deal with the matter. The case was adjourned for Probation reports etc and when he appeared at Court a month or so later he was put on Probation for 12 months. However, his days in the Choir came to an abrupt end shortly after that which brought some shame on the Welshman because, as I understand it, being a member of a Welsh Choir raises ones status within the community and perhaps his real punishment was that of being sacked from the Choir.

Night Duty Call outs were not my favourite days. Crawley CID did not have a dedicated Night Duty Officer as we all worked varying shifts between the hours of 0800-2200hrs each day expect Sundays when we worked 0900-1700hrs. After those times if a CID presence was required by the Night Duty Uniform Section they would have to call out the Night Duty DC or DS. This meant that each CID Officer could expect to be on Night Duty call 2 or 3 times each month. If you were called out during the night you were expected to deal with whatever you had been called out for and then report for duty by 0900hrs that morning and work your normal shift.

For example in the case of the Welshman who was charged with indecent assault I was called around 0100hrs and worked through until 0900hrs after which time I commenced my normal day shift working through until 1700hrs. By that time I would have been very tired and glad to see the inside of my own home. We did have some recompense in that we could claim overtime for payment or time off which was handy. It was always a bonus for me if I had not been called out having been on Night Duty Call out because it meant that I got a decent night's sleep.

John LLOYD

In 1980 I had the opportunity to fly on Concorde. The Concorde fare from London to New York was well outside of my budget but in the early 1980's British Airways offered the occasional Charter flights on Concorde operating supersonic flights over the North Sea or the Bay of Biscay. Unfortunately these were also not affordable for me. However, a work colleague of Jackie's at British Caledonian Airways, Colin French, identified that that BA were also offering seats on a positioning flight on Concorde between London Heathrow and Glasgow prior to one of the Supersonic Charters over the North Sea.

The cost for a seat on this positioning flight was £80.00 (still a fairly hefty sum in those days) one way but Colin and I jumped at this opportunity and reserved our seats. We made our way to Heathrow on the appointed day and boarded Concorde. What struck me was just how small the cabin was, very narrow with just enough space for two rows of seats divided by a narrow centre aisle and no more. The windows were minute although seemingly very thick.

We took our seats and readied ourselves for take-off. The aircraft taxied out to the runway and the Pilot applied full thrust. I have never experienced a take off run quite like this one. I remember being thrust back into my seat with some considerable force. It was not uncomfortable but it was certainly thrilling. The take off run seemed fairly short because the aircraft was flying light due to it carrying no baggage etc. The pilot rotated the aircraft which responded immediately and when the afterburners were engaged up we went at a very steep angle. It felt as though we were conducting a vertical climb such was the power and thrust being used.

Once cruising altitude had been reached the cabin crew served Champagne and canapés during our short 45 minute flight to Glasgow. In what seemed like just a few minutes we began our descent into Glasgow Airport. Because the aircraft was operating over mainland UK we had not flown at Supersonic speed but that did not deter Colin and I from enjoying every minute of the experience.

After landing Concorde taxied to its allotted stand just short of the main terminal building after which we disembarked. I was absolutely amazed

Bundu, the Beat & Beyond

to find that, as we exited the aircraft, there was a very large crowd of people waving and cheering at us from the public areas in the Terminal building. I felt just like Royalty must feel and I almost gave the "Royal" wave before I realised that this vast crowd had not come to greet us mere mortal passengers but had, of course, come to view and welcome Concorde on its maiden flight into Glasgow. Such was the amazing allure of this aircraft that all these Glaswegians had taken the trouble to come out in their thousands just to catch a glimpse of this wonderful aircraft.

Colin and I returned to Gatwick in a British Caledonian BAC 1-11 later that afternoon. What a come down after travelling in Concorde but we did have some wonderful memories.

Later in 1980 I decided to surprise my mother and I set up this surprise by telephoning her at her home in South Africa. I advised her that a friend of mine called John Williams would be flying to Johannesburg shortly and asked her if she would she mind putting him up for a couple of nights? Mum, of course, replied that she would be delighted. I gave her the flight number and time of arrival and she said that she would arrange for a friend to meet John Williams at Jan Smuts Airport in Johannesburg.

My full name is John William Lloyd.

Jackie had managed to arrange a staff ticket for me with Air Zimbabwe flying out of London Gatwick to Johannesburg via Harare (formerly Salisbury). Air Zimbabwe had only recently changed its name from Air Rhodesia and had just commenced operating the service to London.

I flew out of Gatwick on a Thursday evening having finished work a few hours before. I had just started my long week-end off and was not due back to work until the following Monday.

The aircraft used for this flight was a Boeing 720 which was a shorter version of the Boeing 707. This was an extended range variant and therefore did not require any re-fuelling stops en-route.

John LLOYD

The flight and cabin crew were all white and the service was impeccable apart from the locally produced Rhodesian wine served with dinner which I found to be an acquired taste. I only mention the ethnicity of the crew because this situation did change over the following few years or so and standards did change, both within the airline and the country of Zimbabwe which had once been self sufficient but within a few years had become almost a pariah state which had to import foodstuffs to feed the population and widespread corruption became the norm. It was another of Africa's tragedies.

I arrived at Jan Smuts airport in Johannesburg the following day after a short transit stop in Harare. I collected my baggage and proceeded into the Arrivals Hall where there were many people awaiting sight of their loved ones etc amongst the arriving passengers.

I caught sight of one of Mum's friends who I knew called Dougie. He was holding a placard with the name of John Williams written thereon. He caught sight of me about the same time and I could see the sense of shock register on his face, so much so, that all he could repeatedly say was, "Hey, hey, hey hey." etc etc.

After he had calmed down a little I explained what I had done and then, using my Mum's car, he drove me to my Mum's house where I unpacked and settled in. In the late afternoon Dougie drove me to the Thoroughbred Breeders Association where my Mum worked. This was a specialist auction house dealing in thoroughbred horses and my Mum had a key job there and was well known to most members of the Horse Racing fraternity in South Africa including the likes of the golfer, Gary Player, who was also an owner.

I secreted myself behind a bush to one side of the main doors of the building whilst Dougie went inside to collect my Mum. They emerged some minutes later and walked up the path towards my Mum's car. I emerged from my hiding place and followed them up the short path and as they reached her car I said, "Hello Mum."

She turned around and I could see the absolute look of surprise on her face twinned with a mother's joy at seeing one of her sons.

114

Bundu, the Beat & Beyond

We enjoyed a great week-end together and I made the return journey to London on the Sunday where I had a very pleasant surprise waiting for me as Jackie had used the week-end to re-paint our kitchen which had been looking a little tired. To say that I was pleased would be an understatement.

In those days Police vehicles were considered to be almost untouchable in that any Police driver who was responsible for causing damage to one was usually in big trouble. I recall one occasion when Steve Olive and I used a Crawley CID car to travel up to one of the South London prisons in order to interview a prisoner detained there. Steve drove on the upward journey and when we reached Streatham the busy three lane road suddenly became two resulting in traffic vying for position and closing in on one another. As we drove at a fairly slow speed we had a coming together with a car on our offside whose driver was trying to squeeze us out. This caused some scratching and very minor damage to our Police car. In accordance with our Forces Standing Orders we were obliged to report this minor accident to the local Police which, being south London was the Metropolitan Police. A Met Traffic Sergeant duly attended and took notes. Steve suspended himself from driving and I took over.

We reached the prison without further incident and interviewed the prisoner after which we commenced our return journey to Crawley. I was driving and as we approached a chicane in south Croydon virtually the same thing happened as before in that a car on our nearside came too close to us causing scrapes and scratches to the other side of the vehicle. Again we had to call out the Met Police who attended from Croydon. This time it was an Inspector who attended and took notes. Nearing the conclusion of proceedings he said, "Weren't you two involved in a similar incident on Streatham's ground earlier this morning?" I agreed that we had and shaking his head he gave us certain words of advice which included the fact that we should not consider driving within their Police area for some time or words to that effect! Needless to say Steve and I were the butt of office humour for some weeks after that.

In early 1982 I was approached by the Senior CID Officer for North Sussex DCI John McConnell who told me that a vacancy had arisen at Gatwick CID and would I consider moving there to fill that spot?

John LLOYD

I did not take much persuading as he was pushing at an open door because I was fully aware of the potential for very different criminal investigations at the Airport.

I agreed to the transfer but left Crawley with some regrets especially as I would no longer be working with Keith and Nigel which I had found to be very rewarding both on a professional and social basis.

CHAPTER 7

Gatwick Airport CID

I joined Gatwick CID in the Spring of 1982 at which time the personnel were DI Dave Wood, DS John Alderson and DS Bill Smith (ex BSAP) together with Brian Wright, John Burgess, Gerry Cannan, Chris Munn and Brian Cartmell.

The work was quite different from sub-divisional CID in that we did not have many reported burglaries because our Division had few dwelling houses within its boundaries. What we did have in abundance were reports of thefts in transit. These were reports relating to thefts from baggage in transit between Gatwick and elsewhere or from elsewhere into Gatwick.

At that time Gatwick and Heathrow had earned bad reputations as being airports where passenger's baggage would be rifled and some contents stolen. In the main, the property stolen consisted of jewellery, cash and other small easily disposable items. Gatwick had earned the soubriquet of Gatnick whilst Heathrow was known as Thiefrow.

These thefts took place between the time when the passengers checked in their bags and the time when they collected them upon arrival at their final destination.

It was suspected, not without good reason, that the perpetrators of these thefts were the Airline baggage loaders who removed the bags from the baggage belts and loaded them onto the aircraft on departure or off-loaded the bags upon arrival. It was they who had the perfect opportunity to open the suitcases and search them for any valuables.

John LLOYD

The problem we had was trying to identify the exact venue of the theft as it could have taken place at either the departure airport or the arrival airport or indeed at any transit airport down route.

We maintained full reports of these thefts and recorded the names of the members of each Baggage Loaders shifts who were operating each particular flight. After maintaining these records for several months it soon became apparent that the names of certain Baggage loaders appeared more often than others and these became our nominated targets for further investigations. We would arrange for surprise stop checks at the Airport Security Gates when our suspects were leaving work. They were security checked and. on some occasions, stolen property was found resulting in a few individuals being charged with thefts once we had identified the owners and had confirmed that the goods were stolen. This was sometimes a lengthy process and not always successful because of the international nature of these incidents. It was often difficult to identify the owners of the property and thereby prove that any seized item was indeed stolen.

Later we took to placing small covert cameras inside vulnerable areas including the aircraft holds. This was done with the approval of both the Airlines and the Trades Unions after some sensitive negotiations.

This proved more successful and one later operation, targeting thefts from the Royal Mail, led by one of my colleagues, an excellent Detective named Jerry Ormsby, resulted in a number of Baggage Loaders being charged with, and convicted of, a large number of thefts from Baggage.

These were often difficult and protracted investigations and our success rate was often limited by the international nature of the incidents.

We had very good relations with HM Customs & Excise especially their Investigations Branch whose prime role related to the unlawful importation of controlled drugs. We always assisted HM Customs in processing all prisoners arrested for these offences and having them placed before the Crawley Magistrates. This was mainly an administrative task for us although we did become involved in operations relating to Drugs Trafficking but more of that later.

Bundu, the Beat & Beyond

Gatwick Airport has some very large car parks within its boundaries. It is in these car parks that passengers can park their cars for the duration of their travels. The Car Parks are operated by private companies on a concessionary basis from the British Airports Authority (BAA).

Due to their nature these car parks became magnets for thieves from the surrounding areas as there were some very high value vehicles parked there whilst many others had very expensive stereo and audio equipment fitted.

The Car Park companies did have their own security Officers but they seemed to have limited capabilities and incentives. Additionally there were some Close Circuit TV cameras in place but not all areas were covered with this. During the hours of darkness these cameras had limited efficiency because some of the areas were not well lit resulting in poor quality images.

I remember being called out one night around 0200hrs by Chris Standard and his Gatwick Uniform Section who had arrested three young men in their late teens and early twenties who had been caught breaking into cars and stealing radios and audio equipment. Chris and his men had done a really good job in finding and arresting the three suspects as well as recovering a number of Car stereo radios.

This took a very long time to sort out as I had to match each recovered stolen item with a particular car and then await the return of the owner of each car so as to obtain a statement of loss and value etc.

In the meantime I had interviewed each of the youths and some of them made some admissions.

In total I managed to identify thirty vehicles which had been broken into and eventually managed to match up each stolen radio/stereo with the particular vehicle from which it was stolen and within some weeks I had statements of loss from all of the vehicle owners.

The three youths were later charged with numerous counts of theft. They pleaded guilty at Court and were handed suspended prison sentences.

119

John LLOYD

A great deal of work went into that investigation but the end results were worthwhile because all three were convicted albeit that the sentences did not really reflect the impact it had had on the owners of the vehicles they had targeted plus the many man hours it had taken to bring these matters to Court.

A much more pleasant experience came my way when I accompanied my colleague Gerry Cannan to a large Mansion House in Charlwood near Gatwick to assist the occupant with the theft of two small statues which had been removed from the front gate area.

The occupant was none other than Barry Sheene, the world motorcycle champion which impressed me no end. Barry was there with his beautiful model girlfriend, Stephanie. They were both very down to earth naturally friendly people and made us both most welcome and we chatted with them for some time about all manner of different things including the Police work after which we bade them farewell.

There was a positive result for Barry and his statues as Roger Buttle reminded me recently that he managed to recover both items from a house in Crawley as a result of information received.

Barry and Stephanie later emigrated to Australia, I think, but sadly Barry died rather young of the dreaded cancer some years later.

It was in 1982 that the Pope visited the UK and his first point of entry into the UK was at Gatwick where he was met by a large contingent of important people. Sussex Police had formulated a very comprehensive plan to protect the Pope whilst he was within our area of protection and I was part of that plan and was ordered to stand at a round-about near the terminal building through which the Pope-mobile and his entourage would travel on their way to London.

My brief was to report on the size of the crowd at the round-about and to identify any likely troublemakers etc. When the Pope passed my point I was the only person standing at this round-about and as he passed he gave me a lovely smile plus his papal wave.

Bundu, the Beat & Beyond

As previously mentioned Gatwick Division had very few residential burglaries reported due to the relatively few residential houses within the Divisional Boundary however we did have opportunities to investigate a few. One incident that I recall involved two brothers from South London who were seen in suspicious circumstances near Steers Lane just outside the Airport. DS John Alderson and I attended the report together with uniform Officers. We had been issued with a brief description of the two suspects indicating that they were black males, around 20 years of age, slim build and around 6 feet in height.

At that time black people were fairly thin on the ground in the Crawley/ Gatwick/Horley areas so when John and I spotted two black youths making their way towards a parked vehicle whilst carrying a couple of bags under their arms we knew that we were probably on to a good thing.

We intercepted the two who were, by this time, thankfully short of breath. They were arrested and placed into separate vehicles, one into the plain CID car and the other into a Uniform Patrol car from Gatwick which had joined us.

They were taken to Gatwick Police Station and booked into the detention suite. John and I examined the contents of the bags the youths had been carrying and found numerous items of what appeared to be stolen property including jewellery and small electrical items.

With the assistance of Uniformed personnel all the houses in the vicinity of where we had found the youths were visited and inspected. In most cases the occupants were out at work but we did identify three houses which appeared to have been unlawfully entered with a broken window at the rear of each house.

We asked for the attendance of SOCO to examine the outside of each of the houses whilst leaving notes through the front doors of each house requesting the occupiers to contact us at Gatwick upon their arrival at home.

John LLOYD

In the meantime we drove the two youths to their home address in South London and with the assistance of the London Metropolitan Police we searched the premises looking for more stolen property. We did find one or two items which were later identified as being reported as stolen from house burglaries in the South London area. This pleased the Met lads somewhat. The two youths were later charged with offences of burglary and, in view of their previous convictions and the relative serious nature of the current offences, they were sentenced to a term of youth custody.

In the spring of 1983 Jackie and I found out that she was pregnant. We were naturally both thrilled with the news although one downside was that we had to cancel a planned trip to Malaysia (a small price to pay). Our baby (gender unknown) was due in late December around Boxing Day. However baby had other ideas and was not actually born until early January 1984. Jackie was admitted to Crawley Hospital into a ward with about six or seven other women in advanced stages of pregnancy.

At visiting times I was a little embarrassed to see that I had previously arrested two of the other Dads whilst I had been at Crawley CID. We nodded to each other in a semi-formal manner but otherwise contrived to ignore each other's presence.

Jackie had quite a hard time during the last stages of labour which seemed to last a very long time. Our son, Simon, was born eventually and mother and baby were doing fine and both were in a healthy state which is what I was most concerned about. Jackie stayed in hospital for about a week which was fairly normal in those days. In fact I think that she and Simon stayed in hospital for an extra day as I was having full central heating put into our house at the time and the medical staff accommodated us to allow Jackie and Simon to return to a fully heated house.

Some weeks later Simon was baptised at the Friary Church in Crawley after which all the guests adjourned to our house in Crawley for a celebratory party. The party went very well, in fact too well for some of us. My brother Chris had arrived from South Africa the day before and was a little tired from the flight and all the hassle of moving back to the UK after all those years in Africa.

Bundu, the Beat & Beyond

We had a really good time and much strong drink was consumed ably assisted by two gate crashers in the form of the on duty North Division CID officers, Keith Menzies and John Griss.

My brother Chris also had a very enjoyable liquid time until there came a point at which his body said, "no more" after which he gracefully slid down the wall he had been leaning against and collapsed in a gentle heap on the floor.

I wasn't far behind him and I had to take myself off to bed in the late evening leaving Jackie, Keith & Wendy King to tidy up after our other guests had left.

Back at work I began to nurture relationships with the Security Officers employed by each of the Airlines at Gatwick including Ray Searle and his deputy, Tom Cannon, of British Caledonian Airways. They introduced me into the murky world of Airline ticket fraud which I later found out was a global phenomenon and which affected all of the major world Airlines. I knew both these Security Officers from previous times. Ray had been an Inspector with Surrey Police and Tom had been a Sussex Officer when I was at Hove and later at Gatwick before he resigned to take up his position with BCAL.

At that time ticketing fraud was virtually an unknown phenomenon outside the airline and travel industry and was therefore totally unknown to the UK Police with the exception of the Metropolitan Police at London Heathrow Airport who maintained a small squad of Detectives dedicated to investigating Frauds against Airlines.

As I began to delve more and more into this world I realised that if I was going to treat this work seriously I really did need to improve my knowledge of Airline systems and procedures as regards to Ticketing etc.

In those days the vast majority of airline tickets were hand written. This was before the days of full computerisation and E-tickets and the airline systems in place to prevent misuse of tickets and fraud were not particularly robust.

123

John LLOYD

I had been in contact with DS Mick Jones of the Heathrow Ticket fraud Unit over matters of mutual interest as well as seeking his advice on how best to proceed on certain issues. This was necessary at the time at Gatwick as it seems that there was no history of Gatwick Police ever investigating airline ticketing frauds. These issues were global and costing the airline industry a great deal of money especially when you realise that, even in the early 1980's, a blank airline ticket falling into the wrong hands could be valued at around £5,000.00 or more which was a sizeable sum then.

Mick told me of a forthcoming Airline Ticket Fraud course, promoted by British Airways and supported by I.A.T.A. (International Air Transport Association) which was to be held at Heathrow in February 1984. The students were to be a mix of Heathrow Police Detectives and Airline staff.

I approached my Divisional Commander, Chief Superintendent Roy Field, and requested that consideration be given to my attending this course. Roy was an enlightened Officer and could see the value in having an Airport based Detective Officer conversant in Airline ticketing fraud.

Roy had spent most of his career in CID and was, in my opinion, a real Coppers Copper. He knew the score and as long as someone did not try and pull the wool over his eyes he would normally back you to the hilt.

Roy agreed to my request and to funding the cost of the course and my travelling expenses to and from Heathrow for the five day course.

At 0900hrs on 13th February 1984 I presented myself to Room 415 Cranebank Centre at Heathrow which was one of the many buildings used by British Airways for a variety of purposes.

The first presentation and introduction was from Rodney Wallis, the Director of Security for I.A.T.A. and the next five days which followed were crammed full of very technical and intricate data on all the methods of airline ticketing, the meanings and uses of the various common airline documents plus current fraud trends such as Bucket Shop frauds, cross border selling etc. The course included a visit to Aero-print Ltd in

Bundu, the Beat & Beyond

Aylesbury where most of the world's airline tickets were produced and we were able to view first hand all the security features contained within any airline ticket.

The final day included a presentation by Mick Jones of Heathrow CID on current cases being dealt with by his Airline Fraud Unit. Mick Jones would go on to become the Security Officer for Pan Am Airlines at Heathrow when he retired from the Police. Sadly for him that airline ceased operating a few years afterwards.

This course had armed me with knowledge in what to look for in a fraudulent airline tickets twinned with knowledge of investigative techniques which I would find myself using back at Gatwick.

MURDER MOST FOUL

In the late summer of 1984 a member of the public reported a strong pungent smell emanating from a row of cars parked in one of the Multi Storey Car Parks on the south side of Gatwick Airport near to the Hilton Hotel.

A Uniformed Officer was initially delegated to investigate and identified that the smell seemed to be coming from a red coloured VW Derby car. The interior of the car looked clean enough and nothing suspicious could be viewed. Enquiries with the Car Parking Company revealed that the car had been there for some days. The car was not reported stolen and was registered to a person living in Surrey.

In view of the strong and suspicious smell emanating from the interior of the car it was decided to force open the boot. This was done at which time the decomposing body of a young male was found inside.

The matter was immediately reported to the CID at Gatwick and a team headed by DI Dave Wood commenced an investigation.

The body was not removed from the vehicle until the vehicle had been photographed by John Lewis the Gatwick Police photographer and

125

John LLOYD

forensically examined by Roger Mason, the on call SOCO from nearby Crawley.

I was seconded onto the Murder Investigation Team together with one of my colleagues then at Gatwick CID, Jim Campbell, a lively Scot and all round good man.

A full murder team was formed within the next 24 hours which included Detective Superintendent Doug Cheal, Dave Wood, Colin Sparkes, Mark Hayler, Bob Diplock, Kit Bentham together with a number of Officers trained on the recently introduced HOLMES computer system which was a Home Office computerised system for recording all data produced during a major investigation. The HOLMES team included Judy Cunningham (of Bobette fame), Sue Bentley plus Sandra Leader and Lyn Marr who were from Brighton.

In addition we had a full complement of outside enquiry teams all of which were fully experienced Detectives.

One of the first priorities was to identify the body which did not have any form of identity in his now badly stained clothing.

Fortunately the body was fairly quickly identified as that of a man named Jimmy Sergeant from Lower Kingswood in Surrey. The post mortem indicated the cause of death to be from multiple shotgun wounds. Enquiries in the local area of Lower Kingswood revealed that Jimmy Sergeant was believed to have been on the fringes of the criminal fraternity and involved in many things of a questionable nature.

Enquiries also revealed that he had been associating with another man from that area but, in addition, it was believed that Jimmy had been having an affair with his associate's wife.

After gathering all the available evidence, Jimmy's associate was arrested on suspicion of murder and interviewed in custody. He retained a well-known criminal defence lawyer from London who, of course, instructed his client to answer "No Comment" to all questions put to him in interview.

Bundu, the Beat & Beyond

However, during a break from interviews DI Dave Wood spoke with the prisoner, unofficially in his Cell. Certain limited admissions were made but no formal record of the comments and replies were made as this was an off the cuff talk not primarily conducted with a view to gaining evidence.

Shotguns were recovered from the Prisoners home address as were other items which linked him into Jimmy Sergeant.

Our investigations continued with a full Murder Investigation Squad until in the early hours of the 12th October 1984 the IRA detonated a timed explosive device in the Grand Hotel in Brighton in which the Prime Minister, Margaret Thatcher, and her cabinet were staying.

Two Police colleagues who were known to me, Toby Pratt and John Rist, were on duty inside the hotel at the time of the explosion and according to all reports they acted with considerable calm and courage in assisting hotel guests, including the walking wounded, from the remains of the hotel to the safety outside. It seems that their dedication to duty was never formally recognised perhaps because such recognition would probably not be awarded to Police Officers whose Police Force was responsible (in co-operation with the London Metropolitan Police) for the security of the Grand Hotel, the Prime Minister and her cabinet.

This was obviously a very major investigation of national importance which resulted in a large number of Police resources being used. The Gatwick Body in the boot (as it was then known) investigation lost many of the investigative and Holmes team to the Brighton outrage. This was fair enough but it left the remaining team with only the bare necessities with which to operate.

A reasonable case was built against the prisoner but it was mainly circumstantial however it was felt that there was sufficient evidence to support a charge of murder especially when the suspect's wife was able to provide evidence of her husband's involvement with Jimmy Sergeant and her affair with Jimmy etc.

John LLOYD

This was the first time that a wife was able to give evidence against her husband and proved to a turning point in the English Justice system.

Our file of evidence was submitted to the Legal Branch who felt that there was sufficient evidence to support a charge of murder against Jimmy Sergeant's associate.

The limited verbal admissions made to Dave Wood were ruled as being inadmissible in evidence by the Trial Judge.

The man charged with the murder appeared at Lewes Crown Court some months later in 1985 and pleaded Not Guilty. I was the designated Exhibits Officer for the trial responsible for producing all the right exhibits at Court at the right time. The prosecution was lead by a QC who, I felt, did not present the evidence in the best possible manner. Eventually the Jury returned a Not Guilty verdict in respect of the man charged with this murder.

This was a great disappointment to all the murder team and to Jimmy Sergeant's next of kin but try as we might we were unable to identify and secure any direct evidence sufficient to obtain a conviction. "You win some and you lose some" is one way of looking at this but it did not make me feel any better in trying to rationalise things in that way. Sometime you need a stroke of luck in major criminal investigations. Our lucky break never materialised in this case.

An offshoot to this murder investigation presented itself to me a year or so later when a female witness in this case sought me out at Gatwick Police Station and asked to see me. I spoke with her to find out the nature of her call and it soon became apparent that she was having very challenging domestic problems with her husband which often ended in violence. She continually said to me that she "wanted to kill her husband". I told her that she should be very careful of what she said because uttering threats to kill was (and still is) a criminal offence. I tried to offer her some relevant advice on what was really a domestic matter but she was not really in any frame of mind to be either reasonable or accept my advice. She was not prepared to support any official Police action in respect of the alleged assaults on her by her husband.

Bundu, the Beat & Beyond

She continued to make threats to kill her husband and eventually I said to her something like, "Please stop threatening to kill your husband. It is a criminal offence to make such threats and if you continue to do so I will be forced to take some official action."

She continued to make similar threats to kill her husband and in the end I really had little choice but to arrest her and take her to the Custody Suite where the Custody Officer booked her into formal custody. I later interviewed her on audio tape and she was later charged with an offence of Making threats to Kill.

She later appeared at Lewes Crown Court where she pleaded Guilty. I was not present at Court as a Guilty Plea had been anticipated but the Judge saw fit to commend me for the restrained and considerate manner with which I had dealt with the woman and for the sensitive attitude in interview. I had not expected that although I was happy to accept a Judge's commendation which is not handed out lightly. I felt that it complemented my other two Chief Constables commendations I had previously received for involvement in other investigations.

One other occasion I recall saw me investigating a series of thefts at the Airport in which I had partially identified the suspect as a man with the surname of Patel. The only other piece of information I had was that he was due to play in a cricket game at Southgate Playing Fields in Crawley that very day.

Vic Cloney, a colleague at Gatwick CID, accompanied me to Southgate Playing Fields where we saw that there was a cricket match in progress. The fielding team were all Asian men of Indian descent whereas the batting side were all white European men. I therefore deduced that, in view of his surname, my suspect must be one of the fielding team. I went along to the match scorer who was a man of Indian descent and asked him if he could point out a Mr Patel on the field of play. He looked at me, somewhat quizzically and said, "Which one do you want? They are all called Patel. This is the Patel cricket team"!!

John LLOYD

Before I left I recorded the details of all the Patel Cricket team but knowing that I had to make additional enquiries to further identify my suspect.

During my time with Gatwick CID I was elected to be the Police Federation Representative for all Detective Constables in the County. The responsibilities of this part time post included the ability to tender suitable advice to any Detective Officer in the County on all matters relating to Police Regulations and Discipline etc. It also involved me having to attend various Federation meetings around the County including the Joint Branch Board meetings chaired by Tony Byrne ably supported by the Secretary Tony Clarke. It was they who, in the main, negotiated with the Chief Constable and his staff over matters of Officers welfare and rights within the Police Regulations.

I also attended a couple of National Police Federation meetings in Blackpool and Scarborough at which national policy was debated and voted on by delegates from all the English and Welsh Police Forces.

I did defend some of my colleagues who had been charged with disciplinary offences with some success. However there was one specific case which still haunts me today. This involved two Detectives from Brighton, a Detective Sergeant and a Detective Constable, who had been tasked with conducting some criminal enquiries in the Midlands area. These were completed and after their return these Officers submitted claims for petrol used in the CID car having filled up with petrol at a filling station en route.

This was quite normal until it was noticed that the receipt for the petrol was from a Petrol Filling Station located in Warrington in Cheshire, well to the north of their authorised trip. It was further noted that the Detective Constable had relatives living in the Warrington area.

I represented the Detective Constable whilst my colleague, John May, represented the Detective Sergeant. Upon reflection John and I were on a loser from day one in this matter because at no time did either Officer give a satisfactory account to the Senior Police investigators nor to John and I.

Bundu, the Beat & Beyond

I recall that John and I had a meeting with these two Officers at John May's house in central Sussex during which we told them in very straight language that their story was unsatisfactory and not really believable to us. If we had serious doubts as to their honesty and reliability what would the Chief Constable think?

It seems apparent that both Officers had agreed on a story and neither was prepared to come down and change their stance and provide an account of what really happened.

John and I warned the two of the likely outcome should the Chief Constable reach the conclusion that they were being dishonest but they steadfastly stuck to their account of the events.

The eventual outcome at the subsequent disciplinary hearing at Police HQ in Lewes was, from my perspective, a foregone conclusion. The Chief Constable heard evidence from all the relevant witnesses and he heard the accounts of the two Officers subject of the charges who were represented by a Barrister funded by the Police Federation.

They were found Guilty and dismissed from the Police Service.

I have never forgotten this sad situation which was made worse by the fact that these two Officers were highly experienced and well respected Detectives with a very good record of catching villains. From that perspective they were a sad loss to the Police Service but another view was that they deserved the sack due to their honesty, integrity and reliability having been compromised.

During the 1980's it was the practice to hold annual CID dinners to which guest speakers were invited. One year a joint dinner, was held at a Gatwick Hotel, between the North Division and Gatwick CID offices.

A somewhat brave decision was made to invite the internationally renowned actor and all round hell-raiser, Oliver Reed, to be our guest speaker. Oliver lived in a 54 bedroomed mansion in south Surrey and quite close to Gatwick Airport.

John LLOYD

On the evening of the dinner a Detective Sergeant was delegated to drive to the mansion and collect Mr Reed and to bring him to the dinner venue.

All the CID Officers including some very senior CID Officers from HQ were gathered in the bar area of the hotel prior enjoying a chat with colleagues together with pre-prandial drinks when in walked Oliver. Well, walked is not the correct description as he sort of bounced into the room and jigged around a lot whilst making some weird noises. It appeared that he was already well into the spirit of the evening and had something of a very good start ahead of all the other attendees.

I noted that some of the more Senior Officers were not overly impressed with his behaviour but fortunately we were immediately called into the dining room to take our seats for dinner.

Oliver was seated at the top table and tucked into his food with some relish. After the meal there were some speeches and when it was Oliver's turn he delivered a somewhat rambling effort hampered by his inebriated state. The gist of what he was saying that he was a full supporter of the Police and he wished us well in our endeavours in fighting crime.

He then sat down to some applause after which it appears that he became a little bored and suddenly, without warning, he vaulted over the dinner table from his sitting position and landed on the other side in a forward roll. At no time did his body come into contact with the table. This was quite impressive and revealed just how athletic and strong he was.

Oliver was a very well built man and appeared to be physically very strong and his evening with us ended by him challenging some of the CID Officers to an arm wrestling competition.

My good friend, Nigel Godden, who is also very well built and strong, got down on the floor with Oliver and they proceeded to arm wrestle. It was a fairly close contest which Nigel eventually won. This defeat made Oliver somewhat angry and I think that he virtually lost his temper by head-butting Nigel.

Bundu, the Beat & Beyond

Oliver was taken home shortly after that.

Jackie, Simon and I were then living in a three bedroomed semi-detached house in Pound Hill, Crawley. It was situated on a corner plot with fields to the rear. Being a corner plot meant that the rear garden was huge at just over a third of an acre. During the summer months this meant that Jackie and I spent many hours in the garden keeping it under control and neat and tidy.

Because of its size we held several outdoor Barbeques there for Gatwick CID Officers, staff and their families.

As with every other CID office the personnel changed fairly often as people were transferred out or left for whatever reason and over the years I have worked with probably hundreds of different people. Gatwick was no exception to this movement and the continuity of staffing was sometimes an issue.

Some Officers flitted about so often in order to build an impressive CV that they became known as Butterflies. In fact a number of more senior ranks flitted from Force to Force and not just within their home Force. This syndrome supposedly increased the individual's knowledge and expertise but I am not convinced that was the result. The more obvious result was instability in staffing personnel at varying levels and in varying posts. This did nothing for the efficiency of the Police in general apart from breeding a generation of Officers who were solely intent on climbing the slippery ladder of so called success and purely for their own selfish reasons.

During the night of the 15th October 1987 the UK suffered what was to become known as "The Great Storm" The previous evening the BBC TV weatherman had assured viewers that a hurricane was not heading our way. Unfortunately he was very wrong. During that night the southern part of the UK was hit by hurricane force winds which uprooted thousands of trees and caused widespread damage to houses.

John LLOYD

We were fairly lucky in that only one of our trees in the back garden was uprooted and we lost a few roof tiles. One of our kitchen windows blew open but otherwise remained intact. No one was injured so we were fine.

After sunrise the following morning I decided to try and make my way to work using our car and managed to negotiate my way along the Balcombe Road driving around a few upturned trees on the way. I picked up a British Airways Baggage Loader on his way to work and we managed to get into the airport after some very careful driving and avoidance of fallen trees and debris.

I got to the CID office in time for 0900hrs but I was the only CID Officer who made it in to work that day as all the others lived much further away from the Airport than I did and all their roads were blocked by fallen trees. Quite an experience.

My good friend and former colleague at Crawley CID, Keith Menzies, was transferred to Gatwick upon his promotion to Sergeant and although we did not work together it was good to have him around again. Keith later took charge of the Gatwick Anti-Terrorist Unit (ATU) which had a fairly wide remit within the Airport but seemed to concentrate on the Israeli El-Al flights for militant Arab terrorism and the Belfast bound flights in respect of possible IRA activity.

The Gatwick ATU was formed with some good quality experienced personnel including Sue Smith, Steve Scott and Steve Johns. Sue later married Neville Sidebotham from the BAA VIP Lounge and some years later Jackie and I started socialising with Sue and Neville together with Keith and Jackie Menzies and we still see them several times a year at various social events.

My professional life continued as before at Gatwick with my being involved with a series of differing criminal investigations. I continued to make inroads into Airline ticketing fraud at Gatwick and elsewhere.

It was whilst I was investigating one of these frauds that I had occasion to visit the Insurance and claims department of British Caledonian

Bundu, the Beat & Beyond

Airways which was then housed in offices adjacent to the old Beehive control tower. I was directed to a youngish man with very thinning hair who turned out to be Peter Candy who had been a scholar at Broadlands School in South Africa at the same time that I was there albeit several classes below me. What a coincidence. He was more than helpful with my enquiries and I emerged from his office some time later armed with a great deal of very useful information.

Most of the CID Officers would visit Public Houses and Clubs within the airport area with a view to cultivating informants and developing criminal intelligence. Amongst others I often visited the Wingspan Club frequented by airline personnel and had some success with that objective.

Gatwick was then and still is today, a single runway airport and claims to be the busiest international single runway operation in the world. I believe it for, as far back as 1975 when I first went to Gatwick, we were having discussions about Gatwick needing a second runway in order to operate more efficiently and to cater for expansion of business. However this argument was nullified by an agreement between HM Government, West Sussex County Council and the British Airports Authority, that no second runway would be in place at Gatwick before 2019. What a short sighted policy this was.

On the 18th March 1988 the newly constructed North Terminal was opened by HM The Queen. This facility was well overdue as the existing single Terminal at Gatwick had been operating above capacity for some time.

The new North Terminal had been in construction for some considerable time during the previous two years or so and during the preceding year it had been nearing completion. This huge area was essentially one large building site and the only personnel permitted inside were the construction workers and the Security Officers charged with maintaining security within the area. This project employed many thousands of workers at varying levels. It was a very busy place but one in which Sussex Police were, for the time being, not permitted to enter.

John LLOYD

During late 1986 or early 1987 the BAA reported to a Senior Officer of Sussex Police at Gatwick that they had experienced a number of small arsons on the construction site of the North Terminal. Fortunately no one had been injured and damage was minimal.

Prior to reporting these matters to us the affected areas had been cleaned up and any damaged property had been disposed with. This left us with no possibility of any forensic evidence, there was no CCTV evidence and the only witness was a Security Guard who had found the seats of fire and had extinguished the flames and smoke before reporting the incidents to his Control.

I was delegated to investigate these matters and I was fortunate to have the assistance of an excellent Detective called Jerry Ormsby who was then on the strength of Gatwick CID. Jerry had previously been with the Regional Crime Squad and was a very experienced and tenacious investigator.

We decided that the only positive thing to do was to invite the Security Officer who had found the fires in to the Police Station for an informal chat. This we did and he arrived on time at the Police Station early one evening. We took him to the Detective Inspector's office on the first floor where we knew that it would be quiet at that time of day and we would not be disturbed.

This was just before the Police and Criminal Evidence Act was ratified and brought into law which meant that procedures were somewhat easier and less formal.

We sat him down and gave him a cup of coffee and began a general chat about his personal life and his work as a Security Officer at the North Terminal. Nothing too heavy but just very light chat designed to place him at ease.

We gradually introduced the subject of the fires but again nothing too serious. This went on for some time when all of a sudden he said, "I need to go to the toilet". We said that was just fine and he then said, "And I

Bundu, the Beat & Beyond

suppose that you will have to come with me?" Jerry and I looked at each other thinking to ourselves, "We have a right one here". We agreed that we would have to accompany him to the toilet and we showed him the way to the Gents toilet on the first floor situated at the end of a corridor.

We entered the toilet thinking that he wanted to use the urinals but, no, he needed to sit down in one of the cubicles and do what men do when they sit on the toilet.

As he sat himself down on the toilet he then said to us, "And I suppose that I have to keep the door open?" Jerry and I exchanged glances with each other acknowledging silently that we may be onto something. We agreed that he should leave the toilet door open whilst he went about his business.

We continued chatting in a similar vein as before until there came a point when I said to him, "You started these fires didn't you?" Before I had time to say anything else he strained again and said "Yeeeesss"

We said no more at that stage but permitted him to finalise his job with the paperwork after which I told him that he was being arrested on suspicion of arson. He was also cautioned in the required manner which was, at that time, "You do not have to say anything unless you wish to do so but anything you say will be written down and may be given in evidence".

We then took him to the ground floor and presented him to the Duty Sergeant whereupon he was formally booked into custody. He declined to have any legal representation.

He was then formally interviewed by Jerry and me and he elected to complete a statement under caution in which he fully admitted to setting four separate fires on four separate occasions. His motives was mixed but included the fact that he wanted to impress his Superiors within the Security Company. He signed the caution statement after which he was released on bail pending my securing evidence of complaint and estimates of damage etc.

John LLOYD

So we had a real result out of nothing but that was the easy bit.

The hard bit was transforming all that I have described above into a written statement of evidence for use at Court AND to make it believable.

I did my very best and within a week or so I submitted a full file of evidence resulting in the Security Guard being charged with four counts of Arson and appearing at Crawley Magistrates Court for a first hearing. My evidence was never tested in Court because the man pleaded Guilty to all charges.

As he had no convictions and the fires were fairly small in nature the Magistrates decided that they had sufficient powers to deal with the case rather than send him up to the Crown Court. He was sentenced to six months imprisonment suspended for two years. His employment within the Security Industry was over and he was left to get on with his life as best as he could.

I do not want to claim a record for the Guinness Book of World Records but was this, perhaps, the only occasion when a man has confessed to relatively serious matters to Detectives whilst performing number twos on the toilet?

You could not make up a story like this it is so unbelievable but it did happen.

On another occasion I was tasked with investigating a series of threatening letters sent to a female employee of Gatwick Handling. These letters were "posted" through the small vents in her personal locker at the airport. Having interviewed the young lady she was unable to supply any motives for the content of these letters nor was she able to identify any potential suspect who may have been responsible.

There were no other witnesses so I had the threatening letters sent away for forensic handwriting analysis together with known samples of the woman's handwriting. After some weeks I received the results of the

138

Bundu, the Beat & Beyond

handwriting analysis which, although not totally conclusive, suggested that the author of the threatening letters was the alleged victim herself.

I then fully investigated the background of the young woman and it was suggested to me that she may have underlying mental health issues. This was shown to be correct. The young woman did make limited admissions concerning this matter but I felt that in view of all the circumstances it would not be prudent to take this matter any further in any legal sense. She was permitted to resign from Gatwick Handling. I submitted my report and it was agreed not to take any further action.

From time to time the Airlines and/or the Airport would receive telephoned reports of a bomb being on board flight 123 etc. Without exception these calls proved to be false hoax calls mainly made by people with some form of grudge against the airline or one of the passengers on board that flight or on some occasions when a late reporting passenger wanted to delay the departure of their flight to enable them to board and depart. One such incident was reported to me and I managed to track the telephone call which had emanated from a public telephone kiosk in the North Terminal at Gatwick. I had some luck and witnesses sitting nearby were able to give me a description of a young mixed race woman who had been using that telephone a short time earlier.

She was identified as a late reporting passenger on a British Airways flight scheduled to depart within a short period of time. I went to the check in area and found a woman of similar description still trying to check in for the flight even though the flight had closed some time before. I arrested her on suspicion of making a hoax call and took her to Gatwick Police Station where she was formally interviewed on audio tape. She made no admissions and I therefore reported her for the offence and, having verified her home address in London, she was permitted to leave.

I submitted my limited file of evidence but the Crown Prosecution Service declined to proceed with any formal action due to lack of evidence. I thought no more about this until some months later when I was informed that this young lady had made a complaint against me for the manner in which I had dealt with her and for my overbearing attitude in trying to get her to admit to the offence.

John LLOYD

I was not too concerned over this because the number of complaints against Police had risen by quite a substantial number after the criminal classes discovered that they could sue the Police for alleged malpractice and make quite a tidy sum of money in the process.

My file of evidence was submitted to the Police Complaints Authority who were responsible for investigating such complaints and I was later gratified to learn that they had rejected the young woman's complaint on the grounds that, having listened to the full audio tape of my interview, they were unable to establish any overbearing attitude on my part especially when I had said to her words to the effect of "I don't want you to admit to anything that you have not done but etc etc."

In my view she was a chancer who thought she saw an opportunity to make some money out of the Police.

One other investigation of some note which would have some impact on me a few years later involved an American national who had a grievance with Virgin Atlantic Airways which resulted him sending a series of threatening letters to certain well placed Managers within Virgin Atlantic and culminated in him arranging for US College Students to send human faeces wrapped in small clear plastic bags in the mail to various Virgin Atlantic Managers.

He was quickly identified and arrested. In interview he made some admissions and it was clear to me and Mark Eyre who sat in on the interviews that although this man was a little unbalanced he knew exactly what he was doing and that his main intention was to make life as difficult and unpleasant as he could for some employees of that airline.

He was charged with various offences relating to criminal harassment and received a three months custodial sentence before being deported to the USA. I submitted a final report about him to the F.B.I. and thought no more about it. This matter was to resurrect itself a few years later.

During my time at Gatwick our CID personnel fostered really good relationships with representatives of all the airlines operating out of

Bundu, the Beat & Beyond

Gatwick as well as the myriad of different other companies servicing the airport.

Once a year, just before Christmas, it was our practice to hold a grand Christmas party at the Sussex Police facility at Slaugham Manor, a large country house estate about ten miles south of the airport.

It was also our practice to hold a really big raffle with grand prizes at this party and in the few weeks before the party all the CID Officers would visit the majority of their contacts in the aviation and commercial world at Gatwick seeking their assistance in providing suitable prizes for our grand raffle.

To name this event as a grand raffle is something of an understatement because, due to the generosity of our airport contacts, we did accrue a great number of really excellent prizes each and every year.

These prizes included bottles of spirits and wine, food hampers, ladies perfumes and the like up to and including airline tickets for two people and even holidays for two.

Needless to say, invitations to the Gatwick CID party and draw were the most sought after tickets around and we always had full houses.

We sold tickets for the raffle on the night to the invited guests and all proceeds were donated to charity. A good time was had by all and these were memorable occasions for all those who attended.

As far as I know this type of event is no longer held which is a shame because it greatly assisted in fostering really good working relations between the Gatwick CID and the airline and commercial personnel at the airport.

Jackie had, by this time, left British Caledonian Airways just at the time of it being swallowed up by British Airways. She then worked in the Travel Industry with a company specialising in holidays to the USA, in particular Florida. It was there that she met her now good friend, Sheila Mangan.

141

John LLOYD

Purely by chance we later met Sheila, her husband Malcolm and their young son Alex whilst on holiday in Florida. Alex and our son Simon got along very well together as did we four adults. In later years we were to share many enjoyable holidays together in large villas with swimming pools in the area of Javea in Spain.

CHAPTER 8

Singapore

My work in detecting and investigating Airline Fraud continued and over several years I was able to bring many interesting cases to successful conclusions. I was still the sole Detective at Gatwick involved in this type of investigation and had managed to develop a substantial contact base within the industry so that I would receive calls on a weekly basis from at least one Airline Security Officer based in the UK with links to Gatwick or from the Revenue Protection Departments from within those airlines.

In early January 1988 I was summoned to the office of Chief Superintendent Gerry Edwards who was then the Divisional Commander at Gatwick. I had always got on quite well with Gerry and felt that we had quite a reasonable rapport.

I went into the outer Office where his Secretary, Bernie, worked and she bade me enter the inner sanctum. I knocked on the door which was ajar and entered the room. I walked a couple of paces and stood before his desk where Gerry was seated. He was writing on some papers at the time and did not acknowledge my presence nor did he say anything. He continued writing in silence for a minute or so before putting his pen down and looking up at me for the first time.

Without any preamble he said, "I understand that you have been involved in some criminal investigations into Airline Ticket Fraud?" (I knew that he knew full well that I had) I replied that I had and he continued by saying," I have been approached by Brian Wall the Head of IATA Security Section who has requested that we send an Officer to give

John LLOYD

a presentation at a Fraud Prevention Seminar on 23 and 24 February. Would you be interested in doing this?"

I replied that I would and he said, "Well in that case you need to prepare your presentation and deliver it to Superintendent John McKinney (his deputy) so that we can be assured that it will be of an acceptable standard." I assured him that that would not be a problem as I had plenty of material to work with.

Almost as an aside he then said, "Oh by the way, the seminar is to be held in Singapore."

To say that I was elated would be an understatement but I was still somewhat puzzled by his attitude even as I left his Office to return to the CID Office.

I knew Brian Wall from when he had been Head Security Officer for Air Zimbabwe (formerly Air Rhodesia) and I knew him to be a straight talking no nonsense sort of man. We had met when I was at Crawley CID at a time when two of that airlines new in post black stewardesses had been arrested in Crawley charged with Shoplifting. Brian had flown over from Harare to formally dismiss the two women from Air Zimbabwe's employ once they had been convicted of the theft offences.

I later saw Gerry's report submitted to our Headquarters seeking authority for my travel to Singapore. One of the paragraphs read . . ." Detective Constable LLOYD AL605 is experienced in the investigation of ticket fraud and is regarded as an expert in this field at Gatwick. DC LLOYD is the Officer I would nominate to give this presentation because of his background knowledge of the subject and because he has the presence to be able to give a valuable contribution to an international seminar".

I duly developed my presentation and delivered it to Superintendent John Mckinney together with an audience of about thirty other Gatwick Officers who had shown an interest in hearing my talk. John McKinney and I had worked at Hove together years before and I had babysat for his children when I was much younger and single, so we knew each other well and got along accordingly.

Bundu, the Beat & Beyond

That is not to say that he did me any special favours as his critique after I finished my presentation showed. Overall he was satisfied with my effort albeit with a few minor criticisms which I noted.

My presentation was accompanied by a slide show illustrating the various documents I referred to.

I.A.T.A. fully funded my travel and hotel expenses for this trip and I flew out from Gatwick on Cathay Pacific Airlines in Business Class (where else?) which was really comfortable and I was well looked after. The only slight downside was that I had a seven hour wait in Hong Kong whilst waiting for the Cathay connection to Singapore. Oh the sacrifices I made for the job!

The seminar was attended by about 75 Airline Security Officers and Fraud Prevention Officers representing Airlines operating in the Asia, Australasia, Pacific region. I made some very useful contacts.

I reproduce this presentation for your benefit as it illustrates some of the problem issues confronting the Airline Industry in those pre-electronic ticket days plus it also illustrates some of the investigations I had worked on.

I.A.T.A. FRAUD PREVENTION SEMINAR

SINGAPORE—23RD/24th FEBRUARY 1988.

Presentation by:—Detective John LLOYD,
                           Criminal Investigation Department,
                           Sussex Police,
                           Gatwick Airport Division,
                           London, England.

The subject of this seminar is that of FRAUD PREVENTION as distinct from FRAUD INVESTIGATION and DETECTION. This implies, quite correctly, that we are in the business of preventing dishonest acts before they occur but realistically we appear to be more in the business of FRAUD DETECTION.

145

John LLOYD

We all know that Fraud, against the airline industry, covers a fairly wide spectrum of offences from SIMPLE THEFT OF A TICKET and its subsequent misuse through to the obtaining of a ticket using some form of deception to large scale FRAUD, found in the 'BUST OUT' situation involving dishonest Travel Agents.

Clearly, an industry's ability to prevent fraud depends on the commercial systems employed in its day to day operations. Experience indicates that it is loopholes in these systems that permit criminal attacks. It is appreciated that airlines operate in a fiercely competitive commercial market, and are therefore subject to both market and economic restraints. It is also understood that in such an environment expenditure on fraud prevention may not make economic sense in the short term. However, having said this, it is clear that Airlines are now making significant progress in terms of fraud prevention. I nevertheless still believe that much more can be done, and that further expenditure by the industry will show long term economic benefits. (Much applause—they liked this bit).

The use of the Loss Prevention Bulletin is but a small example. There is no doubt that the rationale behind this document is sound. However, we all know that it is not a very effective tool in preventing or detecting the misuse of stolen tickets at the place where it should be most useful, that is, the airport of departure. It is here that the criminal should, ideally, be intercepted. Once the ticket has been used, it is too late, yes if the ticket is recognised as a stolen document post departure, then, yes the offender can be met at his destination by the appropriate authority, but in my submission that is too late, the FRAUD has happened. You have not prevented it, you have merely detected it.

But the question I ask is—HOW OFTEN DOES THIS SCENARIO ARISE? All too seldom I think. I must repeat—THE TIME TO CATCH AN OFFENDER IS BEFORE HE TRAVELS AND NOT AFTER.

I know, as you do, that in practical terms, an airline check in agent has little or no time to recognise a stolen document when presented by a

Bundu, the Beat & Beyond

would-be passenger. Even assuming that the check in agent is sufficiently interested in detecting such a document, the pressures of dealing with a long line of impatient passengers at check-in are such that few such documents are detected. I would argue, though, that this is the very place where they should be detected. The obvious solution would seem to involve a facility at each computerised check-in area for screening each ticket number against daily updated computer lists of stolen or fraudulent documents. The bottom line, I know, is one of expense and a determination by all relevant departments of the industry, and not just security, to initiate such methods of prevention. If cost really is a factor in this, then the estimates of loss in the industry, ranging from US Dollars 200 million to $350 million per annum due to fraud, would appear to be a powerful argument in favour of introducing effective preventative measures.

I propose to illustrate, by example, the varying types of investigations the Police at British Airports become involved with in the context of airline ticket fraud.

In doing so, I would ask that you take one message away with you. Simply that is—INVOLVE US AS SOON AS IS POSSIBLE. The sooner you, as Airline Security personnel, can involve us as a Police Investigative body then, in general, the greater is our chance of success in any investigation. If it is a job we should be investigating, then we should know about it as soon as, or very shortly after, you know about it. Please remember that in this field the Police in general will look to you as the informed experts and will expect you to provide and explain all the relevant data and procedures.

There may be one or two Police Officers who do have sufficient knowledge of your systems and language to conduct an investigation without this type of problem but these are in the minority.

I do not stand before you as an expert on airline systems and procedures but I do have some experience and expertise in investigating airline ticket fraud.

John LLOYD

1. SMALL BEGINNINGS.

My first example involves a young man of only 18 years of age and whilst it only touches on the area of TICKET FRAUD, I believe it will be of interest to you in that it is, in my experience, somewhat unique. It illustrates a situation initially involving a relatively minor fraud which, when investigated, revealed more serious offences.

The young man is what I would term as an "AIRLINE FREAK". His interest, knowledge and ambition in all aspects of the airline industry was such that whilst he was still at school he began writing to companies of airline and security printers indicating that he was in the process of forming his own airline. Needless to say he did not divulge his age, nor the minor matter of his insolvency. He requested the printers to forward samples of their work to him, including airline tickets and security documents. The printing companies were obviously impressed with his in-depth knowledge and naturally not wishing to lose a prospective valuable customer, they duly obliged him by sending specimen documents which were correctly marked with the word "SPECIMEN" and were un-numbered.

The young man continued with his correspondence and later requested further sample documents. Again, the companies obliged but unfortunately one of the tickets although bearing the word "VOID" in the validation box had been numbered.

This was the young man's opportunity. Using a pair of scissors he carefully cut out the word "VOID" from the validation box and then used a cigarette lighter to singe the edges of the cut area to make it appear as if the ticket had been accidently burned.

He then wrote out the ticket to himself for First-Class travel between London-Lagos-London. Later he took this ticket to an Airline ticket desk at Gatwick, requesting the issue of an M.C.O. against the residual value of coupon two.

The Ticket Agent, having examined the mutilated document and relating it to the obvious youth of the holder, became suspicious and informed

Bundu, the Beat & Beyond

the young man that he would have to refer the matter to the airline's refund department. The young man made no objections and went away.

The matter was, much later, referred to me for investigation. In the meantime our attention had been drawn to the youth over quite separate issues. Having produced his own airport I.D. cards he had managed to gain access to some of the restricted areas of the airport and had also talked his way into the offices of various airline Directors and Managers preparing the way for negotiations into his proposed lease/purchase of aircraft in relation to his non-existent new airline. He was seen by Uniformed Police Officers who took the practical step of seizing the I.D. passes and giving him some strong words of advice before sending him on his way.

When the ticket was referred to me for investigation, I arrested the young man who admitted what he had done but stated that he had wanted to test the I.A.T.A. security systems. He claimed to have spoken to I.A.T.A. officials but this of course proved to be false.

From his home I took possession of a large quantity of airline documents, tickets and security documents. I was then able to piece together what he had been up to.

It transpired that he had registered his own company and even had a fanciful name for his paper airline. His initial intentions were to have set up an airline operating business class flights between London and the U.S.A. Using his college's telephone and a commercial telex facility, he made contact with a large number of eminent businessmen and airline executives throughout the world in an attempt to make his company operational. He conducted enquiries and negotiations with several established aircraft manufacturers, airlines, aircraft brokers and individuals, trying to promote and purchase or lease aircraft and recruit personnel for his airline.

He persuaded a local advertising and promotion agent to act as a consultant as a result of which a large amount of promotional work was completed. The young man prepared budgets for his proposed service and tendered them to airline consultants for their comments.

149

John LLOYD

He then appears to have changed direction and decided to operate flights transporting Moslem Pilgrims from West Africa to Mecca during Hadj.

Accordingly he prepared an impressive document entitled "OUTLINE OPERATING PLAN" and together with a photocopy of a Certificate of Deposit in the sum of U.S. Dollars 50 million drawn on an Arabian Bank, he submitted these documents to airline consultants for their comments. These documents were of such a quality that they found favour with these consultants.

His next step was to involve himself with a reputable Travel Agency specialising in travel between England and West Africa. The director of this agency became interested in the scheme. The young man also became involved with some financial backing, although this was never verified. At this point the question of aircraft type was raised and the young man decided that a Boeing 747 would do for a start.

He then made contact with the Managing Director of an airline whose fleet was idle at the time due to civil unrest in the country. He showed the airline executive the Certificate of Deposit for US.50M indicating that his company had financial backing sufficient to fund the lease of a Boeing 747. The negotiations had, by the time of my intervention, reached a stage where a Memorandum of Understanding had been drawn up between the real and the paper airline for the outright purchase of Boeing 747 aircraft.

I discovered that the Certificate of Deposit was a copy of a specimen document which the young man had been sent by a firm of security printers. He had forged the document by photocopying the document many times and by altering the shade control of the copier he had managed to erase the word "SPECIMEN". Having done this he was then able to type onto the document his required details.

There is no doubt that this young man had been able to get as far as he had by his great in-depth knowledge of airline matters and by his habit of dropping names of eminent airline executives into any conversation. His youthful appearance and apparent lack of experience, whilst initially being a drawback, was outweighed by these factors added to the lure of

Bundu, the Beat & Beyond

potential lucrative business. Indeed, even the Judge at his subsequent trial (himself an ex-airline pilot) commented how impressed he was with the young man's obvious talent.

Since I dealt with him he has subsequently been arrested on two occasions for other forms of deceptions in the airline world and has served terms of imprisonment. He is currently wanted for yet another offence of deception and is believed to be in the USA.

2.   PREPAID TICKET ADVICE FRAUD.

My next example involves an ex Travel Agent with great experience of the Travel and Airline Industry. He was dismissed from employment with a London based Travel Agency due to theft of ticket stocks and their subsequent misuse by him for first class round-the-world trips for himself and his girlfriend. After his arrest he was sentenced to a term of imprisonment and upon his release he found himself unemployable within the Travel Agency business. Then, using his knowledge of the airline world he devised a scheme which would feed his need for first-class airline travel and provide him with some pocket money on the way.

The Travel Agency he was last employed with did not open for business at week-ends and so our friend telephoned Airline reservation offices just before midday on a Saturday morning purporting to be an employee of that agency he would quote the correct name and telephone number and their I.A.T.A. code number. He then gave a personal reference and requested the issue of a ticket on departure for a named passenger for first class travel involving multi-sector long and short haul travel. The ticket was to be collected by the passenger that very day at the departure airport (usually Heathrow or Gatwick). He then quoted an M.C.O. number against a major carrier from a series of numbers which he knew to be valid current stock. The M.C.O. was indicated as the form of payment. In order to facilitate this deception he had legally changed his name to that with a double barrelled surname one of which could also be taken as a first name. The ticket request was obviously made in favour of one of the names in his surname. Nearing the conclusion of the telephone call he would indicate that the reservation agent should

John LLOYD

not bother to attempt to ring back to confirm the T.O.D. request as the office was about to close for the week-end and there would be no-one there to receive the call.

The Reservation Agent appears to have accepted this explanation and processed the T.O.D. request in the normal manner. As a result of this all our man had to do was make his way to his chosen departure airport and collect his ticket and fly away undetected. His undoing came when he inadvertently miscalculated a fare for a chosen route. The reservation agent did not pick this up but a sharp eyed ticket agent at Gatwick queried the fare as a result of which an enquiry was made with an employee of the Travel Agency at his home. He confirmed that our man was not a bone-fide employee of the agency as a result of which when our man arrived at the ticket desk at Gatwick to collect his ticket, I arrested him.

He admitted the offence and from documentation found in his possession it was established that the day after his release from prison for his previous sentence he had used this method to obtain a T.O.D. and fly first class to various destinations throughout the world. It was his practice to obtain a re-issue at his first port of call for a different routing from the original issue. In addition, at virtually every stop he would make fraudulent baggage claims against which ever carrier he had just been travelling with.

The method for this was very simple. He always travelled very light and at the airport of departure he would check-in, as hold baggage, a small holdall bag or briefcase, as a result of which he would be issued with a baggage receipt affixed to his ticket. Then, having arrived at the next airport he would collect his small bag from the reclaim area and then remove the baggage label from it. He would then approach the appropriate airline staff and make a loss report in respect of non-existent baggage, thereby indicating that the bag he was carrying had been CABIN and not HOLD baggage.

He used this method many times and within a few weeks he had been paid out sufficient money in cash advances to cover all his personal expenses. During his short periods of residence in England, he booked

Bundu, the Beat & Beyond

himself into good class hotels using a false identity and would leave after two or three days and of course he forgot to pay any of the bills.

In addition to these offences, he was also found in possession of a large quantity of forged hotel vouchers and travellers cheques which he was prepared to use should he find himself stranded at a foreign airport.

Having finalised my enquiries, I established that during his month of liberty this man had obtained and used four tickets from different carriers, causing a loss of revenue of a little under £11,000 and had made ten separate fraudulent baggage claims and had received pre-settlement cash advances against six of these claims, totalling £329.00.

He was charged with various offences and after a period of custody whist awaiting trial, he was sentenced to 21 months imprisonment suspended for two years.

Very shortly after his release he attempted another similar offence against an airline and was again arrested in London. Unfortunately he was later acquitted on a technicality.

He is now free and is not doubt up to his old tricks again.

3. THEFT OF TICKET COUPONS.

My next case involves a lady of Hawaiian extraction who, in August 1987, was arrested at Gatwick Airport. She is believed to run her own travel agency in Hawaii and is therefore familiar with airline procedures.

Her method of obtaining tickets was somewhat different. She is apparently an experienced and proficient thief who simply stole flight coupons from check-in desks, together with boarding wallets and associated rubber stamps. Then, using a stock of validation stickers, she validated one of the coupons for herself and attempted to board a flight to the USA using the identity of the passenger named on the ticket. She was arrested and approximately 3000 other flight coupons were found in her possession, most of which had apparently been stolen by her from

153

John LLOYD

various airports in the USA. These stolen coupons obviously represented a substantial loss of revenue to various American carriers.

From other documents found in her possession it was clear that she had also been involved in thefts of property (including tickets) from fellow passengers on board aircraft in flight.

This lady was charged with offences and appeared at Court where she was fined and released whereupon she returned to the USA.

Our last information is that she was arrested in Los Angeles a few weeks later, where she had been committing similar offences.

A persistent offender who will no doubt continue her activities.

4.   FRAUDULENT STAFF I.D. AND TICKETS.

This type of offence was recently detected almost by accident with, I must add, the invaluable assistance of an airline Fraud Prevention Officer. The substance of this offence is that of obtaining airline staff tickets by use of a deception.

Briefly, this came to light by my investigating the activities of an African man who had used a stolen credit card on board a flight bound for Gatwick. He had attempted to obtain a large quantity of duty-free goods but fortunately an alert Cabin Attendant had become suspicious as a result of which he was arrested upon his arrival at Gatwick. In custody I discovered that he was travelling on a British Caledonian I.D. 90 staff ticket issued in Lagos for return travel between Lagos-London-Hong Kong. He was also in possession of an identity card which showed him as being an employee of Nigeria Airways and thereby entitled to such a ticket.

Having questioned him, he told me that he had left that airline's employ some three months earlier. Communications with this airline proved a little difficult and I therefore decided to charge him only with the offences relating to the misuse of the credit card. He appeared at court and received a short term of imprisonment. In the meantime I had

Bundu, the Beat & Beyond

contacted the Fraud Prevention Officer from British Caledonian Airways on whose paper the ticket had been issued. I explained the situation and voiced my doubts as to the man's right to hold the staff ticket. The Fraud Prevention Officer agreed with my suspicions and arranged to return the I.D. card to Nigeria Airways in Lagos.

This was duly done and we were later informed that in fact our African friend had never been an employee of that carrier. Their subsequent investigation revealed what appears to be a large scale fraud involving the sale of airline I.D. cards to anyone who can afford to purchase them and their subsequent provision of forged written applications for staff travel for the holders of these I.D. cards.

This is an on-going situation which I am sure will continue to cause problems in the future.

5. COUNTERFEIT TICKETS.

In early 1987 poor quality counterfeit tickets began circulating which appear to have originated in West Africa. These documents were never designed with a view for use as a travel ticket but in order to support visa applications and for production to Immigration Authorities to prove possession of a return ticket. However, recent forgeries seized in London, at Heathrow and Gatwick, indicate that these documents are of such good quality that it is highly unlikely that they would be detected in the normal course of events. It is only when these documents are carefully and minutely examined that tell-tale signs can be observed.

These latest forgeries came to light early in October 1987 when an Indian man, resident in the Philippines, flew to Gatwick from West Africa intending to transit through to New York. Upon arrival at Gatwick he presented himself at the airside ticket desk of a British airline and tendered one of their tickets requesting it to be validated for their next flight to New York which left later that morning. This was done. The man then made his way to the Landside ticket desk of the same airline where he presented a B.S.P. ticket plated to Lufthansa for first-class travel between Lagos-New York-Hong Kong-Los Angeles and Frankfurt. All sectors were open. Coupon one of the ticket had already

155

John LLOYD

been used and he requested that coupon two be re-issued for travel between New York-London-Hong Kong. The ticket agent was not happy with the profile of the ticket nor with the manner in which it had been written. It was referred to his Supervisor who was also unhappy although he was unable to identify any particular problem.

The matter was referred to Lufthansa who being unhappy with the validation, declined to issue authority for the re-issue. As a result of that the matter was referred to the British Caledonian Fraud Prevention Officer who examined the ticket and questioned the passenger. The Officer was unhappy with the passenger's replies as a result of which a uniformed Police Officer was summoned. He also questioned the passenger but received confusing and conflicting replies.

In the meantime, I had been contacted and went along to where the passenger was being questioned. The man was arrested and his luggage recovered. At the Police Station a fairly large quantity of tickets, M.C.O.'s and other documents were found in his luggage. Needless to say these were all re-issues of re-issues.

Also found were some rubber stamps amongst which were an Air India stamp and a KLM endorsement stamp. The ticket on which the man had travelled from Africa to Europe was found to have been issued in exchange for coupon 1 of a B.S.P. ticket. The validation box of the B.S.P. ticket was plated to a Travel Agency in the Philippines. These validations, we established, were suspected of being used on counterfeit tickets. Armed with this information, the ticket was carefully examined.

At first glance the ticket appears to be genuine and would certainly pass any cursory examination. However, it was noted that the red carbon on the reverse of the coupons was very weak and was capable of being rubbed away by the use of one's finger. In addition, the red colour of the carbon appeared dull and a darker shade of red than normally found on genuine tickets.

Later, when the forged ticket was compared with a genuine document, it was noted that the background colours of the forgery were extremely weak in comparison with a genuine document whose background colours

Bundu, the Beat & Beyond

are sharp and quite vivid. In addition, the fourth number on the forged document appears slightly larger than the remaining numbers, whereas on a genuine document the numbers are all of a uniform size.

Other differences were also noted later when examined using ultra-violet light. A check was made with the ticket printers by whom the forged ticket purported to have been printed. They were able to verify all the differences and additionally they were able to state that the ticket number had never been issued to the Philippines area on B.S.P. paper.

The Asian man was interviewed in connection with these matters. He admitted that he had bought the ticket in the Philippines but not from a Travel Agency or airline. He further admitted having written out the ticket himself but of course denied any knowledge that the ticket was a forgery. In relation to the airlines rubber stamps, he stated that he was carrying them to hand to a person in West Africa. He was charged with various offences and is currently awaiting trial.

An interesting side issue of this investigation involves an apparent currency exchange manipulation using airline documents. This involved his possession of three M.C.O.'s in his name issued on the paper of a South East Asian carrier. These documents showed the currency to be in U.S. Dollars and the original place of issue to be Los Angeles. However, I managed to backtrack through all the re-issues and finally established that the original issue was by a British airline in Lagos where the form of payment was shown in local currency. In addition, the original ticket issue was for this man's two young children.

The day after this man's arrest at Gatwick, a man was arrested at Heathrow in possession of a forged B.S.P. ticket he was using in an attempt to travel. In his possession were found two blank forged B.S.P. tickets and one Philippine Airline forged ticket. The B.S.P. tickets were of a similar quality to that found at Gatwick. The other ticket purported to have been printed by another printing company. The quality of this particular ticket is so good that the only way of proving it to be a forgery was to use a magic eye scanner which did not react when passed over the security bar codes on the coupons.

John LLOYD

Since that time other good quality forgeries have been picked up in England, the common factor being that they all appear to emanate from South East Asia. This, I am sure you agree, is a most disturbing development, the effects of which can only be harmful to the airline industry.

I believe that now is the time for the industry to take the initiative and take the necessary steps to prevent the problem escalating to epidemic proportions.

In conclusion, I view the problem of airline ticket fraud as an "economic crime ", the ramifications of which are poorly understood by the public. I see this problem as one of public relations and education.

The only way the airlines can cover at least part of these huge losses is to pass them on to the consumer in the form of increased fares and until such time as this "economic crime" is recognised and dealt with as such, then these losses will continue in effect to be subsidised by the passengers.

END

The delegates to this seminar warmly received my presentation and I continued to involve myself with the seminar especially as part of the panel taking questions from the floor in a Q&A session at the conclusion of the seminar.

I would like to be able to confirm that my input had some significant impact on the airline industry who took on board all that I had said resulting in major changes in procedures and protocols to the extent that ticket fraud was minimised. Unfortunately this was not the case, and whilst all the airline security Officers and Revenue Protection departments appeared to endorse what I had said, the airline industry as a whole carried on much the same as they had always done and suffered huge financial losses which were inevitably passed on to the consumer.

Bundu, the Beat & Beyond

The manual handwritten tickets as used then are now virtually obsolete due to the introduction of the E-ticket and I imagine that a great deal of the problems associated with the old style system are now a thing of the past because the airline systems actually generate each ticket resulting in airlines having total control of ticket issues. As far as I know these problems have been replaced by significant amounts of credit card fraud used to pay for the new E-Tickets.

I did enjoy my few days in Singapore and I made some very good contacts from amongst the delegates. Some of these contacts proved useful in the weeks and months ahead.

I returned to Gatwick, courtesy of Cathay Pacific (business class again) where I was met by Jackie and the beaming smiling face of a young four year old Simon which made my homecoming very worthwhile.

I continued with my Airline Ticket fraud investigations and maintained a very good liaison with the Metropolitan Police Airline Ticket Squad at Heathrow and in particular with DS Barry Emmett who was always very helpful and supportive.

I did do some other air travel relating to Police work whilst I was at Gatwick. On one occasion I flew on the flight deck of an Air Europe Boeing 737 from Gatwick to Malta and return. This was part of a joint initiative between Gatwick Airlines and the Police in the context of anti-terrorist training in which we learned some of the problems and procedures involved in flight operations twinned with being able to view at first hand the baggage handling procedures at close quarters both at Gatwick and abroad. This assisted us in a deeper understanding of some of the issues relating to thefts from baggage in transit. I felt really honoured to sit on the flight deck during the take-offs and landings which I found fascinating. This was matched by my inability to spot the runway on approach to Malta and it was only when the First Officer pointed it out to me that I realised what I had been looking at all along.

That flight was also remarkable because on the return leg, as we were crossing the southern coast of France just as it was getting dark in the

John LLOYD

early evening dusk period, a loud bell rang in the cockpit. This resulted in the Captain pushing a button above his head and speaking into his throat microphone. I was unable to hear exactly what he said until he turned to me and said, "There's a call for you" To say I was astonished would be a gross understatement, who would be calling me?

The Captain told me what to do and I donned the spare headset and pressed a button above my head and spoke. I was greeted by the voice of one of my colleagues back at Gatwick CID, Graham Bradley who urgently required to ascertain the location of some document I had been working on.

After the call ended nothing further was said on the flight deck and we proceeded on our way back to Gatwick.

The other occasion I remember flying abroad on duty whilst I was at Gatwick was during a time we had been investigating the thefts in transit of expensive precious stones. As always, one of the problems was trying to establish just where the theft had taken place. Was it at Gatwick or elsewhere?

As part of this investigation it was decided that enquiries needed to be conducted at Frankfurt Airport in Germany. However, due to legal protocols this could not be done on a Police to Police basis but could only be achieved by the Crown Prosecution Service submitting a formal letter of request (otherwise known as a Commission Rogatoire) through diplomatic channels to the relevant German Authorities.

This process was very protracted taking some long months to arrange. Finally, the German Authorities consented to us conducting enquiries at Frankfurt Airport as a result of which another Gatwick CID colleague, Alan Coole, and I flew to Frankfurt where we were met by German Kriminalpolizei (the equivalent of our CID) who looked after us very well. Neither of us could speak German but fortunately one of the German Officers was fluent in English and he assisted us greatly.

The one thing that sticks in my mind about that trip was that it was the height of summer with cloudless blue skies and a hot sun. Alan and

Bundu, the Beat & Beyond

I were dressed in our normal work clothing of suits and ties whereas we were so impressed with the German plain clothes Cops who all wore smart slacks and open necked shirts. Very practical, as whilst Alan and I were sweating and feeling generally uncomfortable, our German colleagues looked very cool and composed.

I also did some internal travel within the UK as part of my job which included a trip to Liverpool where I was royally looked after during my two day visit. One of the local DC's was delegated to look after me and show me around. Her name was Shirley Goodbody who was really delightful and after we had completed some of the enquiries she took me out on the town during the evening. We visited a nightclub (I think it was called the Gladstone Rooms) and as we were parking the CID car a group of young "scallys" approached us and asked if they could look after our car for a small fee whilst we were inside. I suppose that most people would have fallen for this in the fear that their car may have been vandalised during their absence if they had not taken up the youths offer of "protection". Quite rightly, Shirley was having none of it, she produced her Police warrant card and warned the youngsters in clear and somewhat fruity language of the consequences should the CID car be damaged. We returned an hour or so later somewhat relieved to see that the CID car was still in one piece.

I completed my enquiries the following morning after which Shirley took me to the renowned Cavern Club which is really quite small and dingy. I was then taken to Lime Street Railway Station and my return train to London and Gatwick.

CID Detective Training Course 1980. Back row (L-R) John Bishop, John Bacon, Phil Hellyer, Jim Roden, Clive (Yaki) Brind, Barry Gibson, Chris Gillings. Middle row L-R, Ken Scrase, Author, Pete Desborough, Dave Smith, John Watkins, Gerry Cannan, Front Row L-R: Alwyn Evans, DI Ron Bishop, Supt Jack Hirst, Janet Post, Chief Constable George Terry, Det Ch Supt Charles Johnstone, Chief Supt Cyril Leeves, DS Dudley Reynolds, DS George Divall.

Jackie and author at a BCAL party circa 1978.

Ian & Sue Inglis and author, BCAL dinner dance 1981.

Author and Jackie at the wedding of Sue & Ian Inglis, Edinburgh 1982.

Gareth, Jackie and Author 1983.

The author and Jackie with new born son Simon 1984.

My brother Chris at the Christening party for my son Simon 1984.
This was just before he gracefully slid down the wall
after he became tired and emotional

Gatwick CID circa 1985, Back row L-R Brian Stockham, Author, Vic Cloney, Chris Munn, Ben Brittain. Front row (L-R) Julie Phillips (CID clerk), Bill Smith, John Alderson, Dave Wood, Jackie (CID Clerk).

A formal portrait taken in 1991 when I joined Interpol London. This was exhibited on the Bureau wall together with pictures of other Interpol London Officers grouped in crime desk order.

Interpol London contingent at the Australia House Ball 1995. (L-R) Author and Jackie (Sussex), Dave and Denise Hopkins (Sussex), Chris and Debbie Parkin (South Yorkshire), Dave Corrin (Merseyside), two guests, Andy and Carol Walker (Greater Manchester), Terry Baker and Lavinia Shepherd (Bedfordshire).

My first retirement party at Cobalt Square in London 1999 with Alan Shiers and Debby Lofts.

An example of artwork from my friend, Fran Van Vuuren entitled " Birds of a feather ". The monochrome image does not do the work justice due to the lack of the vibrant colours in the original but there is sufficient clarity of the image to appreciate her talent.

CHAPTER 9

Interpol

I should start this chapter by clearly stating that a substantial amount of the matters I became involved with during my time with Interpol were security graded between classified and Secret. This means that I have had to edit down, or omit entirely, some of the work in which I was involved.

In 1990 an advertisement appeared in Police Review, a national Police magazine, which sought suitably qualified Detective Officers for secondment on Central Service for a 2 year period. This secondment was for an attachment to the UK National Central Bureau (NCB) of Interpol in London.

The contents of the advert appealed to me even though, if truth be known, I had little idea of what was involved.

I replied to the advert via my Force's Personnel Department and some weeks later I received an invitation to attend a selection interview at New Scotland Yard in London. Before the date of the interview I took a day off work and visited the Interpol Offices located on the 14th floor of Tower Block at the Yard. I had pre-arranged this visit with one of the Interpol Officers and used this day to familiarise myself with the roles and some procedures in which they were engaged. I found this very useful.

Accordingly, I presented myself for interview at 1000hrs on Thursday 13 September 1990 in Room 1414, Tower Block, New Scotland Yard.

Bundu, the Beat & Beyond

I was interviewed by a panel of three headed by Acting Detective Superintendent Sandy White from Strathclyde Police in Scotland. He was my kind of man in that he obviously did not suffer fools gladly and spoke in a direct manner. He said what he meant which is not something I can say about everyone. I do prefer to know exactly what people are thinking reflected in their speech but so often people say one thing but really mean something totally different.

The interview was quite cordial and, from my perspective, seemed to progress quite well. I was able to answer all their questions in a satisfactory manner. I was expecting to receive the results of the interview at some future time but at the conclusion of the interview Sandy White offered me a position within Interpol London. To say that I was pleased would be an understatement.

Some weeks later I received written confirmation that I was to commence my new duties in a national post with NCB London in January 1991.

This was to be a turning point in my Police career as well as my private life. The only downside, in my view, was that it would take three hours out of my day just getting to and from New Scotland Yard to my house in Crawley. The distance between Crawley and London Victoria Railway Station is only about 30 miles but there are no non stop services available (apart from the Gatwick Express which costs a fortune) so I would be using the commuter services offered by Southern Rail which, door to door, took 90 minutes each way. This was one aspect of my new job with which I was never really comfortable but it is one that I got used to and it became part of my extended working day.

During my last few weeks at Gatwick I had an informant who was supplying information about a prospective case of drugs trafficking by airport staff. The drugs were coming in from abroad and were intended for a UK destination. Due to the nature of these matters I involved the Investigations Unit of HM Customs at Gatwick as this was specifically their area of responsibility. Due to my impending departure I had to hand over the responsibility of handling the informant to my successor, Verna Cannan, who I knew very well from my days at Crawley CID. I

John LLOYD

left this matter in her very capable hands and made my preparations to leave for my new post in London.

I said farewell to my colleagues at Gatwick CID in early January 1991 and we had a small celebratory farewell gathering in the CID office at which I was presented with some farewell cards containing (mostly) some really complimentary remarks twinned with some really humorous and partly ribald comments.

I was sad to say goodbye to such people as Nick Siggs, Danny McCann, Marion Allen, Phil Bottomer, Rex Mathews, Andy Bliss, Kevin Fitzgerald, Kelly McCartney, Mark Eyre, Ian Hands, Martyn (Tosh) Underhill, Phil & Janette Pentney, Les Freer, Chris Standard, Bert Welch, Tony Byrne, Dave Reader, Verna Cannan, Clint Novelle, Mickey Gregory, Steve Scott, Andy Mays, Paul Sellings, Gary Maiden, Christine Hannah and many others too numerous to mention.

Some of these were rising stars of the future, for example Martyn Underhill, who was an aide to CID at Gatwick at that time, went on to achieve the rank of Detective Chief Inspector and was second in command of the Sarah Payne murder investigation. Sarah was a young girl who was abducted and murdered by a Sussex man who was later convicted of this heinous crime. After retirement from the Police some years later Martyn went on to become the first elected Police and Crime Commissioner for the county of Dorset where he now lives with his lovely partner, Debs.

Andy Bliss, a very capable Officer and good all round man, later became Chief Constable of Hertfordshire Police.

I also said my goodbyes to some of the Custody Officers at Gatwick who had been of great assistance to me over the years when dealing with some of the prisoners I had brought into custody. Special mention should be made of Derek Thornton and Ray Pattenden who were particularly helpful and with whom I got along with very well.

Bundu, the Beat & Beyond

I had had very interesting times at Gatwick. I had met and worked with some great people and had travelled to many places both in the UK and abroad.

In mid-January 1991 I presented myself again to Room 1414 on the 14th floor of Tower Block at New Scotland Yard. By this time Sandy White had completed his period of secondment and had returned to Strathclyde Police in Scotland. His position had been filled by Detective Chief Inspector Ann Harrison of the City of London Police. The Head of Bureau at that time was a Metropolitan Police Officer Detective Superintendent Bill Wooding. I met both those Officers that day and they made me welcome.

I joined Interpol London on the same day as another Sussex Officer, Dave Hopkins, who hailed from Eastbourne CID. He and I knew each other previously as we had both worked at Hove albeit on different Sections. Dave was a good all-round man as well as being an experienced CID Officer.

Interpol London was staffed by Officers from all over the UK which had many benefits in that their local knowledge was usually available, when required.

The Bureau was divided into four desks each of which dealt with a different crime category.

1. Drugs.
2. Theft.
3. Fraud.
4. Offences against the Person.

As Office Manager we had DI Graham Dovey from South Yorkshire Police who was a very affable and likeable man as well as being efficient at his job. Working alongside Graham was DI Tom Dorrant, a Metropolitan Police Officer who was our European Contact Officer. Tom was fluent in many languages including French, Russian and Polish and he was often called upon to make direct contact with other European Interpol Bureaux to sort out problems of the moment. At

173

John LLOYD

that time it was Tom's habit to refer to us Provincial Officers as "Carrot Crunchers" This went on for some weeks until one day after he had said it once more I said to him, "Well it's better than being a banana." Tom replied, "What do you mean, a banana?" I said, "Yellow and bent" I did not hear him use the phrase "carrot cruncher" again after that.

As an organisation Interpol operates in four languages, English, Arabic, French and Spanish. Accordingly we had translators fluent in French and Spanish who were able to translate all communications in French and Spanish. Fortunately the Arabic speaking countries normally only transmitted in Arabic to their Arabic speaking partners mainly in North Africa so we did not have the need for an Arabic translator. Heading up this translators section was a wonderful man named Giovanni Ceccarelli who, as you probably surmised, was of Italian extraction. Giovanni, or Joe as he was universally known, spoke many languages quite fluently, and although he did not have a Police background he had developed a great knowledge of how various foreign jurisdictions worked as well as being well versed in the differing legal systems. He was therefore a great asset when trying to identify how best to progress any one enquiry.

As well as the London Metropolitan Police and Sussex Police there were also Officers from Kent, Bedfordshire, Merseyside, Greater Manchester, West Yorkshire, Lothian & Borders, Gwent and the Royal Ulster Constabulary (RUC) in Northern Ireland.

Initially I was placed on the Fraud Desk whilst Dave went to the Drugs Desk.

It is worthwhile me explaining what Interpol is about so there is no misunderstanding of the roles we performed. The correct and full title of the organisation is the International Criminal Police Organisation (ICPO) which comprises 198 member countries around the world.

The title of Interpol came about from the shortened version of the old telex address for the organisation.

Under Article 3 of the Interpol Constitution it is forbidden for member states to become involved in matters of a political, racial, religious or

Bundu, the Beat & Beyond

military character. I fell slightly foul of Article 3 some years later when I was investigating the deaths of two British nationals in the Bosnian war. It was suspected that the first British national had been shot and murdered by one of his own side and the death of the second British national by shooting was unexplained. I had submitted my request to the Bosnian Police and, as was the practice, I had copied this to Interpol HQ in Lyon who asked me for further details before being able to proceed.

I submitted an additional report and Interpol HQ ruled that the criminal investigations into the suspected murder of the first British national could proceed but any investigations into the death of the second one should cease as it was likely that he was killed as a result of enemy action (ie Military action)

Each member country has one Interpol Bureau normally located in the capital city. Each Bureau is normally staffed by experienced Police Officers from that country. The exception to this is France which has two Interpol Bureaux. France has its own National Central Bureau (NCB) located in Paris but it also accommodates the global Interpol HQ based in Lyon.

The main objective of Interpol is the widest possible co-operation in criminal matters including the exchange of criminal information and intelligence.

Due to my background in fraud investigation I believed that I was reasonably well qualified and equipped to deal with matters on the Fraud Desk. How wrong I was. The next six months saw me experience a very steep learning curve whilst I became familiar with the nuances and difficulties involved in International Policing. I had to learn what was possible and what was not. A small example of this would be the obtaining of a simple straightforward witness statement. If I required a statement from a witness in the UK I would simply arrange to see the witness at a convenient venue and time, conduct the interview, and obtain the statement of evidence in written form. I could do this personally (preferable in my experience) or I could ask the local Police in whose area the witness resides to obtain the statement on my behalf.

175

John LLOYD

If an investigating Police Officer wished to obtain a written witness statement from most foreign jurisdictions then normally the only method of being able to obtain such a statement would be by the submission of a Commission Rogatoire (Letter of Request) from a Judicial or legal body such as the Crown Prosecution Service.

A Letter of Request is a letter from one judicial authority to another judicial authority seeking evidence in criminal matters.

The letter has to be translated into the language appropriate to the country in which the evidence is to be obtained. This is not always as easy as it sounds. For example in Switzerland there are three languages spoken in different parts (or Cantons) of the country, French, German and Italian. It is therefore necessary to establish which language is relevant before submitting any Letter of Request.

However, there were exceptions to this as we were able to successfully request the obtaining of willing witness statements from such countries as Ireland, Australia, Canada, New Zealand, South Africa and to a limited extent from the USA. This was mainly because those countries Police and judicial systems operated much the same as we do in the UK. Requests of this nature to the USA could be a bit hit and miss and I recall one so called witness statement from the USA was nothing more than a transcript of a telephone conversation between the US Police Officer and the witness. Needless to say we had to start again with that one as it clearly would not be acceptable in a UK court.

The second problem is that it can take a Judicial Authority (The CPS is no exception) a very long time just to draft the International Letter of Request. (ILOR)

Once the ILOR has been drafted and approved it then has to be submitted to the foreign authority via diplomatic channels which is a further lengthy procedure.

Once the ILOR is received by the Central Authority in the foreign country it will be read to establish that it is a lawful request (according to the relevant laws of that country). Once approved it then has to be

Bundu, the Beat & Beyond

forwarded on to the appropriate Judicial Authority responsible for the area in which the enquiry is to be conducted. Then the ILOR sits in a pile of similar letters from other authorities until such time it is executed. Once executed the evidence is returned to the originator via the same route but in reverse.

This is a weary and time consuming process which can take upwards of six months or more!

Often the UK Letters of Request would include the request for British Officers involved in the investigation to be present whilst the evidence was being obtained. This was for the sake of continuity. In these cases Interpol was tasked with arranging the travel itinerary etc in liaison with the relevant foreign country.

This is just one aspect of international policing in which I, and my colleagues, had to become well versed before we were in a position to give suitable advice to Police Officers of all ranks and from all parts of the UK in how best to advance their particular enquiry.

I will not burden the reader with all the new rules and protocols that I had to learn in the first six months or so but most of it was totally new to me and outside of my previous experience.

The vast majority of our enquiries were received from UK Police Forces or foreign Interpol Bureaux but some were from other agencies and although they related to criminal matters they were, by their very nature, classified as secret.

Being on the Fraud Desk I soon developed, out of necessity, good contacts and relations with the Fraud Units of the UK Police Forces. Our main customers were the London Metropolitan Police Fraud Squad as well as the City of London Police Fraud Investigation Department. These Fraud Squads were staffed by highly experienced and well qualified Police Officers who knew their business very well and appreciated the difficulties of conducting international enquiries. In addition we also had a large number of dealings with the Serious Fraud Office (SFO)

John LLOYD

in London which was staffed by a mix of Police Officers, lawyers and accountants and who specialised in high end major frauds.

Upon receiving a request, say from a UK Police Officer, we would read and fully understand the request before submitting it to any foreign authority. If we had any queries we would send the request back to the originator seeking clarification on certain points. Once satisfied that we had a complete and valid request we would submit it via Interpol channels to the relevant foreign Interpol Bureau.

Upon receipt by the foreign Interpol Bureau it would be translated into the relevant language (if required) and then either dealt with by the staff at the Interpol Bureau or forwarded on to one of their Police or other units for completion. The results of those would then, eventually, be sent to Interpol London where we would have it translated, if necessary, before sending it on to the originating Officer.

We were always kept very busy and when I was fully operational I had around 500 cases on-going at any one time.

In 1991 we were not fully computerised and although we used computers for sending our requests to foreign countries or within the UK we maintained Blue covered paper files in which all correspondence relevant to that particular request was kept. It was also important that each message was properly minuted at the front of the file in order to maintain some order and perspective and additionally so that other Officers reading the file could understand or pinpoint any one particular aspect of the file.

This procedure worked fairly well as long as a file did not go missing which did happen from time to time.

This was, however, quite a Dickensian process but it was what we had until it was supplanted by complete electronic Case Management systems nearly ten years later.

On the Fraud Desk I worked with Terry Imrie from Lothian & Borders Police as well as two London Metropolitan Police Officers, Paul De

Bundu, the Beat & Beyond

Langhe and Jerry Nelson. We all rubbed along well together which was just as well as we were a small team. Paul was an experienced Divisional Detective and was also a Multi Linguist being fluent in French, Dutch and German. This was very useful to our desk and he was often asked to make telephone calls to a Case Officer in a foreign Interpol Bureau seeking an update or chasing a particular case. Jerry was a fluent Spanish speaker and proved very useful when direct telephone calls were need to the Spanish Police or the Interpol Bureau in Madrid.

One morning, shortly after I had arrived, I was sitting at my desk on the 14th floor of New Scotland Yard. Sometime in mid-morning I looked out of the large picture window opposite where I could see the Westminster area when suddenly the building shook and vibrated alarmingly. I then heard the sound of a substantial detonation. I thought that it might be a minor earthquake. I then saw a cloud of grey black smoke rising from the vicinity of Downing Street. The IRA had mortar bombed the Prime Minister's residence. Welcome to London.

I was always kept extremely busy and during the next six months or so I began developing my knowledge and expertise in my new role.

Some of the types of frauds I was dealing with included Advanced Fee Frauds, Long Firm Frauds, high end mortgage frauds, Boiler Room Frauds etc etc. In fact any decent fraud which had some international connection we dealt with.

This was also the time of Asil Nadir and the now infamous massive fraud at Polly Peck. We tracked the prime suspect Asil Nadir as far as Northern Cyprus where the trail abruptly stopped because the UK did not have an extradition treaty with that country which was, at the time, unrecognised as an independent country by any other country except Turkey. It was as frustrating for the Investigating Officers as it was for us. We knew just where the suspect was now located but we were unable to get at him and have him extradited to face justice.

We operated mainly on day shifts but at least one Officer was always delegated to start work by 0800hrs and another at 1400hrs so that the Bureau was staffed by Police Officers between the hours of 0800hrs to

John LLOYD

2200hrs. Outside of those hours any calls were handled by our 24 hour communications unit operating on the 4th floor. This unit was staffed by a mixture of non Police and Uniformed Police staff and most of them had been signallers in the armed Forces which harked back to the days when Interpol used the Morse Code for transmitting and receiving all messages from abroad.

On the days I was rostered to work the 2-10 shifts I always managed to arrange a bed for myself in the Home Office Flats in Ebury Street, Belgravia, where all the provincial Police staff were housed. I did this because by the time I had finished work at 2200hrs I would not have arrived home in Crawley until after 2330 hrs or so depending upon train availability. I always thought that this block of 1950's style flats were a little incongruous being located among the million pound plus town houses all around that very upper class area of London where only the rich and famous could afford to live.

In November 1991 I was selected to go on a two week Interpol Training Course at Interpol HQ in Lyon, France. Also on that course with me were Graham Dovey of South Yorkshire Police and Gareth Hale of Gwent Police.

I had anticipated, wrongly, that Lyon being located a fair way south in France would be fairly warm at that time of year. How wrong I was. It was freezing cold and I had not brought sufficient warm winter clothing with me. I found a French market near to our hotel and managed to purchase some thermal underwear etc which kept my vitals relatively warm.

I found the course to be very enlightening not least of which because it was attended by about one hundred delegates from many countries around the world. During one day we all had to give a solo 10 minute presentation on how our own Bureau operated. I was quite amazed at the differing standards and facilities available to some other Bureaux. The Americans were, of course, full of themselves and talked a very good job and told us about all the state of the art equipment that they used.

Bundu, the Beat & Beyond

At the other end of the scale, I will never forget the input of the delegate from Swaziland in Southern Africa. He was a smashing fellow and I really took to him and his engaging personality. He told us that there was just him in the Interpol Bureau in Mbabane. He had a small office with a table and chair. He had a typewriter and a telephone. If he had to leave the office to conduct enquiries in Mbabane he had to use his bicycle as a mode of transport. If he had to conduct enquiries on our behalf outside of Mbabane then he used the country bus service.

This brought home to me just how diverse we all were and that we did not all have similar facilities and resources.

Being part of Interpol was a bit like being a part of the United Nations and, inevitably perhaps, politics did come into play at some time or other. An example of this was glaringly obvious to me as there were a number of delegates from the Arab countries in North Africa as well as a female Police Officer delegate from Israel. The Arab delegates would not even acknowledge the presence of the Israeli delegate let alone speak to her. Another lesson learned. The Israeli delegate was quite unfazed by this and seemed to accept it as normal behaviour.

On another occasion I was speaking to one of the Irish delegates from Interpol Dublin and we were getting along famously when an Instructor, who should have known better, tried to introduce the subject of Irish nationalism, the IRA and British rule etc, into our conversation. He was being mischievous and trying to stir up a hot debate between us. The Irish delegate and I both blanked him and continued our private conversation. He left our proximity without saying anything further.

I also formed the view that some delegates were more efficient than others which merely highlighted the differing standards then operating in the large number of Police Forces across the world.

I was later able to establish that some Interpol Bureaux were more efficient and reliable than others even though we were all allegedly operating from the same Interpol standards. I knew that certain Bureaux such as Canberra (Australia), Wellington (New Zealand) and Ottawa (Canada) could always be relied upon to provide a first class and timely

John LLOYD

response to most requests for assistance whereas as some of the others were quite unreliable and slow.

Late in 1991 the National Criminal Intelligence Service (NCIS) was formed and brought together many Police units with national responsibility as well as elements of HM Customs, HM Immigration and other agencies.

This brand new Intelligence service was designed to receive information from all sources with a view to developing coherent criminal intelligence which could then be disseminated to the relevant Police Forces or Agencies in the UK.

The UK National Central Bureau of Interpol was one of the Police units which moved over to form the newly created NCIS.

The NCIS was located in a series of brand new Office blocks in the Vauxhall area of London and so it meant that I had to amend my daily travel and instead of using the train into Victoria Station I now changed at Clapham Junction where I got a train to Vauxhall and walked the ten minutes to my new office.

In the higher echelons of the NCIS were two Sussex Officers who I had known in my previous life in the form of John Abbott and Roger Hills. They were both excellent Officers with years of relevant experience. They also had a lot of common sense and were universally liked and respected.

Both these Officers were often seen walking the floors of the various NCIS departments exchanging social chitchat as well as imparting the latest policy or new direction our organisation was taking.

Good men both.

In 1992 an opportunity arose for me to transfer to the Offences Against the Persons Desk which I immediately accepted. Whilst I had enjoyed working on the Fraud Desk I knew that the "Persons" desk, as it was known, would prove far more interesting and challenging because of the wide variety of crimes it dealt with. The following is a brief review

Bundu, the Beat & Beyond

of some of the crimes dealt with by the Persons Desk:—Murder, Sexual assaults, Rape, Physical Assaults, Kidnap, Child Abduction, Human Trafficking, Paedophilia, Terrorism, Aviation offences etc etc.

I began working with Ken Pandolfi, a Metropolitan Officer, Terry Baker from Bedfordshire and Bob Lakin from Hampshire. They were all good men and experienced Police Officers who knew what they were doing. Bob Lakin could be a little eccentric sometimes but he was dedicated to his work and would often go the "extra mile" to achieve a positive result.

Social drinking in the evenings after work was very popular with most Interpol staff and quite often Bob, who lived in Southampton, would wake up at the train's final destination of Portsmouth having slept through most of his homeward journey.

What made the work of this desk so interesting is that we were dealing directly with human behaviour and often it was a case of pitting one's wits against that of the wanted criminal in order to bring him or her to justice. We won most of the time but not always.

In 1994 I was contacted by the FBI Attache at the US Embassy in London requesting that I travel to the USA to give evidence at the forthcoming trial of a US national whose name I recognised from my time at Gatwick CID. I had dealt with this man for criminal harassment offences against some managers of Virgin Atlantic Airways when he had arranged for human faeces to be sent to these managers via the postal system (see Chapter 8). This man had been arrested again, this time in the USA, for waging similar campaigns against some FBI Agents in addition to which he had also made some threats to kill some of the Agents.

The FBI took this seriously and had prepared a file of evidence sufficient to charge the man with serious criminal offences within US jurisdiction. The FBI were also in possession of my report previously submitted to them concerning his activities in the UK and the Assistant District Attorney in Newark, New Jersey, wanted to adduce the UK evidence as evidence of similar fact to add to the weight of the US case.

John LLOYD

In addition to me, the FBI also wanted the attendance of Mark Eyre as well as Tony Hudson who was a former Sussex Police Officer who had worked with me at Gatwick CID. Previously to that Tony had been a BSAP Officer in Rhodesia but was now the Chief Security Officer for Virgin Atlantic Airways in the UK.

I agreed to my attendance in the USA and the US Authorities agreed to fund our Air Travel and expenses whilst we were in their jurisdiction.

A stroke of good fortune was that Tony Hudson was in a position to upgrade our Economy class tickets to their Upper Class cabin and accordingly Mark and I were ushered into the splendid Virgin Upper Class lounge at London's Heathrow Airport where we could choose to have a massage, operate a gigantic train set or simply relax and have a few complimentary drinks in the very comfortable lounge bar area. We met Tony in the lounge and later we boarded the Boeing 747 which was to take us to Newark, New Jersey. We turned left on entering the aircraft and were shown to our seats in the upper cabin just above the bar area.

We were told that the renowned boxer and Heavyweight Champion of the world, Lennox Lewis, was also travelling on the flight in Upper Class but all I ever saw was the figure of a very large man covered in a blanket apparently asleep.

After a really excellent meal accompanied by some fine wine we extended our comfortable chairs to their fully extended position which made a reasonably comfortable flat bed. This was the first and only time that I was able to get a few hours of decent sleep on an aircraft.

We were met at Newark by a female FBI Agent and taken immediately to the offices of the female Assistant District Attorney who was to prosecute the case. She seemed competent enough and seemed very knowledgeable in US criminal law but the file of evidence was a complete mess, so much so, that it would be an insult to call it a file.

She asked for our assistance in getting some semblance of order into the paperwork and during the next hour or so Tony, Mark and I managed to

Bundu, the Beat & Beyond

cobble together a reasonable file of evidence that resembled something akin to a Committal File as we knew them in the UK.

She then went through the evidence that she wanted us to provide and the next day it was straight to Court where I was the first to be called to give my evidence. The Judge had ruled that some of my evidence should not be admitted as it may be prejudicial to the Defence and so I presented an abridged watered down version of my evidence to the Court after which the Defence Attorney gave me a really rough time and, it seems, without me being able to verbally defend myself or give the answers I wished to his line of questioning. The Judge did not intervene so I assumed that this was acceptable procedure in US courts.

Having given my evidence the Court decided that it did not require to hear from Mark Eyre which meant that he had a free holiday in the USA for a few days.

The FBI Agents involved in the case had heard my evidence and congratulated me on my efforts although I thought that these were not as good as they might have been.

We were then released from the Court and in the evening the FBI Agents took Mark and I out for a superb Chinese Dinner. I think that Tony had had to return to London by this time as I do not recall him being with us that night. After the meal we were all handed the Chinese Fortune Cookies and without any ceremony Mark, who may not have experienced these before, popped his straight into his mouth and began eating the Fortune Cookie not realising that they contained a slip of paper detailing his fortune. After a few seconds he began to choke a little and sheepishly had to remove the half chewed mess from his mouth, much to our amusement and his embarrassment.

The FBI Agents we had met were friendly enough and talked a very good job but neither of us was sufficiently impressed with their professional abilities. They gave me the impression of being over-aged College Kids who knew the theory but had little experience. That may be harsh and unfair especially as the FBI has been involved in many very high profile and successful cases since its formation.

John LLOYD

I was once told that the initials FBI stood for "Famous But Incompetent" which was also unfair and probably untrue but Mark and I had seen another side to the FBI.

The following day Mark and I returned to London in our very comfortable Upper Class seats courtesy of Virgin Atlantic and Tony Hudson.

Whilst I was working with Interpol I learned of a staggering statistic about US Law Enforcement which still leaves me a little cold all these years later. Apparently there are in excess of 16,000 separate Law Enforcement Agencies in the USA. Yes, you read it correctly, 16 thousand! In addition a lot of these separate Law Enforcement Agencies do not talk to one another and do not, as a matter of routine, share intelligence and information. I am always left somewhat dumbstruck by this situation but it does go some way, perhaps, to explain just why US Law Enforcement achieves some of the results it does.

It was around this time that bottled spring drinking water became very popular in London with most people travelling to and from work clutching at least one bottle of water. Whilst I am sure that bottled natural spring water is a very good product I have always felt that it is grossly overpriced especially when it is very easy and convenient to drink tap water which in the UK is of a very high quality and cheap. It never ceases to amuse me that if the brand name of one of the more popular brands of bottled spring water is reversed you end up with the word "NAÏVE"

Upon receipt of any request for international assistance either from a UK source or a foreign agency it was always our practice to "add value" to the request. We did this in a variety of different ways but as we had access to some databases not normally accessible to others we were generally able to give some added value to most requests. In addition to this it was also our practice when dealing with requests from abroad to try and identify a UK agency that would benefit from the intelligence potential contained within the request. This was not always an exact science but, with experience, I found identifying a UK Agency or Agencies, who could benefit from the intelligence potential a great deal easier.

186

Bundu, the Beat & Beyond

As our work also included Terrorist related matters we had daily contact with the Anti-Terrorist Command of the Metropolitan Police (SO15) as well as other Agencies.

There were two areas of the work on the Offences Against the Persons Desk in which I developed a special interest and over time I had accrued some expertise as well as success. These were Paedophilia and Child Abduction.

Up until the 1970's and early 1980's paedophiles were mostly active at a local or, at worst, a national level. During this period Police Forces in the UK did not always exchange criminal information and intelligence as a matter of routine. This is just one of the reasons why the likes of Jimmy Savile were able to get away with his crimes. The UK did have a so called national criminal database with the advent of the Police National Computer (PNC) however this was not used by either the Scottish or Northern Irish Police until well into the 21st century. The Scottish Forces could access the PNC but they did not generally contribute to it whilst the RUC in Northern Ireland did not seem to use it at all. This was not joined up Policing.

I identified these loopholes in the early 2000's when I was investigating the background of a Northern Irish man who had been arrested in Australia for murder. Naturally the Australian Police wanted to obtain all his relevant antecedent details including that of any criminal convictions.

I searched his details on the UK PNC with a no trace result. I noticed that the man had been born in Belfast and I made contact with NI.CRO (Northern Ireland Criminal Record Office) in Belfast operated by the RUC. The results astonished me. This man had 44 separate criminal convictions some of which were for serious terrorist related offences.

I did submit a report about this later which, I am glad to say, did have some effect in that the Scottish Forces now all submit details of criminal convictions onto the PNC and some convictions in Northern Ireland are now available on the PNC. Some progress but it could be better.

John LLOYD

By the late 1980's and early 1990's paedophiles were organised not just on a national basis but also on an international basis. They exchanged information on a whole range of paedophile issues including details of vulnerable children who were classed as potential targets for their activities.

These issues and problems were compounded by the fact that the ages of consent for children varied quite widely within Europe let alone the remainder of the world. These ages of consent varied between 12 and 18. In UK the age of sexual consent is established at 16. This age was established as it was felt that a child of 16 is normally sufficiently mature to make an informed decision to engage in sexual activity.

Another factor that affected international paedophilia was the advent of affordable mass air travel which meant that most paedophiles had the opportunity to travel wherever they chose in order to carry out their sexual acts with under-age children.

This, in turn, led to some countries being targeted by paedophiles who identified that economic conditions prevailing in those countries encouraged young children to make themselves available for sexual activity with west European adult males. Countries such as Thailand and Cambodia are just two examples.

These activities were not confined to third world countries but some East European States as well. I had well documented evidence of western European adult males targeting the Czech Republic where young boys were in plentiful supply. This situation did change once the Czech Authorities were made aware of what was going on in their jurisdiction resulting is some high profile arrests and convictions. One of those convicted and who served time in a Czech Prison was a very well-known BBC Radio Disc Jockey.

These convictions often came about because we, on the Persons Desk in London, had developed intelligence on known travelling paedophiles and on some occasions had tracked them on their travels. This intelligence was then disseminated to the relevant countries for their attention.

Bundu, the Beat & Beyond

At that time we were ably assisted by the NCIS Serious Sexual Offences Unit (SSOU) which specialized in collating information from various sources including UK Police Forces which was then developed into hard intelligence. One Officer with whom I was in contact almost on a daily basis from SSOU was Tim Gerrish, a London Metropolitan Police Officer, who seemed to have the knack of being able to identify international travelling paedophiles and developing relevant intelligence which we could use to notify foreign Authorities who would then take relevant action within the confines of their criminal legal system.

Tim and I got along very well as individuals and I was gratified that whenever Tim wanted some help or advice on how best to progress any international aspects of an investigation he would seek me out. We would discuss the ramifications of the case and reach an agreement on how best to proceed. It was an arrangement that worked very well to our mutual advantage.

One travelling paedophile who came to my attention travelled far and wide throughout the world was a British national who, in one three month period, I was able to track and follow his progress throughout the Far East and Australasia and then back to Europe via the Americas. I had circulated his details via the Interpol network and received almost daily reports of his travels until he was finally stopped and arrested in Finland where he had been committing offences against minors. This type of case was never widely reported and seldom came to the notice of the general public but we did conduct a great deal of intensive work in tracking these people and having their movements and activities monitored by the authorities.

One high profile case which did come to public attention some years later was that of Paul Gadd, better known as Gary Glitter, who was arrested and convicted of sex offences with under age children in a Far East Country. After completing his prison sentence he was deported back to the UK where he was immediately registered as a Sex Offender and made subject of a Travel Restriction Order which limited any future plans he may have had as regards to sex offending abroad.

John LLOYD

One of the problems with many paedophiles is that they do not recognise that their activities are wrong. They seem to have the attitude that they have the right to sexually abuse children and fail to recognise that under age children do not have the ability to make an informed decision regarding consent. Neither do they seem to care about the potential psychological effects these children suffer as a result of their actions.

On a family note, my brother Chris, who lived a few hundred yards from Jackie and I in Crawley, met a young lady named Sandra whilst on a foreign holiday. They began seeing each other after their return to the UK and they married in her home town of Cosham in Hampshire on 6th March 1993. They now live in Cosham with their daughter, Robyn, who is currently taking a University Course prior to becoming a primary school teacher.

One other particular case of note that I can refer to was that of a British national named Martin John Scripps. He was a petty criminal in the UK and was mainly involved in frauds, thefts, drugs smuggling and deceptions. In the mid 1990's he was wanted for an offence in the UK but his whereabouts were, at that time, unknown.

In 1995 one of the hundreds of cases I was dealing with was a request from Interpol Singapore relating to a British national who had been arrested in Singapore on suspicion of Murder. The name and date of birth of their suspect was unknown to British Police records and I requested that Singapore supply a copy of their suspect's fingerprints to confirm identity.

This was a particularly gruesome murder in which the body parts of one person had been found in the waters of Singapore Harbour. The victim's body had been dismembered before being put into a number of plastic bags and thrown into Singapore Harbour. The victim was later identified as a man named Gerard Lowe from South Africa. The suspect was believed to have fraudulently obtained money and other valuables from the victim before fleeing by air to Bangkok. From Bangkok he intended to fly to another destination but, unfortunately for him, this flight was routed via Singapore where he was arrested upon arrival, albeit in transit.

190

Bundu, the Beat & Beyond

The suspect was also believed to have murdered two Canadian nationals in Thailand and to have dishonestly obtained monies and other valuables from his victims.

I received a set of fingerprints from Singapore belonging to their suspect and I referred those prints to the Fingerprint Section at New Scotland Yard with whom we had a really excellent relationship at that time.

The results of the fingerprint checks were sent back to me within a couple of days. The prints sent from Singapore were identified as being those of one Martin John Scripps.

I informed Interpol Singapore of this fact and supplied them with copies of his previous convictions as recorded in the UK together with statements of evidence from myself and the fingerprint expert at New Scotland Yard.

Scripps was later charged with an offence of murder and after a trial he was found Guilty and sentenced to death.

He went through the motions of an appeal against his conviction but he withdrew this appeal some days before it was scheduled to be heard. As far as I know, there was no last minute attempt at any intervention from the British Government. It appears that Scripps was resigned to his fate and had not sought Consular assistance in this regard.

He was hanged in Singapore in 1996 and after receiving the official result from Interpol Singapore I submitted a file to the Records Section at New Scotland Yard for "dead" action and his records on the Police National Computer (PNC) were amended to indicate his final fate. A sad case.

The head of Interpol London at that time was a Metropolitan Police Superintendent called Barry Webb who was a very efficient Officer and who was well liked by most of his subordinates. I always got on very well with him and he fully supported me in my endeavours with Child Abduction and Offences against Minors.

John LLOYD

Barry had also invited the entire office staff and their wives/girlfriends/ partners to his large house on the edge of Epsom Downs on Derby Day. We all had a thoroughly wonderful day enjoying the racing interspersed with drinks and eats at Barry's house. Jackie teamed up with Terry Baker, one of my colleagues, and together they managed to place some decent bets with the Bookies and won a few bob.

Barry had a reputation for conducting a good degree of international travel as a result of which he was known as "the world wide webb".

Some years later, Barry Webb retired from the UK police and became the Chief of Police in the British Virgin Islands which sounds idyllic and I am sure that it was until the day when one of his Sergeants who was causing some disciplinary problems stormed into Barry's office and shot him several times with his service pistol. Very fortunately Barry survived this ordeal but his working life as a Police Officer had come to an end.

In 1995 I was nominated to attend an International Missing Persons Conference in Melbourne, Australia. I flew out from Heathrow with a Metropolitan Police Superintendent who had also been nominated to attend the conference. His first action after meeting him at the airport was to try and get us both up-graded into Business class but I could see that his rather blunt and unsophisticated efforts were being blanked by the female Check-in Agent.

We flew firstly to Singapore where we had a stop-over of a couple of hours or so before continuing this marathon towards Australia. I had always known that Australia was a big country but I did not quite appreciate just how large it was until we started flying over mainland Australia. There was hour after hour of flying across what looked to be featureless desert before finally arriving in Melbourne after 24 hours or so. We were both very tired but fortunately the Victoria State Police who were organising the Conference had tipped off the Australian Customs Service who removed us from the very long queue (other passengers in the immediate area thought that we were being arrested) and we were taken to the head of the queue and after a perfunctory, "Do you have anything to declare" conversation we were permitted to proceed to collect our luggage and head towards our hotel.

Bundu, the Beat & Beyond

Our hotel was located in an area of Melbourne called St Kilda and was very pleasant. It was at the time that the Formula One Grand Prix Circuit was being developed there so there was plenty of activity. We had a day spare before the conference and we took a coach tour out to an old gold mining town called Ballarat which had been preserved from its heyday in the late 19th century.

It was really well produced and all the staff were dressed in period costume and spoke in the manner in which their ancestors did in the 1890's. I went into one preserved store in the town and had a good look around at all the items for sale from that era. There was one lady shop assistant dressed in her 1890's finery and I asked her if she would mind if I took her photograph. She looked at me very quizzically for a few seconds before replying, "You mean you want to take my likeness?"

We panned for gold in the ore bearing stream running through the town but I do not remember collecting enough to purchase a soft drink let alone anything else. It was a good day however.

The conference itself was hosted by the Victoria State Police and had about 150 delegates attending including Police from all the Australian States as well as New Zealand.

I presented the international aspects of Police investigations in Missing Persons cases and other speakers gave their presentations with Missing Persons being the central theme. At the conclusion of the conference the delegates voted on a number of motions one of which was that the general public should have direct access to the Interpol files on missing persons. This had not been debated before and had come straight out of left field. I knew quite well that the public would never gain direct access to Interpol files as they contained confidential Police information etc. I informed the conference of this fact but ended by saying that they could access limited information from Interpol Police files via their local Police. This did not go down too well but in the end they had to accept this.

We departed Melbourne the following day en route to London via Perth and Singapore, another 24 hours of tedium but we survived.

John LLOYD

I was nominated for, and became a member of, the Interpol Standing Working Party on Offences against Minors. This working party was organised from Interpol HQ in Lyon and met two or three times a year in various locations. I was lucky enough to be able to attend these working party meetings in various European cities and others such as Ottawa in Canada.

These were really useful in developing a common strategy to tackle the global problems of paedophilia as well as keeping abreast of current trends. As is usual in such matters, the levels of co-operation did vary somewhat depending upon the country involved. I recall attending a working party meeting in Thessaloniki in Greece when the meeting was opened by the Greek Minister responsible for Police and Home Affairs. His welcoming speech was quite an eye opener for, after giving us a really warm welcome and wishing us well in our deliberations he said, "Of course, we do not have this problem in Greece as it is not part of our culture."

This was not well received by most of the delegates including me. We came to the conclusion that either the Minister did not know his subject at all or that he was from another planet.

Through this working party I established a very good chain of contacts in varying countries with whom I could make contact at any time to discuss matters of mutual interest and decide upon how best to proceed in any one case. Whilst I always used the Interpol network to communicate official requests etc I invariably used my unofficial contact lists to smooth the way which helped enormously.

At the conclusion of each of these working party meetings I completed a written report for the benefit of the Head of Interpol London as well as for the information of other interested units.

Later these working party meetings were attended by Brian Drew, head of the NCIS SSOU and Bob Mclaughlin, the head of the Metropolitan Police Paedophile unit. This was extremely useful as they brought their vast experience and expertise to bear. They were more strategic in their thinking whereas I was more tactical and they were also able to steer the working party in certain directions at times when it became apparent that it may be straying off course.

The main thrust of all our deliberations, policy formulation and tactical operations, was the tracking of known paedophiles operating on an international basis and had but one goal in mind and that was the safety of children wherever they might be. Did we succeed? In some ways we did as we raised the bar in so many ways with law enforcement agencies worldwide and we raised the international profile of these awful crimes at the same time. This must always be looked as "work in progress" and I do not think that we will ever win the continuing war but we do win some major battles on the way.

The other area I began to specialise in was in the arena of Child Abduction. This should be viewed as totally separate from the criminal offence of kidnap. Child abduction could be better known as parental child abduction and the offences are laid down in statute in the Child Abduction Act 1984.

In essence the international aspects of child abduction comes about when a person removes a child (under 16) from the UK without the consent of the other parent or guardian.

These situations generally arise with a marriage or partnership between two people (usually a man and a woman) who originate from different countries and/or cultures. It is when these relationships break down that the problems involving child abduction come to the fore.

Before 1984 there was no criminal offence to prevent a parent from removing their child from the UK. There was civil law applicable but unless a court order was already in force there was little that could be done to prevent any child being taken abroad by one of his parents.

The criminal legislation was brought in to fill this gap and it criminalised parents who fell into this category. This also meant that the criminal legislation ran in parallel with the civil law.

John LLOYD

There is an international Treaty called The Hague Convention on Child Abduction in which all signatory countries agree to repatriate abducted children to their country of habitual residence. The only problem with that treaty is that not all countries are signatories to it.

I began dealing with the international enquiries in relation to abducted children with a view to locating their whereabouts so that measures could be taken to return the child to the UK. At the same time enquiries were also made to locate the offending parent so that the CPS could consider applying for their extradition back to the UK to face criminal charges.

These international enquiries were seldom straight forward and were compounded by the fact that some countries do not have any criminal offence involving parental child abduction. This meant that the Police in those countries were less than interested in trying to find a child who was with one of their natural parents.

An addition to that problem was that in many of the Moslem countries the man was considered to be the head of the family who had the right to take his child wherever he wanted. The Moslem wife was often treated as a second class citizen with little or no rights in this context.

I had frequent contact with a charitable organisation called REUNITE which was formed by a lady named Denise Carter whose child had been abducted some years before. (see www.reunite.org)

Reunite was in the business of giving relevant advice to the victim parents in such cases and offering lists of suitably qualified lawyers who could assist in these matters.

I was always very impressed with the manner in which they went about their business. Denise was ably assisted by a solicitor called Ann-Marie Hutchinson who had a great degree of expertise in child abduction matters plus valuable contacts in the legal world.

I recall that on one occasion I had arrived for duty in the Interpol Office at 0630 hrs one morning and was immediately handed a very urgent message received overnight from Interpol Washington which advised that

Bundu, the Beat & Beyond

a 9 year old boy of Indian descent had been unlawfully abducted by his Indian father from his habitual place of residence in the USA and they were currently en route by air to the UK. The boy and his father were due to arrive at Heathrow Airport at 1000hrs that morning so I did not have a great deal of time in which to deal with this matter. They were both booked on an onward flight for Bangalore departing at 1230 hrs the same day.

Unfortunately the US Authorities were not yet in a position to apply for the father's arrest and extradition and an application under The Hague convention procedures had not yet been commenced in the USA. The US Authorities asked for whatever assistance we could provide.

In criminal terms our hands were tied in that we had not received any formal application for the father's arrest and extradition. He had not committed any criminal offence in the UK which meant that the UK police had no power to detain him. Additionally the US Central Authority had not had time to submit any request to the UK for the repatriation of the child to the USA under The Hague Convention.

Initially I did two things: first I contacted a sleepy Ann-Marie Hutchinson on her home telephone number and gave her a verbal summary of the known facts after which I faxed her copies of the relevant correspondence we had received from Interpol Washington. Second, I copied the request from Interpol Washington to the Controller of the Police Ports Office at Heathrow Airport for their information with the request that they confirm with the airline that the father and son were on board the inbound aircraft.

Within 90 minutes of taking that action I had received a copy of a Court Order signed by the Duty Judge in the Children's Division of the High Court ordering that the father be detained and brought to the High Court in The Strand by 1400hrs that very day. Ann-Marie had worked a minor miracle by contacting the Duty Judge and sending him copies of the correspondence with which I had supplied her.

This totally transformed the situation and armed with a copy of the Court Order, signed by a High Court Judge, the London Metropolitan

John LLOYD

Police at Heathrow were now in possession of a legal document empowering them to detain the suspect father and take him to The High Court in London where a hearing was scheduled to take place at 1400hrs that afternoon.

The father and son duly arrived. The father was detained whilst the boy was taken into temporary care of the social services pending the outcome of the hearing at the High Court.

I informed Interpol Washington of the developments and they were suitably grateful

The result of the court hearing was that the father agreed to take the boy back to the USA on the next available flight pending court proceedings there.

This is exactly what happened. The boy remained in local care of social services until the following morning when he was taken to Heathrow where he was re-united with his father after which they were escorted to the waiting aircraft which flew them back to the USA.

In the meantime I had informed Interpol Washington of their impending arrival in the USA and a suitable reception committee was waiting for them when they did arrive. The father was taken into custody pending his criminal trial for child abduction whilst his son was returned to the custody of his mother pending a civil court hearing into custody rights etc.

This was a good all round result for everyone involved, except perhaps for the father. The US Authorities were quite lavish in their praise and suitably grateful because we all knew that if the boy had flown on to India there was little or no chance of him ever being seen by his mother in the US again. It was, in my opinion, a very good example of where the criminal and civil processes combined to produce a very satisfactory result.

Other cases were not so straightforward and tended to rumble on for many months and sometimes years. The initial role we had at Interpol in such cases was confirming the exact location of the abducted child and suspect parent. This was not always easy and was sometimes very

Bundu, the Beat & Beyond

problematic especially in some cases in which the suspect parent moved the child on to yet another location or country in an attempt to evade Police or Authority attention.

I concluded fairly early on that in such cases there were no winners and most of the people involved had their lives altered forever.

Once we had successfully located the abducted child and suspect parent we were in a position to inform the CPS via the Investigating Police Officer. The CPS would then decide whether to seek the extradition of the suspect parent which was fine if the UK had an extradition treaty with that country.

If the abducted child was located in a Hague Convention country the UK Authorities would normally institute civil proceedings in that country for the repatriation of the child which was a relatively straightforward procedure. However if the child was located in a Non Hague Convention country there were little or no other options but for the aggrieved parent to institute civil proceedings in that country. These were normally protracted processes with little prospect of a speedy resolution.

Due to my interest in child abduction matters I was invited to represent Interpol on a Home Office working party specifically tasked with drafting and implementing UK national policy in matters of international child abduction.

This group met about four times a year at the Home Office in London and consisted of representatives from CPS International, the UK Passport Agency, Reunite (Denise Carter), Lawyers specialising in child abduction (Ann-Marie Hutchinson), The child abduction Unit of the Foreign & Commonwealth Office, The Child Abduction Unit of the Lord Chancellors Office (The UK Central Authority for Child Abduction), a Detective Inspector from Greater Manchester Police, the Metropolitan Police Ports Office at Heathrow and myself from Interpol.

199

John LLOYD

The group was chaired by a highly placed Home Office Civil Servant who seemed to have a good grasp of the sometimes complex issues involved and was able to steer the group in a successful manner.

My view is, and has always been, that prevention is better than cure. It is always preferable to prevent an international abduction before it takes place rather than attempt to pick up the pieces after the event. As always the main concern was for the abducted child and our strategy had this in mind in order to minimise the stress and trauma potentially suffered by a child in these circumstances.

We tried taking a holistic approach and developed a strategy which included the creation of a child abduction prevention pack which could be used by any parent concerned that their child might become the victim of abduction. This pack included the facility to produce a full physical description of the child, photographs, a photocopy of the birth certificate, copies of any relevant Court Orders and fingerprints of the child, if necessary, to assist with later identification. The pack also included details of the potential abductor including a descriptive form and photograph and lastly details of the complainant including a copy of any marriage certificate. Once completed these packs could be handed to the investigating Police Officer once an abduction had taken place, thereby saving a great deal of time and anguish. From a Police perspective the information contained in these packs gave the investigating Officer a head start without having to expend a long time eliciting the information from a distraught parent.

Our strategy also involved the UK Passport Agency devising a plan to flag up the child's records with a view to preventing the abducting parent from having a secondary passport issued without the knowledge of the other parent.

Upon receipt of such a report the investigating Police Officer would consider applying for the issue of an "All Ports Warning" to prevent the child being taken out of UK jurisdiction.

At that time parental child abduction was a relatively rare offence, (just a few hundred per year from UK) so much so that most Police Officers

Bundu, the Beat & Beyond

would be unlikely to become involved in investigating such a case. Accordingly we produced a practical guide for Police Officers which listed all the relevant points they needed to consider and action to take.

Whilst this was not perfect it was a great deal better than that which had existed before. This group still exists today perfecting and refining the UK strategy for these offences which continue to rise in number year by year.

Today all Police Forces have their own internal "intranet" in which can be found, amongst other matters, policy and procedures to be adopted in all major criminal matters including child abduction. This is a great step forward from that which existed in the mid 1990's.

Before that many Police Forces failed to recognise child abduction as a crime and would treat such reports as a missing persons case and I spent much time over the years trying to persuade varying Police Forces to treat child abduction as a major crime. This was a battle I did not always win but I am pleased to say that I did get my points of view across most of the time which was quite gratifying.

I was invited to submit a full chapter on the role of Interpol in Child Abduction matters for a forthcoming legal reference book on the subject. I completed this and submitted it to Ken Pandolfi for his approval and I was gratified when he did approve my effort, albeit with one small amendment. (International Parental Child Abduction published 1998 by Jordan Publishing Ltd—ISBN 0 85308 466 1.)

On a very personal note, In late 1997 my eldest son, Gareth, was going out with a young lady called Natasha and around this time they both came to see Jackie and I and announced that Natasha was pregnant. I was delighted for them even though my initial reaction was that I was far too young to become a Grandfather. (I wasn't but it just felt like that I was)

Baby Danielle was born in May 1998 and she was a really lovely baby (I know, I am biased). She has grown up into an even lovelier young teenager (15 going on 25) but she is very sweet and has a most agreeable personality. Sadly the relationship between Gareth and Natasha did not

John LLOYD

survive but Danielle stays with Gareth on a regular basis and matters are as good as they can be in what is always a potentially fraught period.

In August 1998 Jackie, Simon and I took a holiday in Fort Lauderdale in the USA. We had a really enjoyable time and Simon was honing his skills at golf and I had a couple of rounds with him, one of which was at the Sawgrass course. We got back to our hotel quite late one evening and saw on the television news that Princess Diana had been involved in a vehicle accident in Paris and had sustained a broken arm. We were concerned for her but as her injuries did not seem too serious we all went to bed. The following morning we were all very shocked to see on the US Television news that Diana had died of her injuries sustained in the crash. This put quite a dampener on the remainder of our holiday and we returned to the UK some days later in time to witness her funeral on TV. A very sombre occasion and we, in common with most other people, felt sincere sympathy for her two young sons, William and Harry. Another tragic waste of life and at such a young age.

In late 1997 South Africa became the latest country to become a signatory to the Hague Convention on Child Abduction. The South African Authorities, legal profession and Law Enforcement agencies were, however, not well versed in the technical aspects and practicalities of the Convention and they requested some assistance in filling that gap of knowledge.

The UK Authorities agreed to assist and decided to send a delegation to South Africa to deliver a variety of presentations at a two day seminar in Cape Town in January 1998.

I was asked if I would be willing to attend and give a presentation on the national and international Police perspective on matters relating to Child Abduction. My attendance would, however, be at the expense of NCIS because there were no central UK funds or budget from which my attendance at this seminar could be funded.

I agreed in principle and requested that the principal UK delegate, Mr Justice Ward, write a formal letter to NCIS requesting my attendance at this prestigious event.

Bundu, the Beat & Beyond

Upon receipt of this request, the NCIS hierarchy agreed to my attendance with the proviso that I was to be placed on the cheapest flight available.

The cheapest flight that was found for me was with an airline called Caledonian Airways which was the sole surviving offshoot of the now defunct British Caledonian Airways which had been swallowed up by British Airways some years before.

In accordance with NCIS instruction I was reserved a return seat on the Caledonian Airways flight departing London Gatwick on 24th January 1998.

What NCIS had not realised when they booked this flight for me was that Caledonian Airways was now a Charter Airline and only operated the flight to Cape Town once a week. This meant that the NCIS had to fund my accommodation and living expenses in Cape Town for seven days rather than two or three days had I been booked on a scheduled airline such as British Airways. False economy or what?

I did not complain at all, not least of which because Gatwick was right on the door step to my home in Crawley and was therefore far more convenient than trekking up to Heathrow. The small matter that the NCIS was virtually giving me a week's holiday in Cape Town was an added bonus.

On 24th January 1998 I flew from Gatwick to Cape Town via Mombasa in Kenya. Upon arrival in Cape Town I was driven to the Breakwater Hotel on the waterfront in Cape Town within a five minute walk of the Victoria and Alfred Waterfront.

The hotel was a converted prison which may sound pretty grim but it was actually quite comfortable and had all the amenities you would expect in a three star hotel. It was also very well located for all the attractions of central Cape Town. The seminar was to be held at this hotel which was doubly convenient for me.

203

John LLOYD

The remaining UK delegates of High Court Judges, Barristers and family lawyers arrived on scheduled airlines during the next couple of days and we all met up for an evening's social drink and meal at which we all got to know each other a little better.

The delegates included the child abduction specialist lawyer Ann-Marie Hutchinson who I knew very well from my previous involvement in child abduction matters and from the Home Office committee on which we sat.

The seminar was well attended by members of the South African legal profession, judiciary and South African Police Service. Another delegate was David Bruce, the head of Interpol Pretoria, with whom I had some lengthy discussions concerning matters of a mutual interest. He was especially interested to learn of the high caseloads carried by Officers from Interpol London as well as learning of the manner in which we were organised into varying categories of criminality which resulted in developing specialist Officers in those fields which in turn led to a greater efficiency in how these matters were dealt with.

At the conclusion of the two day Seminar I was gratified to learn that the content of the seminar had been well received by all those who had attended and that the South African Authorities were suitably impressed with the level of professionalism displayed by all those giving presentations at the seminar.

The day following the seminar we had organised a trip to a wine estate called Spiers. The journey there was taken by train from Cape Town Railway Station. The train comprised of former Rhodesian Railway carriages from the 1950's/60's era. These carriages had been converted so that the interiors were essentially lounges with comfortable armchairs and table etc. I had previously regaled my companions with stories of travelling by train from Kitwe to Johannesburg during the early 1960's and had told them of our enforced stops at Bulawayo where my brother and I had a bath etc etc.

Bundu, the Beat & Beyond

They were suitably impressed therefore when they saw a sign in one of the carriages advertising baths at Bulawayo Station for the sum of two shillings and sixpence.

We arrived at Spiers Station and were ushered off the train and were seen across the main road by a Traffic Policeman who had been delegated to stop the traffic for us to permit us access to the Spier Estate located on the other side of the road.

At that time the Spier estate was very impressive and catered for its visitors on an almost grand scale. We were given a tour of the winery as well as a presentation on the differing types of wine produced on the estate after which we were at leisure to involve ourselves in various activities. Some took advantage of the horse-riding facilities which were available whilst others, myself included, walked around the Cheetah enclosure viewing these beautiful creatures from close quarters.

We were then summoned to the lunch table located on the main veranda outside the Cape style cottage where the truly impressive Cape Buffet had been put on display. I just love Cape Malay food and there was plenty of that on offer as well as a great variety of other South African delicacies and treats available. We enjoyed a rather lengthy lunch taken at a leisurely pace suitably fortified by ample quantities of great South African wines.

At some time in the mid to late afternoon we were summoned back to the train which was now waiting for us at Spier Station. We reluctantly retraced our steps back to the train where we enjoyed the return journey into Cape Town. A lovely social day enjoyed by all.

That evening we attended a farewell dinner at a Cape Town Restaurant which was splendid and we were suitably entertained by Mr Justice Peter Ward who seemed to be something of a raconteur and wit who gave a very humorous speech of thanks and farewell.

The following day I was left in Cape Town by myself as all the others departed on their scheduled return flights to Heathrow. I was not

John LLOYD

downhearted because this was Cape Town in the height of the summer and I still had two days left in which to enjoy myself and I did.

I did, however, get into a little hot water with my friend Fran because I completely forgot to telephone her at her home near Johannesburg and she, quite fairly, took umbrage at this omission.

On one of those days I took the catamaran trip from Cape Town harbour out to Robben Island where Nelson Mandela and thousands of other political prisoners had been detained over many years. It was quite a grim place although strangely exciting and motivating at the same time.

I stood in the doorway of Nelson Mandela's prison cell and noted just how small it was. This was highlighted by the fact that Nelson Mandela is quite a tall man at around 6 feet two inches, I believe, and so he would have had very little space in which to move in that cell. His cell overlooked the central courtyard of the prison where inmates were put to work breaking rocks.

The guides were all former inmates and they were able to regale us with tales of their incarceration. At the end of one story I said to my guide, "I suppose that it must have helped to have a sense of humour being kept in a place like this"? I thought that I may have said the wrong thing because he looked at me with a very serious expression for a few moments before bursting into laughter. Thank goodness he saw the funny side of that one.

I am very glad that I made the effort to travel to Robben Island even though I found it to be a very sobering experience.

I arrived back to a cold and gloomy Gatwick on the 2nd February 1998 with some great memories of some good people and a splendid city.

During the mid 1990's I met two Police Officers, on separate occasions, who later were to come to national prominence in the UK but for very different reasons.

Amongst a very large number of cases on the Persons Desk I was also dealing with a high risk Missing Persons case involving a young woman

Bundu, the Beat & Beyond

originating from the Thames Valley Police area who had been reported missing and was believed to be in Spain. On behalf of Thames Valley Police I had conducted protracted enquiries via the Guardia Civil in Spain all with a view to tracing the young woman. As I recall we did not have a great deal of information with which to work and the Spanish Police were having difficulties in tracing her whereabouts.

We had issued an Interpol Yellow notice which is a formal international circulation of a missing person but after some months all our leads began to dry up. As far as I was concerned we had done all we could from the UK and to a large extent we were in the hands of the Spanish Authorities.

This situation did not appear to be acceptable to the Officer in charge of the investigation in Thames Valley as a result of which my Superintendent and I received a visit from a uniformed Thames Valley Police Inspector. He was shown my file which he read through but he was obviously dis-satisfied. It was explained to him that we really had done everything possible but that, unless further information was forthcoming from any UK source, we were somewhat in the hands of the Spanish Authorities.

This Officer was still unhappy and disgruntled but eventually he left our Office. His name was Ali Dizae who later achieved a degree of notoriety when, as a Commander in the Metropolitan Police in London, he was convicted of criminal offences of Perverting the Course of Justice and misconduct in a public office. He was sentenced to three years imprisonment.

During my Police career I met with many hundreds of Police Officers and got on well with most of them. I did not take to Mr Dizae and was somewhat relieved that I had little further contact with him.

The other Officer who rose to national prominence was a Detective Inspector in the Metropolitan Police in London who took me out to lunch one day as a small thank you for my assisting him and his team with some difficult and protracted murder enquiries abroad. He was a most affable man and in the short time that I met him he gave me the

John LLOYD

impression that he was a straight forward hard working Detective with a high level of competency.

His name was John Yates and he later rose to become Assistant Commissioner of the Metropolitan Police where he was tasked with investigating some very high profile criminal matters. He was later forced to retire early due to criticism of his role in the phone hacking enquiry. I felt that this was premature and that his departure was a sad loss for the Police service.

During recent years cases of Police corruption have, quite rightly, been featured in the national UK press and media. A number of these cases seem to feature Officers from London's Metropolitan Police. During the course of my work in London I did meet, or come into contact with, many hundreds of their Officers and I can honestly say that not once did I feel that any one of them were potentially corrupt. My feeling was that, in the main, they were hard working honest Cops who were doing their level best to achieve the required result without breaking the rules.

There were one or two occasions in which I felt that an Officer appeared to have too close a relationship with the national press and media but that was purely my feeling.

The London Metropolitan Police has around 32,000 Police Officers and I suppose that from time to time it is inevitable that a few of them will be tempted by the short terms financial rewards offered by the large and active criminal fraternity in London. This does not make that action right and I make no excuses for the dishonest few who fall foul of this temptation.

During the 1990's and into the new Millennium, Jackie and I enjoyed several holidays on the fantastic Kenya coast, initially at the Mnarani Club in Kilifi and later at several boutique hotels on Diani Beach just south of Mombasa. We also managed to include several visits to the Wild Life Game park at Tsavo East where we were able to witness many different species of wildlife in their natural habitat.

Bundu, the Beat & Beyond

It was when we were enjoying a relaxing stay on Diani Beach that we encountered a bit of a problem. After a very enjoyable dinner in the hotel restaurant Jackie and I were strolling back to our accommodation near the beach. We were walking along a dimly lit pathway but looking upwards to the heavens admiring the wonderful light display from the stars which were highlighted against the cloudless night sky.

This was a mistake because as we continued our slow walk we failed to keep an eye out on the path ahead. Without warning Jackie gave a single scream and I looked down at the path just in time to see a smallish dark coloured snake slithering away from our feet towards the bushes and undergrowth at the side of the path.

I realised what had happened and I walked Jackie back to the main hotel reception area and told the management what had happened. They immediately organised a hotel transport to take us to the Diani Beach medical centre and hospital located a few miles from the hotel.

When we reached the hospital Jackie had calmed down and was able to climb out of the hotel transport unaided and get into a hospital wheelchair which was awaiting our arrival together with hospital staff.

We were ushered into an examination area where the Sikh Doctor examined Jackie's foot. We noted that there was one puncture wound on her big toe and that her foot was slightly swollen.

I described to the Doctor what had happened and initially he appeared somewhat sceptical that Jackie had received a snakebite especially as there was only one puncture wound. The snake had been about 18 inches in length and the Doctor concluded that it was probably a very young snake. He said it was a great shame that we had not brought the snake in for identification but I told him in no uncertain terms that there was no way that I would have delved into the dark undergrowth searching for a venomous snake at that time of night. The Doctor concluded that the snake may have been a young black mamba which is one of Africa's most venomous.

John LLOYD

In the meantime Jackie's foot had begun to swell quite alarmingly and the Doctor finally agreed that she had probably been bitten by the snake but due to the sandals she was wearing only one of the snake's fangs had penetrated her skin.

Jackie was then given a general anti snake venom and was kept in overnight for observation. She was later told that she had been lucky because the snake appeared to be an immature juvenile and only one fang had penetrated her skin which had reduced the potential deadly effect. The Ward Sister cheered her up no end by remarking that if her leg became any worse they would probably have to amputate it!

I returned to the hospital the following morning and was gratified to see that Jackie was in good spirits and that her swollen foot and ankle area had subsided.

She was released from hospital the following day and we were able to resume our holiday but it had been quite a scare for both of us.

I was due to retire from the Police in March 1999 at which time I would have completed 30 years Police service which is the normal time for Police to retire. I was not particularly looking forward to this because I thoroughly enjoyed my job with Interpol and felt that I was making a positive contribution to international policing as well as obtaining desired results on specific requests from my UK colleagues.

The following twelve months seemed to fly by and before I knew it my colleagues in Interpol had organised a special farewell dinner for me. My very good friend, Alan Shiers from Merseyside was the driving force behind this and we all enjoyed a hearty (and liquid) dinner. I had also organised the standard Retirement "do" which was held at the Metropolitan Police Staff Restaurant at Cobalt Square opposite Vauxhall Train Station. This was well attended and a lot of people said a lot of nice things about me after which they all tucked into the buffet and drinks I had provided. Jackie was with me and was able to meet some of the people I had talked about so often,

Bundu, the Beat & Beyond

After saying some very fond farewells to my colleagues of long standing we left Vauxhall seemingly for the last time.

1999 also saw the very sad death of my cousin Peter who was just four days younger than me. It appears that Peter had an undiagnosed heart problem which caused his untimely and very sudden demise. He and I had shared many adventures as children and although he could be something of a dare-devil at times we always got along very well together.

I was now a retired Police Officer aged just 52. I had not made any serious plans for my retirement from the Police which, in hindsight, was a mistake. Here I was, a man of relatively young middle age who had just completed a term of thirty years in a job which I had (mainly) enjoyed and I was now looking forward with no strategy in place to fill the void left by my newly status of being unemployed.

I decided that I should apply for a job locally in Crawley but I soon found out that prospective employers were not that interested in employing a person of my age and would rather employ a relative youngster in the 18-25 age bracket for varying reasons. The fact that I had maturity, common sense and experience to offer was not really a consideration. I underwent a number of very unsatisfying application processes and interviews in a variety of fields but without success.

In the end, I decided to revert to type and applied for a job with Sussex Police in a non Police role within the Criminal Justice Unit at the newly built Crawley Police Station. I had an interview with Audrey Dungay who headed this unit together with a uniformed Police Inspector Gary Medland. I had known Audrey for many years on a professional basis and we had always got on very well.

The interview must have gone well because I was offered a position very shortly after the interview which I accepted.

One very positive aspect of my accepting this job was that my old friend and former CID colleague, Keith Menzies, was also working in the CJU at Crawley. It was therefore very pleasing to be able to renew our professional relationship albeit on a different level. Keith worked

John LLOYD

alongside another Police Officer, Bob Binning. Although I had never worked with Bob I did know him on a social level and had always found him to be a very engaging personality. Keith and Bob were primarily responsible for reviewing case files bound for court to ensure that there was sufficient evidence to offer a realistic chance of a conviction. In some cases they would issue directions for the obtaining of additional evidence if the case should warrant that course of action. Keith was responsible for all the criminal files whilst Bob tackled all the Traffic related matters.

My new colleagues at the CJU were quite a mixed bag of non police staff and were quite different in outlook in many ways to that I had been used to within the Police culture. They were all friendly enough and we rubbed along quite well but I never really felt that I fitted in with this new working environment.

To me the work was fairly mundane and routine and partly involved maintaining contact with witnesses in a variety of different crime and motoring offences and ensuring that their contact details were up to date and that they would be available to attend court to give their evidence once a trial date had been fixed.

Just before Christmas 1999 Jackie and I attended a NARPO Christmas Dinner at the South of England Show Grounds at Ardingly organised by my old friend and Best Man, Keith King. Keith was on very good form that night and gave a most amusing speech. Everyone had a most enjoyable evening.

Jackie and I had planned a themed New Year's Eve Dinner to be held at our house for a number of guests including Keith and Wendy King. After Christmas was over we received the dreadful news that Keith had suddenly and unexpectedly died as a result of unforeseen complications arising from a heart by-pass operation he had undergone some years earlier. We were totally distraught at this news especially as he was still a relatively young man. We attended his funeral early in the New Year of 2000 which was held at the Woodvale Crematorium in Brighton. It was necessary to have loudspeakers placed outside the chapel so that the large number of people who were unable to find a seat inside could hear the proceedings. It was a suitable testament to Keith and the life he had

Bundu, the Beat & Beyond

led. He had been an inspiration to many Police Officers and ordinary members of the public who had come into contact with him. He was, and is, sorely missed by all those who knew him.

As part of my retirement celebrations Jackie and I took a holiday at Lily Beach in the Maldives in early 2000. This was a really relaxing holiday. We had a well-appointed Beach Hut with all mod cons overlooking the blue warm waters of the Indian Ocean where we swam daily. We also did some snorkel swimming and marvelled at the large range of different marine life on view. Some of the fish were of absolute stunningly vibrant colours. The resort's restaurant had a sand floor which encouraged guests not to wear shoes which I thought was a really nice touch. Our two week sojourn there disappeared very quickly as time seemed to accelerate even though we were not doing a great deal apart from reading, swimming, sunning ourselves and eating. All too soon we were back in the Crawley winter albeit with some wonderful memories of the holiday and some excellent people we had met.

I do not have too many clear memories of my stay at Crawley CJU apart from one during the summer of 2000 when there was a solar eclipse and most of the staff gathered in the rear yard of the Police Station to witness this event. We used the usual film negatives to view this phenomenon but I must have overdone my viewing efforts although I did not realise this at the time. It was not until ten years later that an eye test revealed that I had a small stigma in one eye which did affect my eyesight quality.

After nearly a year at the CJU I received a call from my old friend and work colleague at NCIS, Steve Glynn, who was a Nottinghamshire Police Officer. He informed me of a vacancy which had arisen for a Case Officer within Interpol London which, due to financial constraints, was being offered to non Police staff. Would I be interested asked Steve? I definitely would.

I applied for the job and was invited for interview at the Vauxhall HQ of NCIS. I was interviewed by Jamie Williamson, Fred Hellon and Hilary Lawrence, from NCIS HR. Jamie Williamson was a Thames Valley Police Officer and Fred Hellon was a former Custom's Officer. I had worked with both of them previously within Interpol London and had got along

John LLOYD

with both of them. I had also known Hilary from the time when she worked in the Administrative section of Interpol London. I was able to answer all their questions in an informed and positive manner which was not really surprising as they were asking me about things in which I was already well versed.

Happily I was offered the position at an attractive salary which I accepted straight away.

I returned to Crawley CJU and tendered my resignation to Audrey telling her that I had been made an offer which I could not refuse. I could see that she was disappointed with my decision but she could also understand the reasons behind it.

It had been the practice of my mother to spend the South African summers in that country and the English summers (such as they are) with us in Crawley. This was so that she did not have to endure any of the winter weather in either country. You may not associate Southern Africa with cold weather but as Johannesburg is at an altitude of nearly 6,000 feet above sea level on the high veld it can get very cold in the winter time and I even recall experiencing some snow showers whilst at school at Broadlands.

Just after Christmas in 2000 we received an airmail letter from my mother in Johannesburg informing us that she was not feeling too well and that she would be returning to the UK early within a week or so.

I collected her from the airport and it appears that she had been feeling poorly for some time and had been diagnosed with cancer.

After reaching home we made an appointment for her with her Doctor in Crawley who arranged for specialist nursing care to visit her daily at home.

Unfortunately we could see that she was not improving and once or twice I became a little frustrated with her because she was not eating very much at all.

Bundu, the Beat & Beyond

We did enjoy frequent chats after I had returned from work each day which I did enjoy immensely. It was during one of these chats that my Mum told me that she had a cousin with the surname of Hugg who ran a jewellers shop in Hampshire. She had visited her cousin on several occasions. Apparently her cousin had a son called Michael who was none other than Mike Hugg, one of the founder members of the Manfred Mann pop group who found fame in the 1960's and are still going strong today as the Manfreds. There is a further family connection here in that my sister-in-law, Denise, is an avid fan of Blues music and frequently attends concerts at which the Manfreds are playing. She is on first name terms with the lead singer, Paul Jones, and is also well known to other members of the band, including Mike Hugg. Mike and I have never met but what a small world we now live in!

There came a time in late February 2001 when Mum weakened so much that her Doctor arranged for her to be transferred to St Catherine's Hospice in Crawley where she remained for the next ten days. I managed to visit her every day after work and I know that she was very happy and content with the superb palliative care she received from the nursing staff at the Hospice.

During the morning of Sunday 4th March I visited her at the Hospice by which time she had been moved to a single bed side ward. We had a really good chat about many things which ended by me telling her that I loved her. She told me that she loved me. I think that this was the first and only time we had said this to each other.

I could tell that she was very weak and I feared that the end was fairly close. I left my Mum promising to return after lunch. When I reached home I contacted my brother at his home in Cosham and told him of the situation. He indicated that he would come up to Crawley that afternoon.

I returned to the Hospice with Jackie in the early afternoon and we went to her side ward and sat beside her bed. She was in a deep sleep and I suspected that it was likely that she would not re-awaken.

John LLOYD

And so it proved because she breathed her last around 2.30pm. I summoned a nurse who, in turn, summoned a Doctor who certified her death.

Sadly Chris did not arrive for another 20 minutes or so but I met him outside the Hospice front door and told him the bad news. Jackie and I then left him to say his farewells to our mother whilst we waited in the main reception area.

She was later cremated and her remains were interred next to my fathers at St John's Churchyard in Hove. Together again after nearly 30 years.

She died just a few weeks short of her 80th birthday.

Upon hearing the news of her Grandmother's death, my seven year old niece, Robyn, said to my brother Chris," Daddy, does this mean that you are an orphan?"

Chris also told me that Robyn wrote on their calendar on the day that Mum died. Her entry was "Nana did" Her spelling has improved since then.

CHAPTER 10

NCIS Re-Visited

On a Monday morning in May 2001 I presented myself to the main security gate at NCIS HQ in Vauxhall and after identifying myself I was escorted to the main Security Office where I was photographed and had my new NCIS Identification Card issued. I then made my way to the International Division of NCIS where I was to resume my career in international policing within the UK National Central Bureau of Interpol.

In the year or so since I had left it was obvious that some of the old faces were no longer there but I was pleased to see that a significant number of people I had known previously were still around. This made my re-assimilation a great deal easier.

I was initially assigned to work on the Fraud Desk with Mike Dixon from Cambridgeshire Police. Mike was fairly new in post but he was an experienced Detective well versed in matters of Fraud as well as all matters relating to computers.

The Interpol Bureau was still as busy as it ever had been, in fact it seemed to be receiving more and more requests for assistance in criminal matters both from UK and foreign Law Enforcement Agencies.

Each Case Officer was, at that time, responsible for dealing with about 500 individual cases at any one time. We were never short of work and sometimes struggled to keep our heads above water.

John LLOYD

Matters improved a little when we were given a bespoke computerised Case Management system from which time all our new cases became electronic whilst the old blue paper files were gradually phased out. However bearing in mind that a significant proportion of Interpol Case Files could still be active many years after being instigated this would mean that some of the Blue paper files were still in use some ten years later.

I renewed some old friendships with colleagues such as Patricia Thompson from the RUC in Belfast. Pat was a hardworking Officer with many years' experience and was one of those people who outwardly portrayed a somewhat hard exterior but was really quite a softie at heart. She and I always got a long together really well and we often bounced ideas off each other as to the best way to progress any one case.

A curious incident took place shortly after my return to NCIS when I was inspecting a notice board within the International Division and I was reading a photocopied article on Child Abduction which had been printed in the national UK Police magazine "Police Review" As I began to read this article I realised that I recognised all the content because I had written it about 18 months earlier and had left it for the Persons Desk information as a reference document when I retired in March 1999. The article in Police Review was attributed to a female Metropolitan Police Officer who had joined Interpol London after I had retired in March 1999. The article was a straight lift from the one I had prepared all that time ago, the only difference is that it purported to have been written by this new Officer. A blatant case of plagiarism. The only saving grace was that it had spread the experiences and lessons to a wider Police audience.

I always hankered to return to the Offences Against the Persons Desk as this was the desk which, in my view, offered the best variety of interesting and diverse cases to deal with.

I was therefore fortunate in being offered a post on the "Persons" desk after being back just short of a year.

Bundu, the Beat & Beyond

I was then able to renew my great interest in dealing with cases of international travelling paedophiles and cases of Child Abduction.

I also became re-acquainted with the Serious Sex Offenders Unit within NCIS and formed strong professional links with the members of that unit which now included Norman Trew who was a UK Customs Officer. Norman and I were able to initiate and progress a great number of international cases involving travelling paedophiles which resulted in the development of quality criminal intelligence and, on occasion, the arrests in UK and abroad of a number of paedophiles which took them off the active list for some time and disrupted their activities.

Norman and I flew to Ottawa to attend a conference organised by the RCMP relating to Child abuse and paedophile activity. I gave a presentation on one of my cases relating to my tracking an active paedophile on his lengthy journey across the world during which time it was suspected that he had committed several serious sexual offences against minors. This operation had a successful conclusion after he was arrested and charged with offences in Europe.

Norman and I made a number of really good contacts whilst at this conference which proved mutually very useful in the time to come. We also had a good tour of Ottawa which is a beautiful city but all too soon we were homeward bound to London.

I met Alan Shiers around this time. Alan was a Merseyside Officer and was seconded to NCIS where he came to work on the Persons Desk. Alan was a very experienced Detective from Liverpool and was very knowledgeable in matters pertaining to Drugs misuse. He had a typical scouse sense of humour which I was immediately attracted to. We got along very well together and formed a friendship which lasted many years. Whilst working on the Persons Desk Alan developed an interest in Firearms and their misuse and was prominent in developing a national strategy to counter the misuse of firearms, especially replica guns which had been converted into working firearms.

Around the same time we also had a couple of other Merseyside Officers join the Bureau with Bill Greenway and Jean Cropper. Bill worked

John LLOYD

mainly on the Fraud Desk and, in my view, was not a typical Scouser in that he had a very dry sense of humour and appeared to have something of a chip on his shoulder concerning his perceived view that all people from the south of England looked down on him because of his Liverpool accent. He was a nice enough man and was also hardworking.

Jackie and I attended numerous social functions in London including several excellent Balls at the Australian High Commission in London which featured large dance bands as well as a formal dinner. These were quite formal affairs with men dressed in Black tie and Dinner Jackets and the ladies in their finery. We were fortunate to share tables with Chris Parkin from South Yorkshire Police who worked with me on the "Persons" Desk. Chris was a very fit athlete and a very competent Police Officer as well as being very good company. Some years later he transferred to Sussex Police but sadly died from cancer after just a few years in post in Sussex.

Also sharing our tables at these functions were Terry Baker from Bedfordshire Police and Lavinia Shepherd his then girlfriend, Alan Shiers and his wife Carol plus Andy Walker from Greater Manchester Police and his wife Carol. Very good times indeed.

For these occasions Jackie and I were able to borrow a flat in the Home Office flats in Ebury Street in Belgravia which was always very convenient (and cheap).

Andy Walker was always a pleasure to work with and he was one of the best problem solvers I ever came across. I believe that I was considered to be one of the more experienced members of staff and I would often be approached by other members of staff (of all ranks) seeking advice on just how they should progress the international aspects of a criminal matter but Andy was at a different level in that although he did not have the same range and degree of international experience as myself he was particularly good at resolving those prickly issues that no one else would look at. In addition he was a really nice man and it was always my pleasure to work alongside him or share any number of social occasions. In later years there was another very likeable man called Chris Bennett

Bundu, the Beat & Beyond

who joined us from Lincolnshire Police who came a very close second to Andy in solving very difficult issues.

After a year or so I was asked if I would transfer to the Research Desk which was responsible for receiving all the international enquiries from both the UK and abroad and act as a sort of filter to establish if the request fell within our remit and was feasible. The desk would then allocate these enquiries to the respective crime desk to deal with but some of the simpler cases and those considered to have a short life would be dealt with by Research Desk staff as a Fast Track case.

This desk consisted mainly of non Police Staff with no law enforcement background and because of this they did require a greater degree of supervision and assistance. The only Police Officer on this desk was Nick (Nobby) Clark from Lincolnshire Police. Nobby was an experienced and well liked Officer and was very competent at what he did. Unfortunately he was not particularly liked by some of the upper management team, perhaps because of his reputation for hard drinking. As far as I was concerned this issue never encroached into his professional life and was therefore not a problem for me.

Nobby and I complemented each other quite well and we tried our best to pass on our knowledge and expertise to the non Police staff that included Rob Drake, Nelita Texeira, Vicky Moore, Colleen Healy and others. They were a good team of people and worked hard to the extent that work which had originally been dealt with on the crime desks was now dealt with on the Research Desk. This obviously had a beneficial effect on the Crime Desks.

The Research Desk was certainly efficient at what it did and it did deflect a good degree of work from the Crime Desks but after a time I did look for a return to the Offences against the Persons Desk which is where I felt that my expertise could best be used.

I did eventually manage a return to the Persons Desk which satisfied me no end. I was again dealing with serious international crime work which included offences of Murder, serious sexual assaults, terrorism etc etc.

John LLOYD

Over the years I had built up quite a network of contacts in most UK Police Forces and other UK security Agencies to the extent that I was normally able to direct or task most of my enquiries to the right agency and at the right level.

Much of this, however, was later superseded by the introduction of the International Police Liaison network where all the UK Police Forces nominated one and sometimes two International Liaison Officers whose responsibility included the receiving of all requests for international assistance from within their own Police Force area or from us in the International Division of NCIS. This was mutually beneficial and worked very well for many years. This system was still in good working order when I finally retired in 2011.

International Police Liaison Officer conferences were organised at which all the ILO's attended and were given a programme of a variety of topics which were of interest to them and which would add to their knowledge and expertise. This also proved to be a two way street in that it was an opportunity for these ILO's to highlight any areas of concern they may have had in respect of the efficiency and operations of the International Division of NCIS.

I was then nominated to become the central trainer for the new International Interpol communications system to be known as I-24/7.

I went on a trainers course at the Interpol HQ in Lyon in France and came away knowing all there was to know (or so I thought) about the new system. It was actually quite exciting and seemed to answer most of the issues we had previously faced.

The system offered the Interpol network a discreet and confidential communications network using what was called a Virtual Private Network (VPN) using the internet. The system has very stringent security features and, to my knowledge, it has never been compromised.

In addition to the efficient and immediate communications between all Interpol Bureaux in the world it also offered the possibilities of access to the various International crime databases such as stolen vehicles, stolen

Bundu, the Beat & Beyond

and lost travel documents, stolen works of art and a terrorist suspect database. It also allowed all Interpol Case Officers wherever they may be to apply electronically online for the issue of the Interpol notices. These notices included Red for wanted persons, Blue for persons whose location was sought, Green for suspected travelling criminals and yellow for missing persons. Later this would also include modus operandi warnings for terrorist matters.

Overall, this was a good system and I could immediately identify the advantages for the UK not least of which was the possibility for the UK Immigration Service to have direct access to the international database for stolen and lost travel documents (passports mainly). I envisaged the use of this system at the point at which it was most needed, ie: the Airports and seaports throughout the UK. Sadly it was to be many years before this came into being.

I delivered presentations on this system to all the UK Police Force Liaison Officers as well as all the staff from the International Division within NCIS so that they could access and use the system.

Eventually all Police Forces in the UK had computer terminals within their Force giving them direct access to the I-24/7 databases and which meant that they could conduct their own checks at Force level without the need to make a request to NCIS.

I also gave a presentation to a high level delegation from HM Immigration Service and they seemed delighted with the system and they appeared to appreciate the potential benefits for the UK if their staff at air and sea ports could have direct access to the worldwide database of lost/stolen travel documents. Sadly for some reason, whether it was bureaucracy or lack of money or both, the decision to request access to this database was not forthcoming for several years and when it was finally requested there were innumerable technical problems in actually getting the system in place.

I am pleased to say that a few years before I finally retired the new UK Border Agency did gain direct access to this system at air and sea ports. It had been a struggle but it paid immediate dividends.

John LLOYD

I must acknowledge the very good work put in by Ken Pandolfi, a former Metropolitan Police Detective Superintendent who managed our unit with innovative skill and tact during the years leading up to the disbanding of NCIS. I had known Ken for many years, since the early 1990's, when he had been a Detective Sergeant in charge of the Offences Against the Persons Desk. He was a Scot of Italian ancestry and always seemed to have a very clear vision of how the Interpol Bureau should be operating. He could be a little prickly at times but overall we all knew that he held the interests of the Bureau and his staff close to his heart. Personally I was sorry that he felt it necessary to leave Interpol when SOCA was formed. Perhaps he knew something that we didn't?

Due to ever decreasing financial budgets the Police staff was becoming a very expensive asset and the inevitable happened when NCIS could no longer afford to employ the number of Police staff then on its payroll.

There came a time when it was decided that a significant number of Police staff would have to be returned to their parent Forces. This had an immediate and direct effect on the Interpol Bureau and almost overnight we lost nearly 50% of our Police staff which had serious consequences on our ability to deal with the volume of work plus it had a negative impact on our efficiency.

The Police staff were replaced by NCIS staff who did not have any law enforcement background and who did not necessarily understand the finer points of the criminal law and criminal offences. This was recognised by NCIS management who devised an in house training scheme in which criminal law and procedures were taught. These courses were very much akin to the Initial CID courses which every Police Detective has to undergo as part of their training.

We struggled on as a unit and the new staff relied very heavily on the more experienced staff for day to day advice on a whole range of matters. Not ideal, but we had to make the best of what was a pretty bad job.

If NCIS as an organisation had a flaw it was that it did not have any operational ability but always had to delegate operational tasks to the

Bundu, the Beat & Beyond

National Crime Squad or to the relevant Police Forces in whose areas action was required.

The British Government had a re-think on these issues and came up with the idea of the Serious and Organised Crime Agency which would draw together elements from a variety of Law Enforcement Agencies plus it would also have its own operational and enforcement arm which would be drawn mainly from the National Crime Squads. The primary role of this new organisation was to target high echelon criminals thereby disrupting their activities.

The theory sounded interesting with distinct advantages and possibilities over and above those which currently existed.

It also produced a myriad of problems not least of which was that of pay and conditions. For example HM Customs Officers were employed with a salary scale below that of the British Police and the terms and conditions of their service were quite different to that of the Police. The question was, therefore, how would former Police Officers be employed alongside former Customs Officers. They would be doing the same job but would be paid and treated differently. This issue was compounded by the fact that SOCA, as it was to be known, would also employ staff from many other former agencies, each of which operated different pay scales and terms and condition of employment.

The answer appeared to be something of a fudge and all staff transferring to the new organisation would be offered a new contract on SOCA pay scales and terms and conditions of employment whilst retaining the right to remain on their current terms and conditions should they wish to do so. I suppose that this was the only sensible option but it did lead to a great deal of anomalies. Some staff would be better off but others would be worse off in the long term.

SOCA was billed as the "all singing all dancing" crime agency aimed at tackling the upper echelons of the criminal underworld in the UK. The intentions were good but would it work?

225

CHAPTER 11

The Serious & Organised Crime Agency (SOCA)

On the 31st March 2006 the NCIS ceased to exist. I was given a certificate signed by the outgoing Director General thanking me for all the work I had contributed to the NCIS.

On the 1st April 2006 SOCA was born and our world changed almost immediately. The most obvious and immediate change was that there was a complete re-organisation of all the former NCIS units, some of which were disbanded and others assimilated into other units.

The other immediate change was that a seemingly large number of former Customs Officers, at managerial level, transferred over to SOCA and went straight into high managerial posts. This displaced many of the former Police managers, but more importantly it also changed the focus and character of the organisation, not all for the better.

These moves may have been influenced by the Governments decision to reduce the amount of posts within the Revenue & Customs Service (HMRC)

A fair number of former Customs Managers transferred over to SOCA probably attracted by the greater salaries and pension benefits. It was interesting to note that quite a number of these former Customs Officers were in their last few years of service before retiring.

Bundu, the Beat & Beyond

This resulted in a very different style of management and one quite removed from that of the British Police Service. I will not go any further as it will seem that I am bitter whereas I was just really disappointed in the manner in which matters were handled. This was a great opportunity missed.

In my opinion the new organisation had a top heavy management structure resulting in over management.

Under the new regime Interpol remained part of the International Division but we were twinned with the International Desks which fed the SOCA Liaison Officers in their various posts throughout the world. The SOCA Liaison Officers had replaced the former Drugs Liaison Officers and, I believe, brought a greater degree of professionalism and expertise in the war against drugs as well as other matters.

At this stage the International Desks in London maintained their contacts with the SOCA Liaison Officers abroad and we maintained contacts with the Interpol Bureaux worldwide. There was little or no contact between our two units which always seemed to be something of nonsense especially when it was discovered that, on occasion, we were dealing with some identical case matters.

The international desks also had contacts with the UK Liaison Bureau of Europol in The Hague and it was not until sometime later when we all commenced using a new joint electronic case management system that the cases of duplication were reduced to virtually nil.

We were fortunate in having a Police Manager in Interpol in the guise of Frank Francis, a former Metropolitan Police Superintendent. Frank was, and no doubt still is, a genuinely nice man but also extremely capable. He always seemed to have the interests of Interpol and his staff at heart but unfortunately his voice was often lost in Senior Management meetings when he was overwhelmed or ignored by more senior managers who appeared to have their own agendas, some of which were not always transparent. He was ably assisted, in the latter years by another former Police Officer named Mick O'Connell.

John LLOYD

We did have some positive advancement, however, when SOCA management decided to create a unit within the International Division, to be known as Multilateral Operations. This was really joined up international law enforcement and the benefits were seen almost immediately.

Multilateral Operations was a coming together of the Interpol Bureau and the International Desks (as previously described) in so far as that although each unit remained a separate entity we were now in a position to utilise and task all the assets available to SOCA. For example, if we, within Interpol London, received a request for assistance from a UK Law Enforcement Agency we could consider all available options before deciding upon the most appropriate avenue to direct the enquiry. This meant that we could use the Interpol route to progress the enquiry but if we felt it to be more expedient we could use Europol if we felt that the matter had criminal intelligence potential or we could task the SOCA Liaison Officer in any particular country if we felt that the content of the enquiry would be of benefit to the SLO as well as giving him/her some kudos within the host country.

In my view, this system worked really well to the benefit of all, including our foreign and domestic partners. It reached a peak of efficiency when all the Case Handlers within the International Division became more experienced in considering the various options available rather than continuing to use a single route for any one enquiry.

During this time I had the pleasure of working alongside some very good staff including Peter Dunnicliffe, Ewa Rzepa (now Cantrill), John Davies, and Jane Whiting. I had the pleasure of sitting beside Ewa for a couple of years. She was a University graduate and intellectually very sharp and I was continually mentally stimulated and challenged by her on a professional level whilst working alongside her. It was a two way street as I was also able to impart some of my law enforcement knowledge to her.

Incidentally, Jane Whiting had responsibility for dealing with the international aspects of the Madeleine McCann enquiry and was a lynchpin contact between Leicestershire Police in UK (then the lead Police Agency in the UK) and the Portuguese Police who led the

Bundu, the Beat & Beyond

investigation. I will not go into any detail of this matter as it would be inappropriate to do so but what I will say is that Jane handled this matter with great sensitivity and skill albeit that, in my opinion, she was fighting a continual battle for a variety of reasons, not least of which were the apparent failings of the Portuguese Police and Judiciary.

This difficult time was made a great deal easier with the arrival on the Persons Desk of David Fowkes, a former Metropolitan Police Detective Inspector who was greatly experienced in Police matters and who was able to shield us from many of the troubling issues emanating from senior SOCA management. David and I got on very well together as we tended to speak the same language and have similar thought processes which was a real benefit.

The year of 2006 proved to be a really good year for romance for both my sons, Gareth and Simon.

Gareth met the lovely Lisa who has a young son called Kieron. It seems that they hit it off straight away and were soon a couple. In 2007 Lisa started a five year course at Guildford University studying for her Nursing Diploma and after graduation she obtained a position as a Staff Nurse on the Oncology Ward at Guildford Hospital. She later transferred to St Catherine's Hospice in Crawley where she remains to this day.

On the 29th February 2012, a leap year, Lisa took the plunge and proposed marriage to Gareth. Fortunately for Gareth he said yes and they were married in Horsham in June 2013. I could not be happier for them both. Gareth has fully committed to this relationship which has finally laid to rest my fears over his apparent commitment phobias. I know that Lisa's parents, Suzanne and Dave, are equally as happy.

A coincidence arose here in that the Registrar who conducted the wonderful ceremony was Sue Watson, a former Police Officer and wife of Andy Watson with whom I had worked many years before at Gatwick Airport.

Also in the summer of 2006 our son, Simon, met the equally lovely Amy who was, at that time, between her second and third years studying Biochemistry at Sussex University. Amy graduated with a first class

John LLOYD

honours degree in 2007 and now works in Cancer Research at the Institute of Cancer Research in Sutton where her post is funded by Cancer Research UK.

We also met Amy's mum, Jane, and her two other offspring, Katie and Joseph Price. Before anyone jumps to any conclusions let me point out that our Katie is the real Katie Price!

Amy & Simon were married in Crawley in July 2009 and are now the proud parents of young Benjamin who was born at the end of August 2011.

I had always yearned for a daughter and now I have two who have dedicated their professional lives at either end of the Cancer spectrum. I am very proud of both of them and love them as if they were my natural daughters.

2006 was also a good year for a splendid holiday which Jackie and I shared with our good friends Nigel and Cherie Godden to celebrate my 60th and Nigel's 50th birthdays. We decided to splash out a little and we reserved first class seats on Nationwide Air from Gatwick to Johannesburg where we were to change aircraft en route to Cape Town.

After boarding the aircraft at Gatwick we were ushered to our seats by the friendly Cabin Staff who even addressed us by our names which quite impressed me. However the thing that impressed me even more was that having consumed our pre-take-off glass of Champagne I was just about to say something to Nigel who was seated immediately in front of me when I noticed that he was already asleep! We were on the taxi-way heading for the runway and this man is asleep? I was impressed because I have always had difficulty in sleeping during flights and here was Nigel fast asleep with the journey only minutes old. He is one of those lucky people who can relax and fall asleep in almost any situation. I envy him that.

After arriving in Cape Town we were driven to a lovely Boutique Guest House/Hotel in Seapoint, which Cherie had found, called the Blackwater Lodge where we were made most welcome and received very personal

Bundu, the Beat & Beyond

service from all the very helpful staff. We stayed in Cape Town for a few days taking in all the sights before hiring a vehicle and heading out of Cape Town towards the Winelands where we enjoyed a splendid picnic lunch and wine tasting session at a winery called Boschendal.

Later we made our way to the coastal town of Hermanus where we hoped to do a spot of whale watching. Unfortunately Nigel was a little under the weather due to a touch of food poisoning and Jackie, who is not a good sailor, did not fancy getting into the relatively small boat which was to take us out where the whales were located. There was something of a sea swell and I knew that Jackie might struggle with that. So, it was just Cherie and I who went out on this fairly small boat and enjoyed an hour or so of getting "up close and personal" with some Southern Right Whales.

We continued up the splendid "Garden Route" until we reached Port Elizabeth where Nigel and Cherie left us for a two day visit to a local Game Reserve whilst Jackie and I took a flight to Johannesburg where we met up with my friend of long standing, Fran and her husband Jim who lived not too far away.

All too soon our holiday was at an end and Nigel and Cherie met up with us in Johannesburg before we took the return flight to Gatwick.

I turned 60 that year as did my friend of very long standing Fran. I had always been aware that she was artistic but it was not until she turned 60 that she began to take up painting and sketching to any serious degree. I have seen some of her work since that time and I have always been impressed by the high standard of her work. I am also the proud owner of four of her paintings which hang on our walls at home in UK. She seems to improve with every painting that she completes and she has been quite successful in selling some of her works in the Johannesburg area. I just wish that she had started earlier in life. Who knows where she might be now?

On the 3rd February 2009 whilst walking to the train station to catch my train to London I slipped on the snow and ice and fell heavily on the pavement. I managed, with some difficulty, to get to my feet and hobble

John LLOYD

the remaining two hundred metres or so to Three Bridges Train Station thinking that I had badly sprained my ankle. Upon arrival at the station I found that all train services had been suspended due to the severe weather conditions. I was not best pleased.

I managed to find a taxi to take me home as I had difficulty in walking. I telephoned Vauxhall and told the Duty Officer that I would not be in to work due to my accident etc. My ankle did not seem to get any better during the next few days and eventually (it's a man thing) I did go to see my local GP who, quite fairly, said that I should go to hospital to have an X-ray on my ankle to establish the extent of the damage. I took a taxi to Crawley hospital where my ankle was x-rayed and it was confirmed that it was broken. I was then wheeled to another department where my ankle and foot was put into plaster to just below my knee and I was told to go home, rest my ankle, and take about three months off work.

Jackie and I were due to fly to Uganda about two weeks hence to visit her brother Eric who now lived there having retired from Kent County Constabulary after 25 years' service. There was little doubt that I would not be able to travel and using an old connection Jackie still had with a former Airline colleague, we managed to change my ticket and transfer it to my sister-in-law Denise. Jackie travelled out to Uganda, together with Denise, Simon & Amy, leaving me at home but she did arrange for our very good friend, Monica Bending, to visit me once every day to ensure that I was alright and had sufficient food etc. I was very grateful to Monica for all her assistance; she is the type of person who is able to cope with just about anything that life throws at her. She is one of life's unsung heroes. Thank you Monica.

It was Monica's practice to visit me daily at around 0700 hrs which was fine by me as I have always been an early riser but I am not quite sure what our neighbours thought about her daily early morning visits. They have been too polite to comment.

There followed many weeks of a gradual return to fitness including sessions at the physiotherapists department at Crawley hospital. Eventually the plaster cast was removed and I began daily short walks outside the house to improve my fitness and strengthen the ankle.

Bundu, the Beat & Beyond

Initially these walks were more of a hobble as my ankle was still sore. Before going back to work I had a couple of weeks relaxing in Mauritius which was very nice although the weather could have been kinder.

The Occupational Health Department of SOCA had been in contact with me before my return to work and they advised that I should have a graduated return to work by starting with just a few days a week and on reduced hours. I tried this for one week but felt that I was able to make a full return to work which I did the following week.

It was a case of diving straight back into the work, the level of which had not reduced and within a few days it was almost as if I had never been away.

Then, guess what? Having experienced several years of progressive and effective working, the SOCA senior management decided that Multilateral Operations should be disbanded and we should revert to being separate units again. This was taking some giant backward steps and did staff moral no good at all.

It was further announced that our Fugitives Unit, responsible for validating all the European Arrest Warrants and assisting the Metropolitan Police's Extradition Unit in locating and arresting wanted offenders in the UK, was to be moved from our HQ complex up to a SOCA facility in Warrington, Cheshire. This was to be a major upheaval because few, if any, of the London based staff intended to re-locate to Warrington which would necessitate the training of all the new staff from Warrington who were to be responsible for operating the unit after the move. Accordingly all these staff from Cheshire were temporarily seconded down to Vauxhall where they were given on the job training for their new roles within the Fugitives Unit.

Matters proceeded along these lines for twelve months or so at which point we had another major change of direction from senior SOCA management. It was decided that, instead of the Fugitives Unit moving to Warrington, the Interpol Unit would move instead.

John LLOYD

A review of the international division was instigated by senior SOCA management to have a look at the International division and just how it would operate in the future. In my mind, those responsible for conducting this review were handed a set of suggestions and guidelines before they began their review and were expected to come to the right conclusions that coincided with those of SOCA management. We were advised that part of this review was to examine the viabilities of moving the Interpol Unit from London to Warrington.

I submitted several reports to those responsible for the review along the lines that it made no sense at all to move an International Unit out of the International hub of London. My reports were ignored.

We were unable to understand the reasoning behind these proposed moves but it was later announced that the entire operations of Interpol London would be moved to Warrington in Cheshire. The reasons we were given for this decision were based around the Lyons Report from some years earlier which encouraged all Government departments to re-locate some of their operations outside of London. This would have made some sense if SOCA had decided to move non international units out of London which they were quite capable of doing.

London was then, and remains today, an international hub for so many departments, units and businesses. In law enforcement terms London has all the Metropolitan Police Units with national responsibilities and with whom we had daily contact. If there was ever an issue which required a face to face meeting we could arrange one inside half an hour or so whereas that would not be possible from Warrington.

London also has the HQ of the CPS International Division and the CPS Extradition Unit (headed by my former colleague from Sandgate, Gary Julian) as well as having all the foreign Embassies, most of which have a foreign Police Liaison Officer based within the Embassy and with whom we could have regular face to face meetings to resolve issues of mutual interest and concern.

Bundu, the Beat & Beyond

From a Persons desk point of view, London also had the one and only office of CEOP (Child Exploitation and Online Protection) Centre and with whom we had virtually daily contact.

As soon as the move of Interpol London to Warrington was confirmed this resulted in all those staff from Warrington who had received twelve months training in Fugitives Unit operations in having to switch immediately to receiving training in the vagaries of handling Interpol Case Files and all the knowledge required in that context.

To compound this error it was announced that the move was to take place within six months which made a total nonsense of the proposed training schedule.

You have to bear in mind that, in my experience, it takes a trained and experienced Detective Officer about six months to fully learn all the "rules of the game" when he/she is new in post in dealing with the international aspects of criminal enquiries. An experienced Police Detective fully understands the criminal law, the Police terminology as well as understanding all the points needed to prove any criminal offence.

The same could not be said of the Warrington staff who were to take over the responsibility for the Interpol functions. None of them, at Case Officer level, had any prior law enforcement background or experience. This placed them at a very distinct disadvantage from day one as well as giving them little or no credibility when dealing directly with UK Law Enforcement Officers.

Most requests we received from our foreign partners contained some intelligence potential for the UK. It was therefore imperative that all Case Officers recognised this potential and were able to decide which UK Agency, unit or individual would most benefit from receiving it. Once having decided at whom to aim the intelligence it was also very important for the Case Officer to add value to that intelligence by conducting relevant research in the various databases available and to then send a more complete package to the recipient. An experienced Case Officer will do this automatically but, unfortunately, the same

John LLOYD

could not be said for the poorly trained personnel in the North West Hub of Warrington.

They had received some theoretical training but what they could not be taught was experience. That takes many years to develop.

It has to be remembered that the work undertaken within the Interpol Bureau is unique in the UK and is not replicated elsewhere. It is a specialist Unit with specialist skills and knowledge required to operate on an efficient basis.

I felt quite sorry for the Warrington staff who were, on the whole, a good bunch of people but who had been placed in an invidious position. They lacked the knowledge, skill and training time and with the calibre of some of their leadership it seemed to be a case of "the blind leading the blind"

During all this time we still had to maintain and progress the large number of international enquiries we were tasked with on a daily basis. In fact our workload increased with terrorist related matters as well as the "Threats to life" requests we were receiving on a daily basis. These cases emanated from the so called Osman ruling in which the Police had a duty of care to any individual who was the target of threats of violence or threats to kill. Often these matters had an international dimension which is where we came in and assisted.

In addition we found that the influx of large numbers of East Europeans into the UK appeared to import some areas of criminality into the UK which had previously been quite rare. One example of this was Kidnap and extortion and we found ourselves dealing with such cases on a weekly and sometimes daily basis. SOCA has an excellent Anti Kidnap & Extortion Unit (AKEU) and with whom we had almost daily contact.

As well as kidnaps we were further dealing with offences of smuggling of human beings for sexual or economic exploitation. These offences came about where young women were trafficked into the UK having been promised some lucrative employment but on arrival their male handler invariably raped the victims and forced them into prostitution.

Bundu, the Beat & Beyond

A variation on this type of crime included cases of vulnerable men being taken abroad and being forced to engage in hard physical work for little or no pay whilst being kept in appalling living conditions and being fed very little food whilst their "handlers" received all the economic benefits of their labours.

Again we found that the majority of offenders in sexual exploitation cases emanated from Eastern Europe, mainly Albania, whereas a number of offenders in the economic exploitation cases seemed to originate from the Travelling community and were mainly Irish.

We frequently received requests from both abroad and the UK to assist in such cases and we did have success in tracing the victims and having them released from their nightmare existence whilst fully identifying the offenders and having appropriate legal action taken.

On frequent occasions we received requests for assistance in locating such victims in the UK with very limited information and we often had to try and identify UK addresses or locations using only partial information. Having identified what we considered to be a correct address or location I would contact the International Liaison Officer for the relevant Police Force area and task him/her with the operation of recovering the victim etc. We did have a good degree of success in such cases but I suspect that these were only the tip of a very big iceberg.

We also had increased contacts with the CEOP (Child Exploitation Online Protection) Centre, based in London, which had taken over the national responsibilities of the former SSOU in NCIS days and we were constantly passing on good grade intelligence to CEOP relating to paedophilia and child pornography links in the UK. CEOP was a unit quite separate from SOCA and made its own policies and set its own priorities. I had always found CEOP to be a most professional outfit with Officers who were dedicated in the pursuit of paedophiles wherever they might be. They had also developed strong relationships with some foreign Law Enforcement Agencies especially in those countries most targeted by paedophiles.

John LLOYD

I understand that CEOP is to be subsumed into the new National Crime Agency (NCA) which becomes operational in late 2013 and will replace SOCA. My hope is that CEOP will continue to develop and direct its attention to paedophiles to the same level.

The time for the move for all the Interpol responsibilities to move to the so called North West Hub in Warrington arrived. This was a sad day for me as I could see that all the hard work we had put in over the years in building up the profile and efficiency of Interpol London both within the UK and abroad had been seemingly cast aside. In the 1990's and early 2000's Interpol London enjoyed a very high reputation throughout the UK and abroad but the same does not apply today.

After the move to Warrington I began to receive numerous telephone calls from disgruntled customers, from all levels of UK Law Enforcement and with whom I had enjoyed a very healthy working relationship, in which they criticised and complained of the sharp fall in the levels of assistance and knowledge from the NW Hub staff. I did explain that this was not the fault of the NW Hub staff but this did not go down at all well with most of the callers.

We had always been told that the brand name of Interpol London, which had existed ever since the UK joined the organisation, which I think was in 1928, would be maintained. Senior SOCA management continually assured us that the brand name of Interpol London would still be retained even though the actual site of Interpol London would be in Warrington. For me, this was the only sensible decision in what was a series of very poor decisions. However, I have recently learned that Interpol London no longer exists as a name and SOCA management have re-branded the name as Interpol Manchester which has caused some consternation and confusion amongst the wider international Policing community. The fact that Warrington is not Manchester seems to have eluded those who made this ludicrous decision.

I suspect that the decision to move Interpol London out of London was because senior SOCA management placed little value on our work as it did not fall directly within the SOCA remit. I suspect that most of

Bundu, the Beat & Beyond

them did not really understand our business together with the real and potential value to the UK.

If any senior SOCA management should ever get to read any of this and deign to respond I suspect that they will issue a typical SOCA management statement justifying their actions and decisions. No matter what sort of response may be forthcoming, I can assure you that most SOCA International Division personnel know exactly what happened.

In early 2011 Jackie and I took yet another holiday in South Africa enjoying a couple of weeks in a rented beach house in Strand in the Western Cape. We hired a car and made the most of each day by exploring more of the beautiful winelands as well as the Cape Peninsula. We spent one glorious afternoon and evening at Newlands watching the Cape Cobras thrash their rival Cape team in a 20/20 competition. We saw many international players on view including Makihya Ntini, Mark Boucher and others.

At the end of our two week idyll in the Cape we treated ourselves to a wonderful trip on the world famous Blue Train from Cape Town to Pretoria which turned out to be 24 hours of luxurious pampering from the dedicated and very attentive train staff. Upon arrival at our Pretoria Hotel we were visited by our good friends, Fran and Jim, who live in nearby Johannesburg and we enjoyed a very sociable lunch together during which Fran presented me with three of her newly painted pictures. What a treasure! The next day we had a return trip to a chilly UK courtesy of Sir Richard Branson and his staff.

I had always planned to retire from full time employment on my 65th birthday in 2011 and accordingly I submitted a written report indicating my intention to do so. SOCA Human Resources Department asked if I would be interested in remaining in post on a yearly contract basis but my mind was made up and I declined their offer.

Once the Interpol unit had moved northwards I had transferred onto the Gateway Desk which was responsible for all the work previously undertaken within NCIS by the old Research Desk. The volume of work

239

John LLOYD

was great and the current staff, some of whom were temporary agency staff, really struggled to keep their heads above water.

I am pleased to say that within a couple of months, with some very hard work on my behalf, their backlog of work had been eradicated which seemed to change the outlook of the staff into a more positive attitude which was beneficial to the desk as a unit.

Due to time accrued and leave owed to me my date for departure from SOCA was set for the 22nd September 2011. My last day was a really mixed one in that I had come in early at 0630 hrs as was my practice. I had set up all the desks work for the day as usual and had even commenced a few new cases but after 0900hrs I found that my desk telephone was ringing on an almost permanent basis. The callers were people I had known and worked with over many years all wishing me well for the future. I even had a call from Mick O'Connell at Interpol HQ in Lyon where he had moved upon promotion. I was quite touched by that kind gesture.

I had a bit of a liquid lunch with some former colleagues, Mike Dixon and Nobby Clark who had come down from Lincolnshire especially for this purpose, plus Angela Jolly who I had known for many years since she had joined the old NCIS as a much younger lady. We had a very pleasant lunch after which I said my goodbyes to Mick and Nick. Angela and I walked back to the SOCA HQ buildings from the restaurant and on the way we met two SOCA managers who immediately jumped to the conclusion that Angela and I must be having an affair. We laughed and returned to the office where I found a small queue of people waiting to say their farewells to me. I was really touched by this kind gesture and I said my farewells to Naomi Twist, Jennifer Wright, Tracey Howells and others.

I then said my farewells to the remaining staff on the floor, including Phil Donaldson who had always been most helpful to me, before making my way downstairs to the International desks where I said a fond farewell to my good friend Jules Jaggers with whom I had shared many a laugh down the years (her laugh is most distinctive). She is a really good person with many years experience on the Europol desk and other similar posts.

Bundu, the Beat & Beyond

I had requested that there be no formal presentation and farewells so I was not really surprised by the lack of any senior SOCA management to wave me goodbye.

My old friend Simone Alleyne walked me to the Security Gate where I handed in my SOCA identity card, said farewell to Simone and headed off to Vauxhall railway station and home.

I was also saddened by the fact that I had been unable to say farewell to my friend of long standing, Tim "Timbo" Dawkins who was on long term sick leave. I had known Timbo since our NCIS days and I was always impressed with his knowledge and expertise. I was honoured to have called him a friend. Keep fighting Timbo!

You will have noted that this chapter on SOCA is somewhat abridged when compared to the preceding chapters. This was intentional because I do not have many fond memories of SOCA and I thought that the manner in which the Interpol Bureau was side-lined and downgraded was an absolute disgrace.

I still miss the nature of the work which I always found to be challenging and interesting. I will also miss the people with whom I worked who were, in the main, a good team of skilled and able people.

I do not miss the senior SOCA management in the same vein that I do not miss the daily three hour train commute.

As previously written I am not bitter but I am greatly disappointed that the Interpol London Bureau, which did have a world class reputation, was downgraded in such a poor way and that my professional life of 42 years within law enforcement had to end in such a manner.

You may not be surprised to read that a new organisation to be called The National Crime Agency (NCA) is due to be launched on 1 October 2013 and will be fully operational by December 2013. It will replace SOCA but will undertake responsibility for the work currently done by SOCA as well as other responsibilities.

John LLOYD

I, for one, will not be sad to see the back of SOCA and I sincerely hope that the new NCA will fully grasp the nettle and tackle national and international crime in a more holistic manner and not be blinkered into fairly narrow points of view and focus. I wish their staff well.

CHAPTER 12

A Retirement Bombshell

I spent the first few months after leaving SOCA on gardening leave using up my accrued time and leave. Jackie and I went on holiday to the Gambia which was very pleasant and we returned home much refreshed after a period of rest and relaxation in the Hotel Karaiba in The Gambia.

On my birthday in 2011 I hosted a retirement lunch for myself to which I had invited fifty guests. I had wanted to invite more but I was unable to do this because of catering restrictions at the venue.

I invited a mix of people including my immediate family, my Aunt Ethel and numerous cousins, family friends and former Police colleagues.

I had a thoroughly enjoyable time and we all devoured a really delicious three course lunch interspersed with numerous bottles of wine, followed by cheese, biscuits and Port.

At the conclusion of the lunch I gave an impromptu speech which seemed to be received very well by all those in attendance. I had not planned to give a speech but I just felt that it was right to do so on this occasion. This was a very special day for me, one which I will always remember and I thank everyone who was able to attend for making it such a grand occasion for me.

I joined Sussex County Cricket Club as a member and have enjoyed many days (weather permitting) of watching first class cricket at the County Ground in Hove or, on occasion, at the smaller grounds at Horsham and Arundel. My cousin, Sheila, and her husband David are

243

John LLOYD

both members and we have sometimes been able to meet up and enjoy a day's cricket together. I took Jackie on her first and, so far, only visit to the County Ground to witness a 20/20 match. Unfortunately the game was rained off and we spent most of the evening in the bar area having a few beers with two former BCAL colleagues of Jackie's we had met there by chance. So it was not an entirely wasted evening.

I have been a member of NARPO (National Association of Retired Police Officers) since I retired from the Police in 1999 and Jackie and I have attended a number of NARPO social events since then at which we meet up with former colleagues and their spouses and generally have a good time. I am a member of the North Sussex Branch of NARPO which is very ably run by Ahmed Ramiz, Colin Moules and Adam Christie together with our Social Secretary who is none other than my former colleague from Crawley CID days, Roger Buttle.

I wrote to a number of local charities and similar organisations in Crawley seeking work as a part time volunteer. I received a reply from Crawley Hospital where I attended an interview. The lady who interviewed me suggested that she should refer me to St Catherine's Hospice in Crawley as she thought that my skills and personality would be best suited to their requirements.

I was then invited for an interview at St Catherine's Hospice where I was offered the position as a volunteer driver. This suited me very well.

I have always found the staff at St Catherine's to be very friendly and caring and the atmosphere within the Hospice is surprisingly jolly and upbeat. I am really pleased to be just a small part of this wonderful organisation.

My duties are quite straightforward and involve me collecting out-patients from their homes in mid and north Sussex as well as south Surrey and driving them to the hospice where they enjoy activities in the Day Centre as well as being supplied with a very good lunch by the staff.

I collect the patients from the Hospice in the afternoon and drive them back to their homes. What has surprised me a little is just how many of the patients open up to me and are quite happy to tell me their life story including details of all their current medical condition. I assume that this is beneficial to those patients and I am quite happy to listen and comment as and when appropriate. Whilst what they tell me is always confidential I do reserve the right to pass on any relevant medical details to the medical staff at the Hospice in situations where I deem it to be relevant and in the interests of the patient.

St Catherine's, in common with most other Hospices throughout the country, provides an excellent service to the community and for those in-patients, who may be spending their last few days before the inevitable end, it is an environment in which they feel at peace whilst receiving the very best palliative care from the dedicated Nursing staff. I am filled with admiration at their levels of dedication, compassion and understanding.

Sadly, my relationship with some of the patients can be of a fairly temporary nature but I am afraid that this goes with the territory and is something which I have had to accept.

I can recall that, when my mother spent her last days in St Catherine's just over twelve years ago now, she was always very grateful for the kindly care and attention she received from the Hospice Staff and I know full well that she was content and at peace when she died.

St Catherine's Hospice is a charitable organisation and relies heavily on donations, gifts etc, to keep the Hospice operating and I am aware that is a continual battle for the Hospice's fund raising team to generate sufficient income to maintain the levels of service they currently provide.

In March 2012 Jackie and I took a flight from London Heathrow to Cape Town where we intended spending a few days before taking a cruise ship back to Southampton. We boarded our Virgin flight at Heathrow and were ushered to our comfortable seats where we were offered a pre-flight drink during which time the remaining passengers were boarding the aircraft.

I happened to look up at the same time that a very elegant black lady was passing our seats. I immediately recognised her and said something like,

John LLOYD

"Who let you on board?" She gave me something of an old fashioned look and then she recognised me and a big radiant smile emanated from her face.

We exchanged quick pleasantries before she continued walking to take her seat behind us.

Later in the flight she came back to where Jackie and I were sitting and we had a lengthier chat. She was Sophia Okpala who worked in the International Division, as I had, in SOCA before I retired. Sophia was travelling to Cape Town to visit her sister in the Newlands area. A small world.

Later in the flight Jackie sighted a Virgin Stewardess who was operating on the flight who she knew through her Parish Church in Crawley and they had an enjoyable chat. Two co-incidences in one short period of time.

As part of my retirement strategy I have also acquired a dog. Apart from the company and love that dogs provide I thought it best to acquire a dog so that I had to get out of the house four times a day in order to walk the dog and at the same time giving myself a bit of extra exercise in order to try and keep my burgeoning waistline in check.

When I was very fit from my teenage years and into my mid 20's I had what was then termed a "washboard stomach". Today they are called "six packs" I regret to say that my former six pack has turned into a rather large "One Pack" so I need all the help I can get from exercising the dog.

We have a chocolate coloured Labrador who we named "Mtoto" (pronounced Toto) which is a Swahili word meaning "Little one" She was very little when we got her as a nine week old puppy but I suppose that she has almost outgrown her name now but it is not something we aim to change.

She is very sweet and affectionate and loves to make friends with every human and every dog that we meet. These feelings are not always

Bundu, the Beat & Beyond

reciprocated. We have found that Mtoto just loves having her tummy tickled, but then, who doesn't?

I meet all sorts of people and other dogs whilst out walking Mtoto. Some are very friendly whilst some are not. Mtoto is a very sociable dog and wants to be friends with all the people and all the other dogs she meets.

I have also encountered one or two amusing incidents whilst out with Mtoto. Two recent ones come to mind. The first happened when I was walking Mtoto along a pavement towards some playing fields. On the opposite side of the road and walking towards us was a young lady walking her very large German Shepherd dog which I noted was not on a lead.

As we got adjacent to one another the temptation was obviously too much for the German Shepherd because he suddenly ran across the road in order to inspect Mtoto who was just as eager to make friends. It was very fortunate that no cars were in the vicinity at the time.

The young woman walked across the road to collect her dog and she did so she shouted, "Bulldozer, get back here!"

I had never heard a dog called by this name before but I managed to keep my mirth in check and stopped myself from bursting out with laughter.

The second occasion was amusing but also potentially sinister. Again I was walking Mtoto along a pavement in the early evening when two young men of mixed race walked towards us on the same pavement. They had a small terrier type dog on a lead but as the Terrier approached Mtoto it became quite aggressive, barking and snapping at Mtoto who only wanted to give the Terrier some big licks. The young man holding the lead said, "Sambo, stop it, get back, come on." The two young men then looked at me and smirked as if to say, "I bet that you could not call your dog by that name."

I made no comment but I did smirk back and we made off in opposite directions. To this day I still do not know if the dog's name as quoted by the young man was correct or whether it was a trap for me to fall into.

John LLOYD

In these days of ultra-political correctness one cannot be too careful.

I am also delighting in observing my Grandson, Benjamin, growing up. He is now (as I write) 20 months old and seems to change a little every time I see him. He is a really lovely boy but he can be a bit of a handful on occasions (the same as most other children I suppose). He has his mother's blue eyes and has blonde curly hair with short ringlets. I know that I am biased but he is a rather beautiful human being.

Whilst researching a fact in connection with this book I telephoned my cousin, Janet, who, as usual was delighted to hear from me. I told her that I was in the process of writing my memoirs and checked the specific fact which I needed. She appears to have identified that this was a very opportune moment and dropped a very large bombshell.

Janet told me that she had been adopted by my Auntie Lily and Uncle Tom when she was only a few days old. I had had no inkling of this previously and this news obviously came as quite a shock to me.

More was to come.

Janet went on to tell me that her natural birth mother was none other than my mother. This was obviously a real revelation to me and I am glad that I was seated at the time she told me.

It may have been that my mother had been something of a "wild child" during her late teens and early twenties which, of course was during the very uncertain times of the Second World War. Being interested in Military History I have read numerous books which often refer to the attitude of many young people during the war of "living for the moment because tomorrow we may be dead"

The identity of Janet's natural father was unknown and subsequent enquiries by my grandparents with the local Army camps proved fruitless.

My Grandparents felt unable to take on the responsibility of raising Janet, mainly due to my Grandfathers poor state of health, but my

Bundu, the Beat & Beyond

Auntie Lily and Uncle Tom, who were childless, generously stepped in and offered to adopt the baby which they did.

In the long term this probably worked in Janet's favour because Auntie Lily and Uncle Tom were very loving parents and were able to assist her with costly music lessons and later helped her way through University and music college whereas had she remained with my Grandparents she may well not have had those opportunities.

I will never know just how well my Mum coped with having her baby adopted but I do know that my Mum and Auntie Lily always kept close to one another for the rest of their lives and they communicated regularly whilst we were living in Africa. I must therefore assume that my Mum was regularly kept up to date with the progress of her first born child.

Janet had known of this situation since before she married her husband, John, in 1969 but my mother had sworn her to secrecy not to divulge this information to any other members of the family including my brother Chris and I.

I was in no way upset at receiving this news but I was genuinely shocked. To be told at the age of 66 that you no longer have a cousin but that you do have a half-sister is quite an amazing revelation.

It has not made me love Janet any less, quite the opposite, as I feel even closer to her now than I have ever done. In fact, I am quite delighted.

I am very thankful that Janet was not adopted outside of the extended family because it is likely that I would not have known of her existence.

I later telephoned my brother, Chris, and told him of this startling news. He re-acted much in the same way as I had. He was not upset in the slightest but he was shocked and somewhat stunned.

My views on my mother have altered, but only slightly. I cannot pass any judgement on her for what happened nearly 70 years ago. Those were very different times from today in the 21st Century and I can never know the full circumstances. These revelations have not made me love my

John LLOYD

mother any less because she was a very good mother and I will always see her in that light but what it has done has made me amend my view of her somewhat but not in any negative way.

I wrote to my friend, Fran in South Africa, and told her this news and I think that her reaction sums up the situation really well. Fran wrote, "John, I bet when you set out on this 'adventure' of writing about your life, you never in your wildest dreams thought that information would be unearthed, which would kind of rock your world. Some funny, some surprising and some pretty well astounding. I think it is wonderful that you have 'discovered' a sister. As you say, what a pity it is so late on in your life. However, the plus of that is that you have always liked this cousin, and are excited now to call her sister.

As far as your mum is concerned. That news must have shaken you, and I think she would be mortified if she knew you now knew of her secret. In this day and age that would never have been so shocking, but back then it was a disgrace and people made a plan to hide it all. I smiled at you saying your mum must have been a 40's wild child. Yes, I think that about sums it up. But you know, she lived her life to the full. Probably following her heart more often than her head.

As you said, you grew up in a loving home and that's all that matters. I think a lot of families have skeletons in the cupboard, and of course it would shock the foundations of all you believed in, on discovery."

I am still coming to terms with this new situation and I suppose that it will take some time before I can fully take in and appreciate the new dynamics of my family which I view in a positive manner.

In the last few years Jackie and I have discovered the delights of cruising and have enjoyed some really wonderful cruises including one around the UK as well as a Caribbean cruise with a sail back to Southampton, a cruise from Cape Town to Southampton and more recently a cruise from San Francisco southwards down to Mexico then to Central America where we transited the Panama Canal (a really fascinating day) where we marvelled at the engineering and effort that had gone into the

Bundu, the Beat & Beyond

construction of that facility, then through the Caribbean before heading back to Southampton via the Azores.

We have also been blessed in meeting some lovely people on these cruises including Vivienne and Marcus Priest (from UK) and Gary and Christine Cooper (from Australia). We were privileged to share a dining table with those four and we got on so well together which really helped make our cruise so memorable.

My sons, who are both movie buffs, were mightily impressed that we had shared a table with Gary Cooper!

It is said that life is all about choices. It is also about "what ifs" and "Maybes" For example, what would my life had been like had I not chosen to come to England in 1966 but had elected to remain in Africa? What would Janet's life have been like had my Grandparents and my mother been in a position to raise her especially as within a couple of years my father was on the scene and was apparently a little disappointed that Janet could not be part of his new family? There are no answers to these questions because, although to some extent everyone has a say in their own destiny, a person's destiny can also be governed by circumstances prevailing at the time.

I have made some good choices during my life but some choices I have made could have been handled in a better manner but then it is always easy to be wise after the event.

So far, my retirement has been full of activity and interest. I have no reason to believe that it will change in the near future, that is assuming there are no further bombshells to come!.

I am enjoying life and looking forward to the next chapter.

THE END

John LLOYD

The content of these lists are in no particular order.

FAVOURITE ACTORS.

1. Jack Nicholson
2. Michael Caine
3. Laurence Olivier
4. Jack Hawkins
5. Tom Hanks.

FAVOURITE ACTRESSES

1. Meryl Streep
2. Kathy Bates
3. Helen Mirren
4. Helen Hunt
5. Judy Dench

FAVOURITE MALE SINGERS

1. Simon & Garfunkel
2. Scott Walker
3. Elvis Presley
4. Bob Dylan
5. Johnny Cash

FAVOURITE FEMALE SINGERS.

1. Judith Durham
2. Skeeter Davis
3. Helen Shapiro
4. Dusty Springfield
5. Heather Small

Bundu, the Beat & Beyond

FAVOURITE AUTHORS.

1. Leon Uris
2. Alan Mallinson
3. Wilbur Smith
4. Frederick Forsyth
5. Stephen Ambrose

FAVOURITE FILMS

1. The Young Lions
2. As good as it gets.
3. The Cruel Sea.
4. Lawrence of Arabia.
5. The life of Brian.

FAVOURITE POLITICIANS (there is only one)

Nelson Mandela

SPORTING HEROES

1. Jimmy Greaves.
2. Hashim Amla.
3. Jesse Owens.
4. Steve Redgrave.
5. Ian Botham.

THE GRUMPY LIST.

1. Cyclists riding on footpaths and/or at night without lights.
2. Reality TV shows.
3. Selfish and inconsiderate behaviour.
4. Misuse of the Human Rights Act.
5. Militant Islamic extremism.

John LLOYD

THE BUCKET LIST

1. Tour New Zealand
2. Attend my Grand-daughter's wedding
3. Experience Queens Grill on a Cunard cruise.
4. Take Jackie to the Victoria Falls.
5. Experience a trans-Canada or USA train ride.

Lightning Source UK Ltd.
Milton Keynes UK
UKOW05f0419140813

215352UK00001B/46/P